The Elizabethan Club of Yale University

Members' Issue
300 copies reserved
for members only

The Elizabethan Club Series 8

Elizabeth I, attributed to Zuccaro.
Gift of A. S. Cochran

THE ELIZABETHAN CLUB
OF YALE UNIVERSITY
AND ITS LIBRARY

Stephen Parks

Introduction by Alan Bell

Yale University Press, New Haven and London

Published with assistance from the foundation established in the memory of Oliver Baty Cunningham of the Class of 1917, Yale College.

Copyright © 1986 by Yale University. All rights reserved. This book may not be reproduced, in whole or in part, in any form (beyond that copying permitted by Sections 107 and 108 of the U.S. Copyright Law and except by reviewers for the public press), without written permission from the publishers.

Designed by John O. C. McCrillis and set in Bembo type by Brevis Press, Bethany, Connecticut. Printed in the United States of America by The Meriden-Steinhour Press, Meriden, Connecticut.

Library of Congress Cataloging-in-Publication Data
Parks, Stephen.
   The Elizabethan Club of Yale University and its library.

   (The Elizabethan Club series; 8)
   1. Elizabethan Club (Yale University)—Library—Catalogs. 2. Rare books—Bibliography—Catalogs. 3. Rare book libraries—Connecticut—New Haven—Catalogs. 4. English literature—Bibliography—First editions—Catalogs. 5. Cochran, Alexander Smith, 1874–1929—Library—Catalogs. I. Elizabethan Club (Yale University) II. Title. III. Series.
Z881.N559P37   1986   011'.44   86–7789
ISBN 0–300–03669–8

The paper in this book meets the guidelines for permanence and durability of the Committee on Production Guidelines for Book Longevity of the Council on Library Resources.

10 9 8 7 6 5 4 3 2 1

A Note on the Illustrations

The frontispiece shows the club's portrait of Queen Elizabeth, attributed to Federigo Zuccaro, which was part of the founder's original gift to the club in 1911. The portrait of Alexander Smith Cochran on page 2 was painted by Bayard H. Tyler. It was given to the club in 1977 by Mrs. Sherman Ewing, in memory of her husband, a nephew of Mr. Cochran. Both portraits are reproduced from photographs by Joseph Szaszfai of the Yale Audio-Visual Center.

   The two photographs of the interior of the clubhouse on page 9 were taken in 1986 by T. Charles Erickson, University Photographer, and the view of the exterior of the clubhouse on page 8 is taken from a drawing by Theodore Diedricksen, reproduced as "A View of the Elizabethan Clubhouse at Yale University" by the Yale University Press in 1920.

*Dedicated to the
Memory of Alexander Smith Cochran,
Founder of the Elizabethan Club,
and Charles Beecher Hogan,
first cataloger of its library.*

CONTENTS

Introduction by Alan Bell	1
Catalog by Stephen Parks	37
Index	275

Introduction

Alexander Smith Cochran, by B. H. Tyler.
Gift of Mrs. Sherman Ewing

INTRODUCTION

The standard account of the foundation of the Elizabethan Club is by William Lyon Phelps, who in a few brief paragraphs described how he had been approached by a dimly remembered Yale alumnus, an unremarkable but grateful member of his Elizabethan drama class of a decade and more previously. He offered to send a list of some interesting books he had amused himself by collecting while in England for the fox hunting.[1] Phelps, alerted to the possibility of a benefaction by the astonishing quality of his former pupil's choice collection, maintained the correspondence and was eventually visited by the potential donor. The books were offered as the nucleus of a literary and social club for Yale students, to be founded in premises that would be bought and especially endowed for the purpose. The story, told with an élan characteristic of Billy Phelps, may seem somewhat dramatic and oversimplified; but even in the absence of the complete correspondence, letters surviving in the Elizabethan Club's archives show that the surprise offer made by an impulsive benefactor is in fact accurately recounted.[2]

The donor was Alexander Smith Cochran, born in 1874 and a member of the Yale class of 1896, who was from 1902 to 1910 president of his family firm, the Alexander Smith and Sons Carpet Company, of Yonkers. Vastly wealthy by both inheritance and his manufacturing interests, with a fortune estimated in 1903 at some $50 million, he was of course reckoned by the press to be America's most eligible bachelor. (Phelps had apparently not recognized the wealth, as indeed he had

---

[1] W. L. Phelps, quoted in Gilbert M. Troxell, "The Elizabethan Club: Its Origins and Its Books," *Yale University Library Gazette* 27 (1952): 19–28, at pp. 19–20; see also Phelps, *Autobiography with Letters* (New York, 1939), 292–293. Charles Beecher Hogan's Yale M.A. thesis of 1933, "A Catalogue of the Books Printed before 1700 in the Elizabethan Club, Yale University," should also be mentioned here.

[2] Elizabethan Club Archives, deposited in Yale University Archives, Sterling Memorial Library, box EC4.

been unaware of the keen interest, of his inconspicuous class pupil.) It was on 3 November 1910 that Cochran, after preliminary correspondence (now missing), paid his decisive visit to Phelps, a couple of hours' conversation and lunch at the professor's house settling the scheme in outline. The following day Cochran acknowledged Phelps's hospitality with the offer of a rough card catalog of his books, adding that "I really think that the idea of the Club, not a faculty institution, a place where men with literary tastes may come freely and use as a club socially as well as for study—will be a real 'true note' in Yale life. I'm glad you feel about the undergraduate side of Yale as I do."[3]

This is not the place to rehearse the story of the initial opposition the notion encountered on the part of the president and other Yale dignitaries, nor the timely hint that Columbia University might prove a more welcoming and compliant recipient of the benefaction; that story is told briefly in Gilbert M. Troxell's short history. From a bibliographical point of view it is more significant to note the way in which Cochran, encouraged by reported interest in the Elizabethan Club scheme, soon showed himself eager to develop the collection. "It really looks as though we should be able to make something worthwhile," he wrote to Phelps on 8 April 1911, adding that "there are several important sales of books coming soon." Bernard Quaritch, Ltd., his London agents, had already been in touch with him about the imminent Hoe auction in New York (due to start on 24 April) and the forthcoming Huth sale. Consultation was necessary to ensure that the existing stock was suitably complemented: "Needless to say I don't want to go in at once carte blanche and purchase."[4] Nevertheless, Cochran appears at first to have had some reservations about the Hoe sale, Quaritch having had to encourage him to reconsider an intention not to bid: "It is rarely that such opportunities occur to purchase the early English plays," they had urged.[5] A list was drawn up, however, and Andrew

---

3 Cochran to Phelps [4 November 1910], dated by Phelps to Andrew Keogh, 21 April 1937, with a brief account of Cochran's visit: Club Archives, EC4.
4 Cochran to Phelps [8 April 1911]: ibid.
5 Quaritch to Cochran, 14 April 1911: ibid.

Keogh of the university library, in consultation with Phelps, advised on some seventy-eight Hoe lots, for which backing was subsequently assured. "I saw Cochran yesterday—he says Buy things at this sale, *if we need them,* no matter if they are high," Phelps reported to Keogh on 26 April.[6]

As a result, Keogh was able to report happily to his benefactor: "I was very glad indeed to get your word of approval as to my action at the sale. I really did my best to spend your money, but my conscience would allow the purchase of only 11 items, at a total cost of $2,225. While the prices of most of these books were high, they were not absurd; the books are all first editions, in fine condition, and in beautiful bindings; and the fact that they came from the Hoe library adds to their interest."[7]

Cochran showed a commendable caution about minor purchases, preferring to wait for a really big opportunity. Such a chance soon occurred when the third Huth sale (15 November 1911, the first of a twelve-sale series to cover books in the Huth collection) was announced. Cochran, in Austria taking a cure at Semmering, wrote to Keogh on 23 September: "When in London a week or so ago I saw Quaritch and find the Huth library is to be sold there in November. There is a very fine lot of Shakespear. Probably such a lot won't come up again for a long time and they will bring big prices perhaps. My idea for the Elizabethan Club collection now is to confine ourselves principally to really well known and rare books. That is, not to get a lot more of the lesser writers but fewer of really well known ones."[8] A consultation in London was proposed (at Cochran's expense), but a list had to be sent instead, sufficient for estimates to be requested from Quaritch. "I don't know that I shall do anything about the sale," Cochran wrote, tantalizingly, while he made up his mind.[9]

Only three weeks before the sale, the potential purchaser still dis-

---

6 Phelps to Keogh, 26 April 1911: ibid.
7 Keogh to Cochran, 10 May [1911]: copy, ibid.
8 Cochran to Keogh, 23 September 1911: ibid.
9 Cochran to Keogh, 18 October 1911: ibid.

played a disconcerting infirmity of purpose. Rejoicing to Keogh that the clubhouse itself was so satisfactorily advanced, he reported that "the only books I was really tempted with at Huth sale were the five or six 1st Ed Shakes[peares]. But Quaritch seemed to think the five I selected would bring about £12,000 or more. So I decided to drop the question. Perhaps it is as well to go slow now, get straightened out and decide along what lines to work."[10]

It seemed alarmingly likely that even after tentative inquiries had been made of the principal London salesroom agent, discretion would prove the better part of valor, though Cochran's Yale beneficiaries had already had ample opportunity to expect a certain degree of indecisiveness in all his transactions with them. The firm of Bernard Quaritch, who had enjoyed Cochran's intermittent custom since the end of 1908, must also have become used to his unsettled intentions. On 11 December 1908, Cochran—apparently on the spur of the moment—had bought seven Interludes from Quaritch's stock, and "that day decided to form a dramatic collection," which was to contain only first editions of individual works and would (except, of course, for the Shakespeare folios) avoid collected editions.[11] At the time of the presale publicity for the Huth collection he was still not exclusively decided on collecting drama. Absence in Austria had decided him "not to do much if anything about Huth sale," as he wrote to Quaritch in late September, when asking— out of general interest—for estimates on various lots, including the whole Byron section. At that time, however, it seems to have been Persian illuminated manuscripts that were engaging his attention. "Will you send me here any translations (that is worth while sending here for reading) of Persian poets to read?" he asked Quaritch (an appropriate firm to consult, since in an earlier generation they had put out the small first edition of Edward FitzGerald's translation of *Omar Khayyam*). "Also please," he added, "if you come across any illuminated manuscripts like what I purchased (none worse) I'd like to have opportunity to purchase. It seems with such a start I ought to *only* get the finest

10   Cochran to Keogh, 4 November 1911: ibid.
11   Notes on an interview with E. H. Dring of Bernard Quaritch, 9 February 1928: ibid.

and try to make a small collection of the finest in the world(?) or available—Always from the artistic view."¹² (Phelps's teaching, though it had inculcated an intermittent delight in Elizabethan drama, had not impressed itself on Cochran's epistolary style, and the composition of his letters is—to put it politely—simple and unadorned.)

E. H. Dring of Quaritch's was soon able to find a good collection of Persian manuscripts (belonging to a Dr. Martin of Paris, and including a fine *Poems of Nizami* at £6,000), which he offered to bring out for inspection, mentioning that the proposed visit to Semmering would give them the opportunity of discussing a new development in the Huth business. "Would you care to consider the purchase of the Shakesperes en bloc before the sale?" Dring asked in a letter of 3 November, offering to take over any unwanted items from such a transaction for Quaritch's own stock. "A hint has just been given to me that such a private sale would be considered by the executors, but I did not feel justified in spending so much money myself as it would have incommoded me in buying other items in the sale. . . . If such a purchase could be effected I am sure you would save a great deal, as the valuations would be on a very conservative basis."¹³

The hint had undoubtedly come to Quaritch's in their dealings with Mr. Hodge of Sotheby, Wilkinson, and Hodge, the auctioneers, who on 7 November reported that "it is very much as I feared, [Mr. Huth] does not care to sell privately and will not allow me to accept less than £31,500 (thirty thousand Guineas). I understand that Sotheran offered (their letter is now existing) the late Mr Alfred Huth fifty thousand pounds for the Quartos alone and he refused to sell."¹⁴

Hodge's letter nicely mingles apparent reluctance to trade and a reminder of (authenticated) competition at an earlier date, with a definite financial proposition. Cochran soon started showing himself keen, and the telegraph wires between London and Semmering were humming.

12   Cochran to Quaritch, received 30 September 1911; a letter of 15 October 1911 also refers. I am grateful to Bernard Quaritch, Ltd., for permission to quote from the annotated copy of the Huth sale catalog in their archives, with the relevant correspondence bound in.
13   E. H. Dring to Cochran, 3 November 1911: copy in Quaritch archives.
14   Tom Hodge to Alfred B. Quaritch, 7 November 1911: ibid.

The exterior of the clubhouse, engraved by Theodore Diedricksen.

Two interior views of the clubhouse.

At first it was only selected items that were asked about, but Cochran before long agreed (on 9 November) to take the entire collection, paying an immediate deposit to secure the whole set. Quaritch's, with their wide knowledge of the market, were soon able to inform their customer that "your numbers would have realised much more at auction, owing to two serious rivals wanting exactly those that you wanted. They are undoubtedly the cream of the lot."[15]

And so at thirty thousand guineas was concluded a major transaction in the history of book collecting; at a single stroke were acquired forty-two prime lots from the grandest library then available, and secured to the manifest frustration of other dealers and collectors. The purchases were later rounded off by the Huth copy of Bacon's *Essayes* 1597, which Quaritch bought for £1,950 on the second day of the sale, reporting it to Cochran immediately as an exceptionally important book that was unlikely to be available again. A note was added that "I mentioned to Mr W. A. White of Brooklyn that you would be on the Lusitania. He is an enthusiastic collector and tells me that he has frequently lent books to Yale. Although he was disappointed that he had not the opportunity of competing for some of the quartos he was delighted to learn that you had secured the collection for Yale. I think there will be some excitement in book-collecting circles tomorrow, when it is known what you have done. There will be many people envious of Yale's good fortune."[16]

The local management of the Elizabethan Club project had been told of their good fortune by Cochran's simple message wired on 10 November 1911: "Confidential have secured entire collection Huth sale Shakespeares."[17]

No more lavish or appropriate opening gift to the club could be imagined. The news took some time to reach Phelps, who was then on leave in Europe. On Christmas Day 1911 he wrote to Keogh from Munich: "I am simply struck dumb with amazement when I heard of

---

15 Undated draft telegram, [November 1911]: ibid.
16 E. H. Dring to Cochran, 17 November 1911: ibid.
17 Club Archives: EC4.

Introduction

those wonderful Huth purchases, for I realised immediately that it puts Yale at the head of the Western Hemisphere in Eliz things. . . . Little did I guess when I started giving my course in the Elizabethan dramatists years ago, that it would come to this."[18]

Alexander Cochran's subsequent involvement with the club and its library was limited and sporadic. Once the duplicates (including an inferior First Folio) had been sorted out and disposed of through Quaritch, bibliographical references in the club's correspondence with Cochran indicate his growing reluctance to develop the rare-book collection, though the old pattern of eleventh-hour decisiveness still occasionally shows. In April 1915 two contradictory telegrams show that at first the prospect of further purchases at the General Brayton Ives sale was firmly rejected, but the purchase of the Florio translation of Montaigne's *Essayes* 1603, in a binding bearing Queen Elizabeth's arms, was reported a couple of days later: "Couldn't resist pleasure of bidding Florio's translation for the Club for it seemed so appropriate."[19]

Some miscellaneous donations followed in 1916, but the Huntington duplicates sale of 1917 aroused no interest in Cochran, nor is any response recorded to Keogh's having sent a copy of the Lord Mostyn sale catalog (Sotheby, 20 March 1919) temptingly marked with Yale's holdings. Pleased though Cochran seems to have been at occasional reports of the success of his foundation, his interest in it seems to have regretfully decreased. Keogh reported a conversation with Cochran's lawyer in 1921, in which he heard that the founder believed "that his gift was not appreciated. . . . he was greatly disappointed at the reception he had from the [university] administration in 1911." In such circumstances it would not have been prudent to ask for money for further books.[20]

Nevertheless, Cochran's interest in the club was rekindled when further endowment was needed to maintain the building and to avert the

---

18 Phelps to Keogh, 25 December 1911: ibid.
19 Cochran to Keogh, 8 and 10 April 1915: ibid.
20 Memo by Keogh, 22 February 1921: ibid.

imposition of a charge for membership, freedom from dues being a matter on which he remained adamant.[21] Contributions to make up deficits are recorded from time to time, but in bibliographical terms at least the founder's work toward his club had been done.[22] "Well," as he had commented on a favorable report from Gilbert Murray about the foundation, which reached him in 1919, "it was done right."[23]

Book collecting had failed to retain Cochran's volatile interest long enough to establish a settled habit of patient study, competitiveness, and expenditure that building a collection demanded. The main passion of his life was for yachting, although in 1920 he became married secretly to Madame Ganna Walska, an opera singer, the divorce settlement in 1922 being large enough to attract widespread press coverage. In 1914 he had built the *Vanitie* to defend the America's Cup against the British merchant Sir Thomas Lipton's *Shamrock*. Such patriotic gestures do not come cheap, but Cochran had the means to indulge them to the full. He appears to have been a model employer of the work force of seven thousand at his Yonkers factory, who were generously remembered in his will when he died in 1929. "Mr. Cochran was extremely democratic," an obituary recalled, "and would stop in the street to chat with persons of modest circumstances. The people of Yonkers greatly admired him, and his employees adored him."[24] Local philanthropic gestures (which included the endowment of Phillipse Hall Manor, Yonkers, as a museum of American furniture and portraits) and anonymous national endowments (including the foundation of a College of Preachers at the National Cathedral, Washington) scarcely diminished his fortune. His estate was announced at \$38,977,227,[25] though the books in the inventory were valued at a mere \$8,988: but one half-pennyworth of literature to this intolerable deal of wealth.

Considering the willingness Cochran had briefly manifested to follow a book-collecting whim, and to back his fancy with highly skilled

21 Cochran to Keogh, 22 March 1925: ibid.
22 See, for example, Cochran to Keogh, [April 1926]: ibid.
23 Cochran to Keogh, 31 December 1919: ibid.
24 *New York Times*, 21 June 1929, 25.
25 Ibid., 6 August 1932.

advice and full prices for first-rate wares, it is a matter for great regret that his bibliophilic phase was so brief. He had the potential and the means to develop into a major collector on a very grand scale indeed, equipped to take advantage of some very important opportunities the market presented in the second part of his life. He chose instead the sponsorship of international competitive yachting, and his fame was literally cast to the winds. His memory will endure more lastingly in the library he had merely started to collect. Regret at Cochran's failure to continue as a serious book collector must however be tempered by the fact that his volatile fancy was once caught by the notions of founding a literary sodality for the students and faculty of his old university and placing at its center the fruits of his brief excursion into the world of rare books.

Cochran's venture at this rarified level of bibliographical expertise, literary judgment, and financial investment had been a short one, but he had the good fortune to hit the market at a time when such signal opportunities were available. By placing his collection in the custody of a permanent foundation and thus beyond the possibility of further exposure to the market, he became the last private owner in some very distinguished sequences of provenance. His place is therefore secure in those chains of ownership so important to the history of bibliophily and of literary taste, which through the accumulated evidences of former possession can provide so much additional information about books, libraries, and literary history. As Edwin Wolf II remarked when discussing some early English provenances of books in the Library Company of Philadelphia, "A provenance is at once a cachet of excellence and a sentimental link in a cultural chain which binds one age to another. A copy of a book which has come from a distinguished collection of the past has been accorded respect beyond that given to just 'another' copy of the same edition. How we love the roll-call of pedigree when we speak of the Farmer-Heber-Britwell-Jones-Clawson copy of a rare Elizabethan play. The respect is heightened when the former owner was not merely a collector of note—no denigration of the honourable title of 'collector' is intended—but was a famous author, a renowned historical figure, or a person of nobility or notoriety."[26] For an Elizabethan Club example in the same vein, we might refer to the Second Quarto of *Romeo and Juliet* 1599, with its Steevens-Roxburghe-White Knights-Daniel-Huth-Cochran provenance, each link in this distinguished chain having its special importance to the historian of book collecting.

Looking initially at the principal opportunities available to Alex Cochran in the bookshops and auction rooms during his brief concentration of interest, four groups deserve special comment. Two of them—the "Irish Find" and Mostyn books—belong to rather obscure corners of the annals of collecting, but their constituent volumes are still accorded a special cachet as a group; the others, from the Hoe and Huth sales, belong to the mainstream of collecting history. The so-called Irish Find books sold at Sotheby's on 27 June 1906 as the "Property of a Gentleman in Ireland" derive from one of those infrequent incidents that from time to time quicken the pulse of scholarship. The owner of a house in Ireland came upon an old black-letter volume while his property was being demolished, and he tore out a specimen leaf to send to Sotheby's for opinion. On his being assured by the auctioneers that it was indeed of interest, the tattered volume was posted to London without even the benefit of wrapping paper, but the bare string held together what turned out to be a group of seven pre-Shakespearean plays, or Interludes, which were bibliographically even greater rarities—because less obviously estimable—than early Shakespeare texts themselves.[27] Disbound and separately lotted in the sale (lots 955–971), they fetched £2,602 for their uncomprehending owner. Quaritch bought them all, one each for the British Museum and for the Brooklyn collector W. A. White, but five of them were still in stock when Cochran paid his fortunate visit to the shop. These, now at the Elizabethan Club,

26 *Book Collector* 9 (1960): 275.
27 Seymour de Ricci, *English Collectors of Books and Manuscripts (1530–1930) and Their Marks of Ownership* (Cambridge, 1930), 177–178. It should be noted that some of Cochran's purchases from Quaritch may have been on the firm's shelves very much longer than the Irish books. Paynell's *Conspiracie of Catiline* 1557 (48) bears Dring's collation note of 13 August 1880, and other volumes have notes much earlier than the Irish Find sale.

E. V. Utterson (EC 53)

Perkins arms (upper cover of EC 115)

Sir J. H. Thorold and Syston Park (EC 84)

Robert Hoe (EC 148)

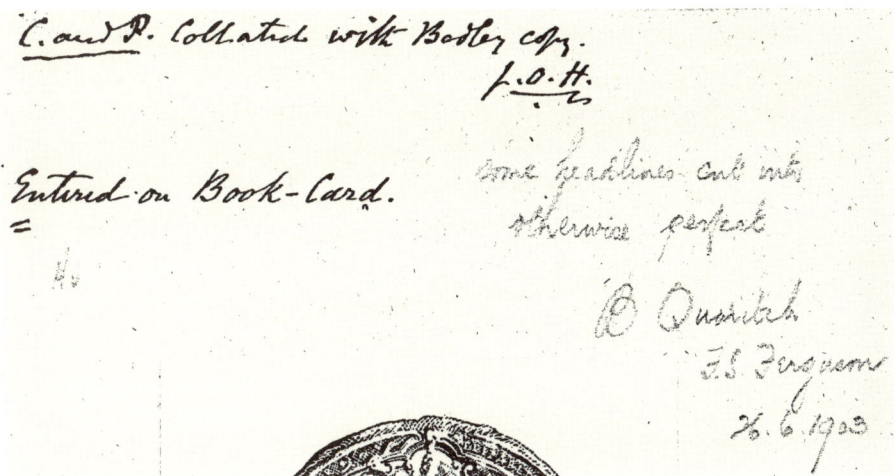

Collation notes of J. O. Halliwell-Phillipps and F. S. Ferguson of Bernard Quaritch Ltd. (EC 119)

include the two most expensive in the sale: Thomas Ingelend's *A Pretie and Mery New Enterlude: Called the Desobedient Child* [?1570] (103), and *The Enterlude of Youth* [1557] (246) at £233 and £230, respectively.

A much more buoyant, knowledgeable, and competitive market makes it highly improbable that any dealer could nowadays hold for very long a large stock of such quality, but at that time Quaritch also had on their shelves for the delectation of their new customer a group of purchases from the Sotheby sale of 31 May 1907, "The Property of a Nobleman," soon identified as coming from Lord Mostyn, of Mostyn Hall, North Wales. He had consigned a sample of his large family library, lotted by the auctioneers as sixty-eight individual sixteenth-century plays. The discovery recalled for the world of rare books the batch that had turned up at Lamport Hall, Northamptonshire, in 1867 (most of which later formed part of the celebrated Britwell Park library collected by the Christie-Miller family): like the Lamport books, the first group of Mostyn plays was of unusually high quality. Quaritch bought twenty of the sixty-eight lots, of which eight are now in the Elizabethan Club collection.[28]

These Mostyn books and the further and much larger portion sold at Sotheby's in 1919 (by which time, as we have seen, Cochran had lost interest) remain a historically tantalizing problem. A final sale of books and manuscripts from Mostyn Hall held by Christie's in October 1974 provided an occasion for examining the early manuscript library catalogs which were included in the sale (lots 1075–1077), but the auctioneers were able only to report inconclusively that "it is not clear when this remarkable assemblage [of plays] was put together or by whom, but the main part was probably in existence by 1650; there are no signs of later provenance."[29] Early though this date is, the Mostyn library was even older than that, "a considerable library" having been collected by the first Sir Thomas Mostyn (1535–1617). Arguments about provenance centering on the Sir Thomas Mostyn of the late seventeenth century are inconclusive, since the four hundred plays may

---

28 Including nos. 4, 9, 10, 47, 85, 91, 156, and 232.
29 Christie's sale catalog, 9–10 October 1974, foreword.

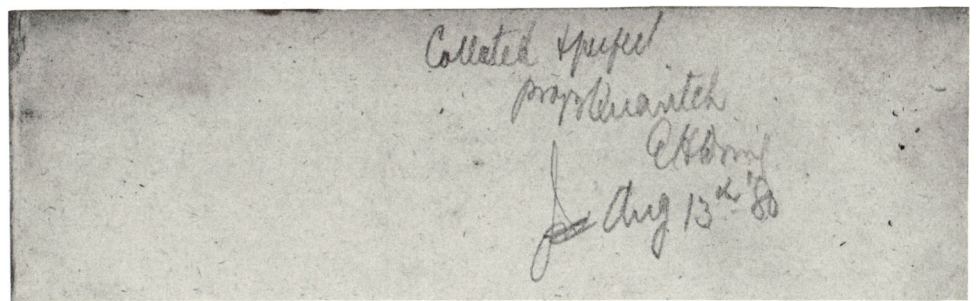

Collation note of E. M. Dring of Bernard Quaritch Ltd. (EC 48)

Frederick Locker (Jester, EC 160)

Frederick Locker (1874, EC 14)

Henry Huth (EC 197)

well have been excluded from the listings if their owner (a serious collector whose important Welsh MSS. are now in the National Library of Wales) had, like Sir Thomas Bodley himself, regarded plays merely as riffraff "baggage books," not worth serious consideration. The Mostyn Hall library still held minor surprises even at its final dispersal sale, but the secret of the seventeenth-century origins of the dramatic collection was not then revealed.

Both the so-called Irish Find and the Mostyn plays provided Cochran with welcome opportunities for high-quality acquisition through the retail trade, but he was even more fortunate in the timing of the dispersals at auction of the two very large general collections, also of the highest quality, the Hoe and the Huth libraries. The collection formed by the American printing press manufacturer Robert Hoe was the first of these to be offered, in sales by the Anderson Auction Company, New York, beginning on 24 April 1911 and continuing through November 1914. The dispersal is important as the first sale in New York of a library of international stature, for Hoe's collecting technique combined (as John Carter has described it) "the inclusive approach with operation on a really massive scale."[30] The series was notable for the emergence of Henry E. Huntington as a major force in the salesroom, and for the regular appearance of Dr. A. S. W. Rosenbach as a persistent underbidder; the rare-book world would not be the same again after such powerful elements combined.

Hoe's books were already well known, not least from the excellent sixteen-volume catalog he commissioned and had privately printed between 1903 and 1909. The sections on "Books by English Authors Who Lived before the Year 1700" were particularly attractive to collectors, and the subsequent sale presented them with some rare opportunities; prices even for the first part exceeded all previous auction records. The sixteen Hoe books now in the Elizabethan Club collection (all but one of them donated by Cochran) are mainly dramatic texts, including some of the club's Beaumont and Fletcher, and Thomas Heywood, as well as Bacon's *Essayes* 1625 (7) and Spenser's *Prothalamion*

---

30 John Carter, *Taste and Technique in Book-Collecting* (Cambridge, 1948), 62; see also Wesley Towner, *The Elegant Auctioneers* (New York, 1970), 258–262.

1596 (224), but they fail to give more than an inkling of the unusual range and quality of the Hoe library in its many categories. Whether in incunabula (from a vellum Gutenberg Bible onward), medieval manuscripts, Americana, literary autographs, or (especially appropriate in a founder member of the Grolier Club) books from Jean Grolier's library, the quality is strikingly high. So very accomplished a collection is it, and so unusual in its range and achievement when compared with other American private libraries of its day, that one wonders whether a permanent home might not have been found for it, putting so much bibliographical richness beyond the possibility of scattering. Whatever the probabilities this offered of an institutionalized posterity, this was not the collector's wish. He had apparently been unimpressed on his travels by European standards of corporate custody and believed that private libraries offered the best chance of books being well cared for. Besides, he argued, "if the great collections of the past had not been sold where would I have found my books?" His will therefore decreed that his own collections should be sold at auction. "He loved his books," his friend Beverly Chew commented, "and wished them to pass after his death to those who would continue to cherish and care for them, and that they in their turn should transmit them to the booklovers of the future."[31] The Elizabethan Club need not feel unduly guilty, however, about amortizing its small quantity of Hoe books; plenty of others are available bearing his ex libris, with its device of a tiny handpress to indicate the origins of the collector's wealth and interests, as a warranty of quality.

The disposal of an even grander library formed by the London merchant banker Henry Huth (1815–1878) and continued by his son Alfred Henry Huth (1850–1910) was rather differently arranged. The younger Huth directed in his will that the British Museum Library should be allowed to choose fifty Huth volumes for its collections, specifying also that any duplicate or imperfect volumes involved in the transaction should be exchanged with those from the Huth library. (This last provision accounts for the fact that the imperfect 1597 Quarto of *Richard III*

---

31 Beverley Chew, foreword to Anderson Auction Co. catalog 905 (24 April 1911), v.

at the Elizabethan Club [+33] is stamped as a discarded British Museum duplicate.) The volumes selected by the trustees of the Museum were appropriately commemorated in an impressive folio *Catalogue* which they published in 1912; it includes some exceptional manuscripts, blockbooks, and incunabula; an improvement to the museum's first dated Caxton; three Shakespeare Quartos to add to the museum's already established richnesses, which derived from the Garrick and King George III collections; and the group of seventy Elizabethan ballads that Henry Huth had acquired in the 1864 sale of George Daniel's collection. After this magnificent bequest to the nation, plenty remained to keep the salesrooms busy for a long time, and for the distinctive label EX MUSAEO HUTHII, added for the sale, to be broadcast among private and institutional libraries as a guarantee of interest and excellence.

The extent and value of the Huth library can be gauged not only from the catalog of these fifty chosen items or from the auction catalogs of the series of sales extending from 1911 to 1922. Toward the end of his life, Henry Huth had arranged for the compilation of a five-volume catalog, *The Huth Library,* which was issued posthumously in 1880 under the care of W. Carew Hazlitt and the bookseller F. S. Ellis, both of them careful scholars. The catalog, which was bibliographically innovatory in giving full titles and collations, raised the standard of reference books of its kind, as well as providing a full record of an individual library, which had moreover long been generously available to serious scholars.

Henry Huth, who had assembled the greater part of this remarkable collection, was a consummate bibliophile, whose attention had been engaged as a schoolboy by the contents of a bookshop at which he was selling unwanted volumes to pay for some amateur chemistry experiments. After early travels for his family banking firm, during which he bought a few books, he settled in London and made daily visits to the principal booksellers on his way to and from work, concentrating his main business in the hands of Joseph Lilly, who acted as his agent in the rooms. F. S. Ellis recalled Lilly as a curmudgeonly and parsimonious character,[32] but he was a knowledgeable broker who did well

---

32 In Bernard Quaritch, *Contributions Towards a Dictionary of English Book-Collectors* (London, 1892), 2:2–3; but see also Nicholas Barker, *Biblioteca Lindesiana* (London, 1977), 154.

for his patron (by all accounts absolutely his opposite in character) at the George Daniel sale (1864) and the series devoted to the library of Thomas Corser (compiler of *Collectanea Anglo-Poetica*), which extended from 1868 to 1873. It was from these libraries that much of Huth's better old English literature came. It was Lilly, too, who negotiated the sale to Huth of the 1604 *Hamlet* (168), which had been sent to Hatchard's from a country house in the Scottish borders: the price was £150.

Henry Huth's range was very wide, but one of his main requirements in all his collecting was that his books should be bibliographically perfect and in good condition. Imperfect books he regarded as "the lepers of a library." Huth's attitude to the range of his collection had been formed with the achievements of the Grenville library—then only recently bequeathed to the British Museum—in mind, but he showed less interest than Grenville in the early editions of Greek and Latin classics, which had been a prime concern of an earlier generation of English book collectors. His preference extended beyond Shakespeare Folios to the Quarto editions, and those of Shakespeare's contemporaries as well, which received due place in a library conceived in so broad a way. As A. W. Pollard noted in the commemorative catalog of the museum's books: "In the same spirit he devoted much attention to early editions of English poetry, extending his interest to the works of the lesser men as well as the greater, and valuing the brushwood and undergrowth of the forest in addition to the tall trees. Thus his collection of English poetry and imaginative literature was probably second to none in private ownership save that at Britwell Court, while the inclusion of the Elizabethan drama made it, in this respect at least, more representative."[33] Alfred Huth had continued his father's work, adding Restoration plays and further seventeenth-century English literature to a collection that when cataloged for sale provided the best possible grouping of fine early Shakespearean texts of impeccable provenance, and a unique opportunity for another collector able and willing to negotiate a preemptive coup.

---

33 In introduction to *Catalogue of the Fifty Manuscripts and Printed Books Bequeathed to the British Museum by Alfred H. Huth* (London, 1912), xii.

One further collection, conceived and assembled on principles very different from the all-embracing Hoe and Huth libraries, should be mentioned as a direct source of Cochran's purchases. Seventeen volumes at the club bear the various labels or characteristic markings of Frederick Locker (later Locker-Lampson) (1821–1895), the well-connected English man of letters and writer of vers de société, particularly of *London Lyrics* (1857 and often reprinted). Not a particularly rich man, Locker contrived on a limited outlay to be a prescient as well as a discriminating collector, assembling a choice cabinet of masterpieces of English literature "from Chaucer to Swinburne," which he had cataloged by the young A. W. Pollard (later to be so distinguished as a Shakespeare bibliographer) in *The Rowfant Library* (1886; with an *Appendix,* 1900) named after the collector's house in Sussex. Locker-Lampson's collection, "notable for its compactness and unity . . . , in which every book appears to have been bought for a special reason and to form an integral part of the whole,"[34] may seem to less refined collectors to be rather chillingly exclusive, but in his concentration on the earliest, rather than the finest or grandest, editions, he helped set a trend in the history of collecting that has been very influential to this day.

The Rowfant library was sold en bloc in 1905 to E. Dwight Church of Brooklyn, and some of it was included in the sale of Church's books to Henry E. Huntington in 1911 (another of the blockbuster purchases by which Huntington consolidated the position of his library); others were disposed of through Dodd, Mead & Co. The seventeen identifiable Rowfant books in the Elizabethan Club collection all fit into the category of "little volumes of poetry and drama from about 1590 to 1610," which Locker-Lampson described with justifiable pride in his reminiscences, noting that "these shabby-looking little fellows now form a limited but curiously rare and highly interesting library of imaginative literature—a dukedom large enough for me."[35]

Shabby-looking the books might have seemed—internally—to a fastidious collector like Locker-Lampson; externally they are notably dap-

---

34 Carter, *Taste and Technique,* 20.
35 Frederick Locker-Lampson, *My Confidences* (London, 1896), 195–196.

per. Each of Cochran's sources shared the prevailing taste for thorough and well-finished rebinding. Huth used the London craftsman Francis Bedford; Hoe had the resources of the Club Bindery of New York (established by Grolier Club members to ensure high-quality workmanship); Quaritch had of necessity to send to the binders the various slim pamphlets that had been separated for the salesroom and used the London firm of Rivière. Their similarity of technique gives the smaller books shelved in the Elizabethan Club vault a uniform appearance to the modern eye, though it conforms to more opulent Victorian and Edwardian taste. The student of provenance is led to wonder, however, what additional indications of former ownership may have been discarded in the process of tidying up these "shabby-looking little fellows" when they were encased in highly polished morocco with crisply cut and well-applied lettering. Bedford, who had a reputation for washing and resizing the older books that passed through his workshop,[36] once remarked to Locker when a volume was sent back for adjustment because it did not shut properly, "Why, bless me, sir, you've been *reading* it!"[37]

The earliest links in the various chains of provenance that now terminate at the Elizabethan Club begin of course with the contemporary ownership inscriptions or (more rarely) armorial bindings, such as the arms of Queen Elizabeth I displayed on Phileomon Holland, *The Romane Historie* 1600 (+19), and of James I on Richard Greneway's translation of *The Annals of Cornelius Tacitus* 1604 (+35), both of them noted here with the proviso that such royal attributes do not necessarily indicate personal ownership by the monarch. The collection contains only two authorial presentation copies, but both are distinguished ones: the folio Ben Jonson, *Works* 1616 (+13), inscribed with the tag, "Namque tu solebas / Meas esse aliquid putare nugas," significant in view of Jonson's elevated intentions for the collected edition of his works, and Sir Henry Wotton's *The Elements of Architecture* 1624 (244), "Ex dono

36 Carter, *Taste and Technique*, 86.
37 Locker-Lampson, *My Confidences*, 197.

authoris," signed by Thomas Jermy, presumably the owner who wrote many notes on the front endpapers. Single early signatures abound, sometimes (especially on Continental imprints) with quite elaborate mottoes. Only rarely are their owners identifiable, and even when their identity can be inferred (as with John Hull, the early seventeenth-century theologian, presumed owner of Wilson's translation of Demosthenes, *Three Orations* 1570 [64]), nothing is known of their other books. No library can be definitely ascribed to such isolated cases, tantalizing when one would have liked to know so much more of the books, reading habits, and theatrical interests of the Scipio Sqyer who wrote his name and the date "5 Maij 160[9]" on the title page of the 1609 *Pericles* (188).

Other inscriptions may be only schoolroom scribblings, as with the eighteenth-century owner of Chapman's *Homer* 1598 (101): "In time of old as I have been told amor vincit omnia / But now in days as most men says valebit plus pecunia." There is, however, a special charm and interest in the first of the many recorded owners of the 1599 *Romeo and Juliet* (191), who wrote on the verso of H3: "Elisabeth Rotton / Her lot is to b neat." This demure anagram thus inaugurated the career of a bibliophilically distinguished volume that will recur throughout a general discussion of some of the features the Elizabethan Club books display in the rich variety of their proveniential evidence.

The lavish treatment the rebinding owners of the later nineteenth century accorded to their single Quarto texts would, even for Shakespearean volumes, have struck the great book collectors of an earlier period as rather inappropriate. It was a long time before such material ceased to be mainly the concern of the literary antiquary and came to form part of the mainstream of collecting fashion. For long the great libraries and many of the great collectors thought it beneath their dignity to venture beyond Shakespeare in Folio and to pursue the early texts systematically. Thus two major benefactors of the British Museum, Cracherode and Grenville, did not collect Quartos, though Grenville did admit some of the poems to his library. Of the three earliest major collectors of Shakespearean literature, the Elizabethan Club does not

Introduction   25

hold any relevant volumes from the libraries of David Garrick,[38] nor is anything from the editor Edward Capell (1713–1781) to be found there. The reason for these omissions is simple: the bulk of their collections had been bequeathed elsewhere. Garrick's collection of old English plays, assembled in fulfilment of "his lifelong mission to establish the pre-eminence of Shakespeare," was bequeathed to the British Museum, being received there in 1780. Hannah More, visiting Mrs. Garrick at the time, watched the books being removed: "Though they were not things to be read, and are only valuable to antiquaries for their age and scarcity, yet I could not see them carried off without a pang."[39] Capell's collection, brought together in connection with his ten-volume Shakespeare (1768, with later commentary) was handed over in 1779, probably influenced by Garrick's bequest to the nation, to Trinity College, Cambridge, where it still forms one of the best Shakespeare collections in Britain.

The Garrick and Capell collections are important in indicating changing attitudes to the collecting of early dramatic texts and must be mentioned, even though no volumes from these pioneering assemblages were available for the club. Only one volume survives there attributable to the third of the important early collectors, Charles Jennens, of Gopsall, Leicestershire, best known perhaps as the librettist of *Saul* and *Messiah* for his friend Handel. Though he is negligible as an editor of Shakespeare, he surely deserves some additional celebrity as a vain and wealthy poseur "who, were he in heaven, would criticise the Lord Almighty . . . verily an English 'Solyman the magnificent.'"[40] The club's copy of Ben Jonson's *Volpone* 1607 (108), a Cochran donation,

---

38   Though his elegant bookplate engraved by I. Woodinot appears on a set of the fifth edition of Smollett's *Peregrine Pickle* 1773, the bequest of James M. Osborn.

39   See J. F. Arnott's edition of Garrick's 1823 sale catalog in *Sale Catalogues of Libraries of Eminent Persons,* ed. A. N. L. Munby, vol. 12 (London, 1975), 1–3. Johnson's characteristic dispraise of Garrick's library is worth mentioning. When Garrick protested that Johnson's rough and contemptuous handling of his books would spoil them, he received the retort, "No, Sir, I have done nothing but treat a pack of silly plays in fops' dresses just as they deserve. But I see no *books*" (W. Cooke, *Memoirs of Samuel Foote,* 1805; conveniently in C. Hibbert, *The Personal History of Samuel Johnson* [London, 1971], 334).

40   Quoted by S. Schoenbaum, *Shakespeare's Lives* (Oxford, 1970), 284.

is from Jennens's collection, via Earl Howe, through whom the books descended.

George Steevens (1736–1800), whose neat signature—after Elisabeth Rotton's—provides the first name in the main sequence attached to the 1599 *Romeo* (191),[41] among his other services to Shakespeare compiled a catalog of the Capell collection at Trinity (1799). Its thirty copies were circulated with the injunction that no bookseller should be allowed to see them, lest the market price of Shakespeareana should be increased by the availability of such systematic knowledge. An acute editor and commentator on Shakespeare, Steevens occupies a special place in the history of textual and biographical scholarship, but his infinite capacity for quarreling with associates is almost equally memorable: he was reputed to have only three friends, one of them himself.[42] He amassed a very considerable collection, and the sale of his library in London on 13 May 1800 was the first exposure of a large Shakespeare collection on the market. He owned some fifty Shakespeare Quartos, and the prices they fetched (ranging from £20 to £30, ten times the previous results) marked a major step upward in commercial terms.

Among the major purchasers at the Steevens sale were Edmond Malone, J. P. Kemble, and the Duke of Roxburghe, each of them important in early nineteenth-century collecting. Malone (1741–1812), at one time associated with Steevens in scholarship but later raucously spurned, built up an excellent collection (inlaid, alas, leaf by leaf, in large volumes), which is now at Oxford, his brother having presented it to the Bodleian in 1822. John Philip Kemble (1757–1823) was, like Garrick, an actor-collector who formed a very large gathering of English plays that he intended should be used by a "Grand National Theatre," which at one time he had cherished the ambition of establishing in a rebuilt and much enlarged Drury Lane Theatre. The main collection of Kemble's plays (an inlaid set, mounted in imitation of Malone's practice, in some seven hundred volumes) was sold in 1821, for an annuity of £400,

---

41 He also owned the Elizabethan Club *Lycidas* (133), the provenance of which is discussed later.

42 Schoenbaum, *Shakespeare's Lives*, passim.

to the Duke of Devonshire (from whom it was acquired by Henry E. Huntington in 1914, at a price of £140,000). One Kemble volume at the Elizabethan Club, Jasper Mayne's *The Amorous Warre* 1648 (126) has, regrettably but characteristically, been inlaid; it has Kemble's armorial stamp on the boards.

John Ker, third Duke of Roxburghe (1740–1804) was the next owner of the club's *Romeo* (191), which bears his armorial stamp on the title. His acquisition of it at the Steevens sale, at which he was a major purchaser, came late in his life, but he was also busy at that of Samuel Ireland, father of the forger, in 1801 (Ireland was owner of the club's Rowley, *The Noble Soldier* 1634 [160]). The Roxburghe collection was dispersed at auction in summer 1812, its sale the apogee of a frenzy rhapsodically recorded by the amiably enthusiastic clergyman Thomas Frognall Dibdin, whose *Bibliomania* recaptures the aristocratic excitements of the period. The Roxburghe Club, that august bibliophilic society, was founded in the course of the sale, commemorating the purchase by Lord Blandford of the 1471 Venetian printing of Boccaccio's *Il Decamerone*; the book was sold for £2,260 after a memorable battle in the rooms and set a record for a printed book that stood for the next seventy-two years. The book, as John Carter pointed out, was more significant than the mere record, as the Roxburghe First Folio fetched £100, and first Quartos of *Much Ado*, *The Merchant of Venice*, and *Richard II* made £2.17s., £10, and £7.7.0, respectively. "If the Roxburghe sale was the first great sale of modern times," Carter concludes, "it was also the last manifesto of a closing era of taste, in which the effective criteria of the great collectors were not so much literary as physical. They paid a good deal of attention, certainly, to *editiones principes* of the classics and to the rare early romances: but the main objectives of the majority were the splendours of early printing and illumination, fine bindings by the great masters, early illustration, vellum copies, Aldines and tall Elzevirs and the like."[43]

Shakespeare Quartos, then, were included in such a collection, but they did not attract the exaggerated premiums that finely bound classics

---

43 Carter, *Taste and Technique*, 14.

commanded. The developed antiquarian taste for early English literature had yet to establish itself as a major preoccupation of the fashionable collector. The Marquess of Blandford did, however, buy lot 3860, the *Romeo and Juliet,* at £7.10.0, an advance of a quarter over the 1800 price at the Steevens sale, along with his Valdarfer Boccaccio. Blandford (later Duke of Marlborough) (1766–1840) was with Earl Spencer and the Duke of Devonshire one of the noble buyers who dominated the Roxburghe sale. He bought extravagantly for years, building up a considerable library at his Berkshire house, White Knights (the estate is now the center of Reading University), but he overstretched himself and had to sell his books in June 1819. The celebrated Boccaccio brought only £918.15.0; Lord Spencer, underbidder in 1812, acquired it at a vastly reduced price. Lot 3957, the club's *Romeo and Juliet,* fetched even in that disappointing sale a respectable 10 guineas, an advance of £3 over its Roxburghe figure.

Two other early nineteenth-century collections from which a few Elizabethan Club books are drawn deserve special mention here: Syston and Britwell. "Syston" is one of those names commanding special respect in the history of book-collecting, but the contemporary preoccupation with classical texts means that few volumes are likely to be found among the club's books. Nevertheless, two volumes do have this distinguished name in their pedigree: *L'anthropologia* of Galeazzo Flavio Capella, 1583 (27), and Giovanni Francesco Fortunio's *Regole grammaticale della volgar lingua* 1552 (84), both Aldine printings and therefore characteristic of the library from Syston Park, Lincolnshire. By the time of the Syston sale in 1884 the rationale of the library had come to look decidedly old-fashioned. The books had been collected by Sir John Thorold (1734–1815), the ninth baronet, and his son Sir John Hayford Thorold (1773–1831) who succeeded him in the title and developed the parental collection particularly in the period 1824–1831.[44] The first Thorold owned a famous Gutenberg Bible and Mainz Psalter, which were the high spots of the 1884 sale. His successor, whose monogrammed label with the armorial Syston bookplate is in both volumes, had the

---

44 De Ricci, *English Collectors,* 159–160.

unfortunate habit of sending his books to a local binder in Grantham, Lincs., who tooled the bindings with a provincial version of the famous Aldine anchor device. The *Anthropologia* (27) is so adorned, grand full green morocco with brocade doublures—heavily overdone, but entirely characteristic of the Syston Park library.

The main dispersals of the Christie-Miller family library from Britwell Court, Buckinghamshire, took place between 1916 and 1927.[45] They were thus too late for the principal benefactor of the Elizabethan Club. Had Cochran's taste been sustained a decade longer he would have had some fine opportunities in the sale of one of the most important of all collections of rare early English books, though the prominent role of Dr. Rosenbach and Henry E. Huntington throughout the series might well have stretched even Cochran's resources. Formed mainly by W. H. Miller of Craigentinny (1789–1848), known as "Measure Miller" from the pocket foot-rule which he carried to all bookshops and salesrooms to check the dimensions of his purchases, the library had been added to sporadically by later members of the family at Britwell Court, who had also compiled catalogs that made it very well known. Even after the main series of sales some books (including important nineteenth-century English literature) still remained for subsequent disposal, and the one Britwell volume in the Elizabethan Club collection, Churchyard's *The Miserie of Flaunders* 1579 (250), purchased in 1979, derives from the Sotheby sale of this last portion (29 March 1971). It is fitting that the club should hold at least one volume to commemorate an unusually interesting library.

Richard Heber (1773–1833), a heavy purchaser at the Roxburghe and White Knights sales, is a conspicuous figure in the annals of English collecting history, not least for the sheer bulk of his collections. He owned about a quarter of a million volumes in his various dwellings—four houses in England and others on the Continent. Heber was wont to remark that "no gentleman can be without three copies of a book,

---

45 De Ricci, *English Collectors*, 111–112, lists the sales; *The Britwell Hand-List* (London, 1933) conveniently summarizes their contents.

one for show, one for use and one for borrowers,"⁴⁶ and he was celebrated for his omnivorous buying habits and catholic range. The series of sixteen sales that took place between 1834 and 1837 marks the end of the glamorous boom period of which Dibdin had been the enthusiastic laureate. The market, already glutted, was falling, and few new buyers were available. Many of the best English plays went to Miller and the sales had a special place in the formation of the Britwell library; but the next generation of collectors, including Corser, Daniel, and Halliwell, had not yet established themselves. The Elizabethan Club has four Heber books, the *Henry V* 1600 (175) bearing both his characteristic stamp and some detailed notes (large though his libraries were, Heber was attentive to individual copies). *A Midsommer Nights Dreame* 1600 (183), *Othello* 1622 (186) and *The Puritaine, or The Widow of Watling Streete* (1607) (203) are also Heber books and, like the *Henry V,* were to pass through the hands of George Daniel before finding their way into the Huth collection. Heber had bought *A Midsommer Nights Dreame* and *Othello* at the 1819 sale of James Bindley, another of the more interesting early nineteenth-century collectors.

James Orchard Halliwell (later Halliwell-Phillipps) (1820–1889) is a key figure in the revival of interest in Shakespeare in the mid-Victorian period. Most of his life's work was connected with the subject of Shakespeare, "to which he abandoned himself with passionate archaeological zeal."⁴⁷ Industrious in his collecting as well as in his scholarship, he formed several collections (one of them bought in his lifetime by the British Museum, another now in Edinburgh University Library), but litigation and financial pressures at various times in his life enforced the sale of other treasures. His career is regarded askance by historians of bibliophily, not least for his early involvement in the removal of manuscripts from his college library (Trinity, Cambridge) for subsequent sale to the British Museum, and for his stormy relationship with his father-in-law, the omnivorous collector of manuscripts Sir Thomas Phillipps. Yet despite the shadiness and implausibilities of some

---

46   De Ricci, *English Collectors,* 102.
47   Schoenbaum, *Shakespeare's Lives,* 396–432.

of his dealings, his biographical and antiquarian achievements in the cause of Shakespeare are considerable.

At least four volumes in the Huth-Cochran group at the club passed through his hands, including three history plays and a *Sonnets* 1609 (194). *The Merchant of Venice* 1600 (180) is probably ascribable to him, too. Most of the volumes bear his characteristic notes on provenance, though the indications of price have been neatly erased—whether by Huth or by Halliwell-Phillipps it is impossible to say. Most of the volumes are traceable to a sale in May 1857 in which Halliwell disposed of a good many Quartos.

A number of other sales of this period should also be mentioned, auctions of antiquarian collections rather than the large-scale ducal dispersals of an earlier generation. E. V. Utterson (1776–1856) was one of the last survivors of the generation that had flourished at the Roxburghe sale; his library was disposed of in various sales between 1852 and 1857. He was the owner of Samuel Daniel's *Certain Small Poems* 1605 (53), which came to the club from William A. White. The Reverend John Mitford (1781–1859), another antiquary (editor of the *Gentleman's Magazine* from 1834 to 1850) is another scholarly collector of the period whose library and career is at present ill recorded. He was inscriber and annotator of three volumes in the club, dating his signature and writing textual notes on the endpapers (52, 93, 228). His library dispersal in 1860, undiscussed by the standard commentators, may well be worth investigation. The Elizabethan Club also holds three volumes from the collection of John Bellingham Inglis, many of whose books were sold in 1871 (187, 200, 207). They include an *Othello* 1630, and *A Yorkshire Tragedie* 1619; his characteristic binding, unusual in being flush at the edges, with a cruciform decoration of four acorns can be seen on them.

The most important event of the mid–nineteenth century for the development of the Huth (and thence the Cochran-Elizabethan Club) collection was, however, the dispersal in 1864 of the library of the miscellaneous writer, erstwhile satirist, and literary antiquary George Daniel (1789–1864). It is also important in showing the growing attention paid to literary criteria in collecting—not that financial considerations were far from Daniel's mind, either, for he was an accountant by calling, with an eye for an investment as well as for a rarity, and had the reputation in the trade of driving a hard bargain. His shrewd purchases did well for his estate: the entire Elizabethan and Shakespearean library, 2,278 lots, fetched £15,865. Daniel's very fine First Folio, with a Rokewode-Pickering provenance, bought around 1842 for £100, went to Lady Burdett-Coutts for £716 (at her sale in 1922 Rosenbach had to pay £8,600 to acquire it for H. C. Folger).

Daniel was recalled for his "portly figure and florid good-humoured countenance," with a suggestion of Mr. Turveydrop in his manner and Regency affectations, but booksellers found his manner "too supercilious, condescending, and pompous, to inspire any warm-hearted remembrances in those who knew him"; but they also spoke of his skill and taste as a collector.[48]

There are eight volumes from his library at the club, all obtained in Cochran's preemptive scoop of the Huth Shakespeare. Some of them bear his scrolled GD monogram on the binding. His copy of *Lucrece* 1594 (179) carries his characteristic neatly written note at the front: "This volume is of the most extraordinary rarity. Only two other perfect copies are known to exist. One is in the Malone Collection at Oxford. The other copy is also at Oxford—it was bequeathed to the Bodleian Library by the late Mr Caldecott. . . . An indifferent copy, wanting the last leaf, was sold by Mr Evans . . . 1837. The purchasers were Messrs. Payne & Foss, for the Honble. Thomas Grenville. George Daniel, Islington." Detailed references to catalogs are included, demonstrating his thorough and meticulous attitude to the assessment of "most extraordinary rarity," which certainly still remains true of the 1594 *Lucrece*. His four rarest Quartos found their way to the British Museum, one in the 1864 sale and three in the Huth bequest of 1911 that preceded Cochran's purchase; the remainder at the Elizabethan Club are all of special quality.

The library of the antiquarian clergyman Thomas Corser (1793–

---

48 F. S. Ellis in Quaritch, *Contributions 10* (1897), unpaginated entry on Daniel.

1876), sold in eight sales between 1868 and 1873, was another important source of the Huth collection. He (along with Daniel) is another of those who developed a literary approach to collecting and a systematic bibliographical approach for work on his collections, which he put to scholarly use in his *Collectanea Anglo-Poetica* (Manchester, 1860–1883). Four Corser volumes at the Elizabethan Club include *Romeo and Juliet* 1637 (193), with his usual collation note (C and a tick), and a unique variant of Nathaniel Woodes, *The Conflict of Conscience* 1581 (243).[49]

Frederick Perkins, a brewer by trade, put together between 1825 and 1860 a good Elizabethan collection which was sold in July 1889; his ownership of three of the club's volumes is recorded (41, 115, and 153): Chapman's *The Revenge of Bussy D'Ambois* 1613 has his arms stamped on its covers. Two volumes in the collection came from the wide-ranging library of W. H. Crawford of Lakelands, County Cork, sold in London in 1891; his armorial bookplate appears in both (51, 98). Collections like the Daniel, Corser, Perkins, and Crawford libraries provided opportunities in the market for Huth, Hoe, and others; but by the time of the last of this set of examples the transatlantic collector was showing himself an increasingly strong force in the market, with eager and well-funded buying in a field of common interest. American purchasing was slow to arouse British misgivings when conducted mainly in single lots (Lenox's purchase through Henry Stevens of a big batch of Quartos in 1855 is an exception). By the time the Bartlett and Pollard *Census* was published in 1916,[50] however, resentment had been aroused by the bulk purchases of Huntington, Folger, and indeed Cochran himself. British commentators were alert to a cultural threat, and it was necessary for the preface to the *Census* to adopt a partly defiant, partly self-justificatory tone. It was not long, however, before British criticism was somewhat muted by a recognition that the new owners accorded their collections due reverence—witness the monumental

---

49 The Corser-[Carew] Hazlitt copy; see W. A. Jackson in the *Times Literary Supplement*, 7 September 1933.

50 Henrietta C. Bartlett and A. W. Pollard, *A Census of Shakespeare's Plays in Quarto, 1594–1709* (New Haven and London, 1916), xxxiii.

Huntington and Folger libraries—fully worthy of their principal subject. The stability of location that the increasing institutionalization of so many previous volumes at last enforced, though it brings to an end the provenances that are so important a part of their history, created conditions in which the intensive comparative textual analysis of the next generations could flourish.

Cochran, though donor of fully three quarters of the Elizabethan Club's major holdings, was of course not the only benefactor. His gift stimulated others, though there was some pardonable diffidence about offering further material while the riches of the Huth Shakespeare collection were still being digested by the infant foundation. One benefactor who proved generous, and whose holdings show how Cochran might have developed further as a collector, has been mentioned already. William A. White of Brooklyn was a Harvard graduate and a wide-ranging collector of Elizabethan literature whose library appears to have been founded on the Perkins sale of 1889. In December 1911 White wrote, when sending a volume to Keogh: "I do not know how particular you are as to additions to your library—I shall not feel hurt if you return it as not up to a high standard of quality. I think that intrinsically it is a rather interesting book."[51] So Henry Buttes's *Dyets Dry Dinner* 1599 (22) entered the club's collection, to be followed by six more volumes (all with interesting provenances) in 1916 and 1918, and eventually the bequest (received from White's estate in 1929) of John Milton, *Justa Edouardo King Naufrago* 1638 (133). This last donation (the first appearance of *Lycidas*) bears I[zaak] Walton's signature, followed by the eighteenth-century bookplate of the Wiltshire collector John Bowle (sale 1790), the signature and endpaper stamp of George Steevens (sale, as mentioned, 1800), and signed notes of T. Caldecott, the Oxford bibliophile and editor (sale 1833); Quaritch bought it at the 1887 sale of Henry Fletcher Hance, and White acquired it on 11 September 1892. *Lycidas,* with a characteristically long and well-recorded provenance, was a fine donation from a good friend of the club, who built up a

---

51 White to Keogh, 19 December 1911, in Troxell's working files in the Elizabethan Club.

considerable collection not just of Elizabethan books (his own Shakespeare Quartos are at Harvard) but also including a major William Blake section.

White's collection was twice cataloged by Henrietta C. Bartlett, herself a benefactress (donor of 1, 17, 69, and 234, of which 69, Fletcher, *Christ's Victorie,* 1632, had been given her by John Drinkwater), in *Catalogue of Early English Books Chiefly of the Elizabethan Period Collected by William Augustus White* (New York, 1926). Miss Bartlett was, of course, also the compiler (with A. W. Pollard) of *A Census of Shakespeare's Plays in Quarto* (New Haven and London, 1916), published under the auspices of the club and especially important for the detailed attention it gives to the provenance of the individual volumes discussed; her annotated copy is now in the Beinecke Library.

A number of other books were given in the first few years of the club's existence, four from Alfred E. Richards (professor of English at the New Hampshire College), including *The Knight of the Burning Pestle* 1635 (11). The two surreptitious editions of Sir Thomas Browne, *Religio Medici* 1642 (18, a Hoe copy, and 19) came in 1912 and 1913 from Anson Conger Goodyear and Walter Belknap James, respectively. Other well-wishers and early members contributed single volumes. There has never been any expectation that incoming members should contribute books to the club's library, and Heywood's *The Exemplary Lives . . . of the Nine Most Worthy Women of the World* 1640 (94), in an elaborate Rivière binding, is probably unique in its inscription: "Oliver Burr Jennings on his being made a member of the Elizabethan Club at Yale 1917." This family present was, appropriately enough, passed on to the club later.

Some of the later gifts have special bibliophilic connotations or are associated with other libraries. A. Conger Goodyear of Buffalo, mainly known as an autograph collector, also donated (in 1916 and 1922, respectively) *Godfrey of Bulloigne* 1594 (229) and Taylor's *The Olde, Old, Very Olde Man* 1635 (231), both from Locker-Lampson's Rowfant Library, the Godfrey coming from the Osterley Park (Earl of Jersey) library sale of 1885. Sir William Osler, the great physician and a book collector himself, gave in 1913 a copy of Napier of Merchiston's *Mirifici*

Logarithmorum 1614 (144), which had been sold as a duplicate by the library of Christ Church, Oxford; Osler had bought it at five shillings from Blackwell's in 1912. Henry E. Huntington withdrew a copy of *[Comus,] A Maske* 1637 (135) from intended sale with other duplicates from his overlapping bulk purchases, and presented it to the club in 1918. Philip Hofer, the distinguished collector and Harvard benefactor, donated Camden's *History of Princesse Elizabeth* 1630 (+7) in 1933; it carries the bookplate of Sir Thomas Hanmer, whose edition of Shakespeare (Oxford 1744) had earned the comment from Johnson that "its Pomp recommends it more than its Accuracy."[52] Another benefactor connected with a distinguished library, Carl H. Pforzheimer, was the donor in 1952 of Ascham's *Toxophilus* 1545.

It is invidious to pick out donations from Yale alumni and club members, a roll in which club officials and faculty are well represented. A few selections include the 1915 bequest of the big folio Beaumont and Fletcher *Fifty Comedies* 1679 (+3) and Davenant's *Works* 1673 (+9, copy 2; the gift of Mrs. T. R. Lounsbury in memory of her husband); Chauncey Brewster Tinker was the donor of Bunyan, *The Pilgrim's Progress* 1683 (21, the Huth copy). A couple of volumes came from Andrew Keogh, the club's first librarian, who had played so prominent a part in the negotiations with Cochran: Chapman's *Andromeda Liberata* 1614 (32) with its *Justification* (37). The second librarian, and the club's historian, Gilbert McCoy Troxell, is commemorated in a copy of Suckling's *Fragmenta Aurea* 1648 (27), given by Charles A. Ryskamp in 1966. Mrs. Valerian Lada-Mocarski is the donor of White's *The Rarities of Russia* 1662 (247), and Warren Hunting Smith of Geffray Fenton's translation *The History of Guicciardin* 1618 (+38); and there have been other gifts in recent years. Thanks to the initiative of the present librarian, the club has in the past decade made a number of significant purchases (including the Britwell volume mentioned earlier, which added an important provenance to the collection as well as a book of intrinsic interest). These judicious purchases established strong recent precedent for the acquisition of the manuscript "mock charter" from

---

52 Harry Carter, *A History of the Oxford University Press* (Oxford, 1975), 301–305.

the Theobalds Entertainment of May 1591. No fitter commemoration of the club's seventy-fifth anniversary could have been made than the purchase of this document, with its intimate personal connection with Her Majesty and its significance as the only surviving prop from the courtly entertainments of her reign.

Every addition made to the club's collection contributes usefully to a choice accumulation of literature developed in accordance with principles that would surely have had the founder's approval. The Elizabethan Club books are valuable as a concentration of Tudor and Stuart literary texts; they are salutary as the treasured core of a flourishing club; and they are of considerable interest in documenting the history of book collecting itself.

Floreat sodalitas.

Alan Bell

Catalog

Catalog Note

Four standard works have been cited in an abbreviated form:

Arents: Jerome E. Brooks, *Tobacco its History, Illustrated by the Books, Manuscripts and Engravings in the Library of George Arents, Jr.* (New York: The Rosenbach Company, 1937–43).

Greg: W. W. Greg, *A Bibliography of the English Printed Drama to the Restoration* (London: The Bibliographical Society, 1939–59).

STC: A. W. Pollard and G. R. Redgrave, *A Short-Title Catalogue of Books Printed in England, Scotland & Ireland and of English Books Printed Abroad, 1475–1640* (London: The Bibliographical Society, 1926). Second Edition, Revised & Enlarged, Begun by W. A. Jackson & F. S. Ferguson, Completed by Katharine F. Pantzer, volume 2, I–Z (London: The Bibliographical Society, 1976). (Volume 1 of the revision is not yet published.)

Wing: Donald Wing, *Short-Title Catalogue of Books Printed in England, Scotland, Ireland, Wales, and British America and of English Books Printed in Other Countries, 1641–1700* (New York: The Index Society, 1945–51). Revised and enlarged editions of volume 1 and volume 2 were published in 1972 and 1982 by the Modern Language Association of America. (Citations of titles listed in volume 1 follow the numbers assigned in the original volume 1.)

CATALOG

ANDREWES, LANCELOT, 1555–1626

EC 1
A Sermon
1606

A sermon preached before the kings maiestie, at Hampton Court, concerning the right and power of calling assemblies, on Sunday the 28. of September, anno 1606. By the Bishop of Chichester. Imprinted at London by Robert Barker, printer to the kings most excellent maiestie. 1606

4°. A–G⁴H² 17.3 cm.

The first edition. Bound in nineteenth-century marbled-paper-covered boards, leather spine. Pagination, in upper margin, cropped. Signatures of Richard Jennings, Fr. Gardiner, and Danl. Crisp, dated 1772, on flyleaf.

Gift of Henrietta C. Bartlett.

STC 615

APPIANUS, of Alexandria

EC 2
Roman Wars
1578

An auncient historie and exquisite chronicle of the Romanes warres, both ciuile and foren. . . . Imprinted at London by Henrie Bynniman. Anno. 1578.

4°. A²★⁴★★²B–Eee⁴Fff²[-]²¶⁴a–oo⁴Pp⁴Qq² 18.3 cm.

The first edition in English, with cancel general title in first state. Contains additional title pages to the continuation and to the second part, with Ralph

Newbery's name added to the imprint. On the title page to the second part, the translator is identified by the initials W. B. Bound in calf, blind tooling on cover, title on label on spine.

Gift of Alexander S. Cochran, December 1911.

STC 713

APPIANUS, of Alexandria

EC +1
Appian
1679

The history of Appian of Alexandria, in two parts. . . . Made English by J. D. London, printed for John Amery at the Peacock against S. Dunstan's Church in Fleet-street. 1679.

Fol. [-]²a³B–Ii⁴Kk²Aaa–Llll⁴Mmmm¹   30.7 cm.

Translated by John Davies. The first edition. Bound in half dark blue goatskin. Signature of William Wolseley on title page and on the first page of text.

Gift of Alexander S. Cochran, December 1911.

Wing A 3579

ASCHAM, ROGER, 1515–1568

EC 3
Toxophilus
1545

[Toxophilus] [Colophon:] Londini. In aedibus Edouardi Whytchurch. Cum priuilegio ad imprimendum solum. 1545.

4°. A⁴a⁴A–Y⁴   18.6 cm.

The first edition. Bound in full speckled calf, blind tooled on cover. Signature of Anthony Earbery and date 1696 on flyleaf and on the page bearing the armorial woodcut. Bookplates of William Charles de Meuron, Earl Fitzwilliam, and Carl H. Pforzheimer. Carl H. Pforzheimer Library stamp. Collation note of B. Quaritch, Ltd. Edward Hubert Litchfield sale, Parke-Bernet Galleries, New York, 3 December 1951, lot 29.

Gift of Carl H. Pforzheimer.

STC 837

AULNOY, MARIE CATHERINE JUMELLE DE BERNEUILLE, Comtesse d', d. 1705.

EC 261
Novels of
Elizabeth
1680

The novels of Elizabeth Queen of England; containing the history of Queen Ann of Bullen. Faithfully rendred into English by S. H. London printed for Mark Pardoe, at the Black Raven over agianst [sic] Bedford-house in the Strand, 1680.

[Volume II:] The novels of Elizabeth Queen of England. Containing the history of Bassa Solyman, and the Princess Eronima. The last part. Englished by Spencer Hickman. London, printed by E. T. and R. H. for Mark Pardow, at the Black Raven over against Bedford-house, in the Strand. 1681.

[Volume I:] 12mo. B–D^{12}D–F^{12}
[Volume II:] 12mo. A–F^{12} (lacking E$_9$, pp. 113–114)
13 cm.

The first edition in English. Two volumes bound together in contemporary paneled calf. Signature of Elizabeth Weld, 1685, on front flyleaf.

Purchased 1984.

Wing A 4221, A 4222

B., R.

EC 4
Apius and
Virginia
1575

A new tragicall comedie of Apius and Virginia, . . . By R. B. . . . Imprinted at London, by William How, for Richard Ihones. 1575.

4°. A–E⁴   18 cm.

The first edition. Bound by Rivière in red goatskin, gold tooling on cover and spine, gilt edges. The Mostyn copy, sold at Sotheby's, 1 June 1907, lot 426.

Gift of Alexander S. Cochran, December 1911.

STC 1059   Greg 65

B., W., *translator*

See APPIANUS, of Alexandria

BACON, SIR FRANCIS, Viscount St. Albans, 1561–1626

EC 8
Advancement
of Learning
1605

The twoo bookes of Francis Bacon. Of the proficience and aduancement of learning, diuine and humane. . . . At London, printed for Henrie Tomes, and are to be sould at his shop at Graies Inne gate in Holborne. 1605.

4°. [-]¹A–L⁴M²Aa–Ggg⁴Hhh²   21.5 cm.

The first edition, second issue. Bound in original sheep, blind tooled on cover. Signatures of A. Seaton and Thos. Grove inside the front cover; bookseller's note on the first flyleaf; and inscription on the title page: "Sampson Shelley his booke beinge the gift of Bromley of Hampton the 22th March 1643." A further ownership inscription is written inside the back cover: "Jo. Hasleworth Ejus Liber." Among other annotations the following is written on the recto of Hhh_2: "About y^e 15th: year of y^e Reign of King Henry the vi^{th}: it happened y^t: divers things were newly brought in to England, where upon this Rhime was made

"Turkes Carps, Hoppes Piccarell & Beere
Came into England all' in one year."

Gift of Alexander S. Cochran, December 1911.

STC 1164

BACON, SIR FRANCIS, Viscount St. Albans, 1561–1626

EC +40
Advancement
of Learning
1674

Of the advancement and proficiencie of learning: or the partitions of sciences nine books. Written in Latin by the most eminent, illustrious and famous lord Francis Bacon. . . . Interpreted by Gilbert Wats. London, printed for Thomas Williams at the Golden Ball in Osier-lane, 1674.

Fol. $[-]^1[A]-[K]^4[L]^2[\chi]^2[\chi]^1 A-Vv^4(Vv_3=\chi_1)$ (lacking Vv_4, blank) 29 cm.

This edition is a translation of Bacon's *De augmentis scientiarum*, 1623, which was an enlargement, translated into Latin, of his *Advancement of Learning*, 1605. Armorial bookplate of William Northey on verso of title page. Inscription on front paste-down endpaper: "Ex dono Reverendi viri Johannis Newborough mei praeceptoris."

Essayes.

Religious Meditations.

Places of perswasion and disswasion.

Seene and allowed.

At LONDON,
Printed for Humfrey Hooper, and are
to be sold at the blacke Beare
in Chauncery Lane.
1597.

Bacon's *Essays*, 1597 (EC 6)
One of nine surviving copies of the first edition

Gift of Allison Silver, in memory of Helen P. Silver, 1984.

Wing B 312

BACON, SIR FRANCIS, Viscount St. Albans, 1561–1626

EC 5
Baconiana
1679

Baconiana. Or certain genuine remains of Sr. Francis Bacon. . . . London, printed by J. D. for Richard Chiswell, at the Rose and Crown in St. Paul's Church-yard, 1679.

8°. [-]¹[-]¹b–h⁴A⁴B–S⁸ (lacking S_8, blank)   17.3 cm.

Edited, and with an introduction, by Thomas Tenison, Archbishop of Canterbury. Bound in original sheep, rebacked. Signature of John Pettite, dated 1723, on page 184 and on the general title page.

Gift of William A. Speck, 1912.

Wing B 269

BACON, SIR FRANCIS, Viscount St. Albans, 1561–1626

EC 6
Essays
1597

Essayes. Religious meditations. Places of perswasion and disswasion. Seene and allowed. At London, printed for Humfrey Hooper, and are to be sold at the Blacke Beare in Chauncery Lane. 1597.

8°. A⁴B–G⁸   13.8 cm.

The first edition. Bound in green goatskin, gold tooling on cover and spine, gilt edges. The Huth copy (with bookplate), sold at Sotheby's, 17 November 1911, lot 385. Collation note of B. Quaritch, Ltd.

Gift of Alexander S. Cochran, 1912.

STC 1137

BACON, SIR FRANCIS, Viscount St. Albans, 1561–1626

EC 7
Essays
Newly Written
1625

The essayes or counsels, civill and morall, of Francis Lo. Verulam, Viscount St. Alban. Newly written. London, printed by John Haviland for Hanna Barret. 1625.

4°. A⁴a²B–Vv⁴Xx² (lacking A₁, blank)   17.8 cm.

The twelfth edition; second issue, with cancel title page (remargined). This is the first complete edition and the last to appear in Bacon's lifetime. Bound by W. Pratt in red goatskin, gold tooling on cover and spine, gilt edges. The Hoe copy (with bookplate), sold by Anderson Auction Co., New York, 24 April 1911, lot 155.

Gift of Alexander S. Cochran, December 1911.

STC 1148

BALE, JOHN, Bishop of Ossory, 1495–1563

EC 9
Chief Promises
of God
[1547?]

A tragedye or enterlude manyfestyng the chefe promyses of god unto man. . . . Compyled by Johan Bale, anno domini M.DXXXVJJJ.

4°. A–E⁴   18 cm.

The first edition. Bound by Rivière in crimson

goatskin, gold tooling on cover and spine, gilt edges. The Mostyn copy, sold at Sotheby's, 1 June 1907, lot 427.

Gift of Alexander S. Cochran, December 1911.

STC 1305   Greg 22

BARBARO, DANIELLO, Patriarch of Aquilea, 1515–1570, *translator*

See VITRUVIUS POLLIO

BARCLAY, ALEXANDER, 1475?–1552, *translator*

See FELICE, COSTANZO

BARNES, BARNABE, 1569?–1609

EC 10
Devil's
Charter
1607

The divils charter: a tragaedie conteining the life and death of Pope Alexander the sixt. As it was plaide before the kings maiestie, vpon Candlemasse night last: by his maiesties seruants. . . . At London printed by G. E. for Iohn Wright, and are to be sold at his shop in New-gate market, neere Christ Church gate. 1607.

4°. A–M⁴   18 cm.

Printed by George Elde. The first edition. Bound by Rivière in crimson goatskin, gold tooling on cover and spine, gilt edges. Signature of Griff. Williams(?) on title page. The Mostyn copy, sold at Sotheby's, 1 June 1907, lot 430.

Gift of Alexander S. Cochran, December 1911.

STC 1466   Greg 254

BEAUMONT, FRANCIS, 1584–1616

EC 12
Masque of the
Inner Temple
[1613]

The masqve of the Inner Temple and Grayes Inne: . . . presented before his maiestie, the queenes maiestie, the prince, Count Palatine and the Lady Elizabeth their highnesses, in the banquetting house at White-hall on Saturday the twentieth day of Februarie, 1612. At London, imprinted by F. K. for George Norton, and are to be sold at his shoppe neere Temple-bar.

4°. A–D^4 (lacking D$_4$, blank)   17.5 cm.

Printed by Felix Kingston. The first edition, with the cancel title omitting Beaumont's name. Bound by Rivière in crimson goatskin, gold tooling on cover and spine, gilt edges.

Provenance not traced.

STC 1664   Greg 309(a)

BEAUMONT, FRANCIS, 1584–1616, and John Fletcher

EC +2
Comedies
and Tragedies
1647

Comedies and tragedies written by Francis Beavmont and Iohn Fletcher Gentlemen. Never printed before, and now published by the authours originall copies. . . . London, printed for Humphrey Robinson, at the Three Pidgeons, and for Humphrey Moseley at the Princes armes in St Pauls Church-yard. 1647.

Fol. [-]^{1}A^{4}a–c^{4}d^{2}E^{2}f^{4}g^{2}B–K^{4}L^{2}Aa–Ss^4 3X^{4}4A–4I^{4}5A–5R^{4}5S^{6}5T–5X^{4}6A–6K^{4}6L^{6}7A–7C^4

7E–7G⁴ 8A–8C⁴ 8*D² 8D–8F⁴   33.5 cm.

The first edition. Bound in contemporary calf, blind tooling on cover. Collation note of Bernard Quaritch, Ltd., on rear paste-down endpaper.

Gift of Alexander S. Cochran, December 1911.

Wing B 1581

BEAUMONT, FRANCIS, 1584–1616, and John Fletcher

EC 257
Cupid's
Revenge
1630

Cvpids revenge. As it was often acted (with great applause) by the Children of the Reuells. Written by Fran. Beavmont & Io. Fletcher Gentlemen. The second edition. London: printed for Thomas Iones, and are to be sold at his shop in Saint Dunstanes Churchyard in Fleet-street. 1630.

4°. [A]² B–L⁴ (lacking A₁ and L₄, blanks)   18.4 cm.

The second edition (first, 1615), without the heading on A₂v. Bound in half calf, marbled-paper-covered boards. Bookplate of Nathan T. Porter, Jr., and signature of W. K. Simpson, 1947.

Gift of William Kelly Simpson, in memory of Nathan Todd Porter and Kenneth Farrand Simpson, March 1984.

STC 1668   Greg 328(b)

BEAUMONT, FRANCIS, 1584–1616, and John Fletcher

EC +3
Fifty Comedies
1679

Fifty comedies and tragedies. Written by Francis Beaumont and John Fletcher, Gentlemen. All in one volume. Published by the authors original copies, the songs to each play being added. . . . London, printed by J. Macock, for John Martyn, Henry Herringman, Richard Marriot, MDCLXXIX.

Fol. [-]²A–4D⁴4E²A–4A⁴ (lacking 4A$_4$, probably blank)   36 cm.

Bound by Demander in half blue goatskin. Signature of T. R. Lounsbury, May 1872, on front free endpaper.

Given in memory of Thomas Raynesford Lounsbury, by Mrs. Lounsbury, May 1915.

Wing B 1582

BEAUMONT, FRANCIS, 1584–1616, and John Fletcher

EC 265/1
Island Princess
1717

The island princess. A tragi-comedy. Written by Mr. Francis Beaumont, and Mr. John Fletcher. London, printed for J. T. and sold by J. Brown at the Black Swan without Temple-bar. 1717.

4°. A–H⁴   22 cm.

The fourth edition (first, 1669). Disbound.

Gift of Eugene M. Waith, November 1984.

Greg 650 (the earlier editions)

BEAUMONT, FRANCIS, 1584–1616, and John Fletcher

EC 265/2
King and
No King
1676

A king and no king. As it is now acted at the Theatre Royal, by his majesties servants. Written by Francis Beaumont and John Fletcher Gent. London: printed by Andr. Clark, for William and John Leake at the Crown in Fleetstreet, betwixt the two Temple-gates. M. DC. LXXVI.

4°. A–K⁴ 22 cm.

The seventh edition (first, 1619). Disbound.

Gift of Eugene M. Waith, November 1984.

Wing B 1591 Greg 360(g)

BEAUMONT, FRANCIS, 1584–1616, and John Fletcher

EC 11
Knight of the
Burning Pestle
1635

The knight of the bvrning pestle. Full of mirth and delight. Written by Francis Beaumont, and John Fletcher. . . . As it is now acted by her majesties servants at the private house in Drury Lane. 1635. London: printed by N. O. for I. S. 1635.

4°. A–K⁴ (lacking A₁, blank) 17.3 cm.

Printed by Nicholas Okes for John Singleton. The second edition (first, 1613). Bound in three-quarter calf. This play was printed as Beaumont and Fletcher's, but it is now considered to be by Beaumont alone. Bookplates of Alfred E. Richards and John William Atkinson. Signature of Alfred E. Richards, 8 March 1906, and presentation inscription to the Elizabethan Club, on front flyleaf.

Gift of Alfred E. Richards, January 1913.

STC 1675   Greg 316(b)

BEAUMONT, FRANCIS, 1584–1616, and John Fletcher

EC 265/3
Maid's Tragedy
1686

The maids tragedy, as it hath been acted at the Theatre Royal, by their majesties servants. Written by Francis Beaumont and John Fletcher, Gentlemen. London, printed for R. Bentley and S. Magnes in Russel-street in Covent-garden. 1686.

4°. [A]²B–H⁴I²   22 cm.

The ninth edition (first, 1619). Disbound.

Gift of Eugene M. Waith, November 1984.

Wing B 1597   Greg 357(i)

BEAUMONT, FRANCIS, 1584–1616, and John Fletcher

EC 265/4
Scornful Lady
[1695?]

The scornful lady: a comedy. As it is now acted at the Theatre Royal, by her majesty's company of comedians. Written by Francis Beaumont and John Fletcher. Gent. The tenth edition. London: Printed for J. T. and are to be sold by G. Harris and J. Graves, in St. James's-street. J. Barnes in Pall-mall. D. Newman in Leicester-fields. J. Harding in St. Martin's-lane. W. Lewis, and T. Archer in Covent-garden. B. Lintot and E. Sanger at Temple-bar. J. Knapton in St. Paul's Church-yard. R. Smith and G. Strahan, at the Royal-exchange. Price one shilling six pence. [1695?]

4°. [A]⁴B–I⁴K² 22 cm.

The tenth (?) edition (first, 1616). Disbound.

Gift of Eugene M. Waith, November 1984.

Wing B 1613   Greg 334(l)

BEAUMONT, FRANCIS, 1584–1616, and John Fletcher

EC 14
Woman Hater
1607

The woman hater. As it hath beene lately acted by the Children of Paules. London printed, and are to be sold by John Hodgets in Paules Church-yard. 1607.

4°. A–K⁴   17.7 cm.

The first edition. Bound by T. Aiken in calf, gold tooling on cover and spine, gilt edges. Trimmed, with slight loss of catchwords and text in signature F. This play is now considered to be by Beaumont, partly revised by Fletcher. Bookplate of Frederick Locker (*The Rowfant Library,* p. 43), and acquired by Mr. Cochran at the dispersal of that library in 1905.

Gift of Alexander S. Cochran, December 1911.

STC 1693   Greg 245

A leaf of the Gutenberg Bible, *ca.* 1450 (EC +39)

BEAUMONT, FRANCIS, 1584–1616, John Fletcher, and Phillip Massinger

EC 13
Thierry and
Theodoret
1621

The tragedy of Thierry King of France, and his brother Theodoret. As it was diuerse times acted at the Blacke-friers by the kings maiesties seruants. London, printed for Thomas Walkley, and are to bee sold at his shop in Britaines Burse, at the signe of the Eagle and Child. 1621.

4°. A²B–K⁴ (lacking A$_1$, blank)   17.4 cm.

The first edition. Bound by W. Pratt in full calf, gold tooling on cover and spine, gilt edges. Trimmed, with some loss of catchwords and text in signature K. The Hoe copy (with bookplate), sold by Anderson Auction Co., New York, 27 April 1911, lot 1333.

Gift of Alexander S. Cochran, December 1911.

STC 11074   Greg 368(a)

BIBLE, LATIN. GUTENBERG, *ca.* 1450–1455 (42 LINES)

EC +39
Gutenberg
Bible
1450

"A noble fragment being a leaf of the Gutenberg Bible 1450–1455 with a bibliographical essay by A. Edward Newton." New York, Gabriel Wells, 1921.

[4] leaves   41 cm.

Leaf of the Bible contains parts of Chapter VII of Micah, Chapters I–III of Nahum, and parts of Chapter I of Habakkuk.

Gift of R. B. Adam, January 1922.

BLOUNT, CHARLES, 1654–1693, *translator*

See PHILOSTRATUS, FLAVIUS

BOCCACCIO, GIOVANNI, 1313–1375

EC 15
Decameron
1573

Il decameron di Messer Giovanni Boccacci Cittadino Fiorentino. . . . Nvovamente stampato. . . . In Fiorenza nella stamperia de i Giunti MDLXXIII.

8°. ★-★★★★^{4}a–z^{8}Aa–Nn^{8}Oo^2 20.5 cm.

Bound in plain contemporary vellum. Presentation inscription to the Elizabethan Club from Barrett Wendell, 29 November 1912, on the front endpaper, and note by Mr. Wendell on the title page that the book had been given him by "J. K. G." on 9 November 1909. On the inside of the front cover Mr. Wendell has written: "This is the curious edition expurgated by the authority of the Church—by changing all ecclesiastical misconduct into similar behavior on the part of the laity. So far as I can discern little else is altered. . . ."

Gift of Barrett Wendell, 1912.

BOCCACCIO, GIOVANNI, 1313–1375

EC +4
Decameron
1620

The decameron containing an hundred pleasant nouels. Wittily discoursed, betweene seauen honourable ladies, and three noble gentlemen. London, printed by Isaac Iaggard, 1620.

Fol. [Volume I:] A–V^{6}Aa^{8}Bb–Nn^6 (lacking Nn$_6$, blank)   28.1 cm.

[Volume II:] [-]⁴¶–¶¶⁴¶¶¶²B–Zz⁴Aaa⁶   28.1 cm.

The first edition in English (the translator is not known). Bound by Rivière in red goatskin, gold tooling on cover and spine, gilt edges.

Given to the club in 1912.

STC 3172

BODIN, JEAN, 1530–1596

EC 15A
Demonomania
1590

Io. Bodini Andegavensis de magorvm daemonomania. . . . Libri IV. . . . Francofvrti ex officina typographica Nicolai Bassaei. M. D. XC.

8°. A–Z⁸a–z⁸Aa–Dd⁸ (lacking Dd₈, probably blank) 15.9 cm.

Bound in paper-covered boards. Bookplate and signature of Alfred E. Richards, 25 October 1908, and presentation inscription to the Elizabethan Club, 27 January 1913, on front flyleaf.

Gift of Alfred E. Richards, January 1913.

BRENDE, JOHN, *translator*

See CURTIUS RUFUS, QUINTUS

BRETON, NICHOLAS, 1545?–1626?

EC 16
Old Mans
Lesson
1605

An olde mans lesson, and a yovng mans love. By Nicholas Breton. London imprinted for Edward White, and are to bee solde at his shop neere the little north-doore of S. Paules Church at the signe of the Gun. 1605.

4°. A–F⁴G² 16.7 cm.

The first edition. Bound in half brown goatskin. This copy is imperfect, lacking ten leaves: A_{1-3}, C_4, E_{1-4}, C_{1-2} (supplied in facsimile). Signature of Robt. Whitton, K.B., on A_4. Bookplate of Frederick Locker (*The Rowfant Library,* p. 7), and acquired by William A. White at the dispersal of that library in 1905. Presentation inscription to the Elizabethan Club from W. A. White, 10 November 1918.

Gift of William A. White, November 1918.

STC 3674

BRISSET, GEORGE

EC 17
Apology of
G. Brisset
1610

The apologie of George Brisset, Lord of Gratence. Written vpon consideration of the inhumane murther of the late French king. . . . Translated out of French into English. Printed for William Barley, and Iohn Baily. 1610.

4°. A–D⁴ 17.9 cm.

Unbound; stitched, as issued, with its original price ("iijᵈ") marked on the wrapper.

Gift of Henrietta C. Bartlett, 1934.

STC 3791

BROWNE, SIR THOMAS, 1605–1682

EC +5
Pseudodoxia
Epidemica
1650

Pseudodoxia epidemica: or, enquiries into very many received tenents, and commonly presumed truths. By Thomas Browne Dr of Physick. The second edition, corrected and much enlarged by the author. . . . London, printed by A. Miller, for Edw. Dod and Nath. Ekins, at the Gunne in Ivie Lane. 1650.

Fol. A–Xx⁴Yy² 27.8 cm.

The second edition (first, 1646). Bound in modern half calf. Signature of Danl. Costeker on front flyleaf. Signature of Max Förster and date, 9 January 1909, on the title page.

Gift of Max Förster, 1935.

Wing B 5160

BROWNE, SIR THOMAS, 1605–1682

EC 18
Religio
Medici
1642

[*Religio Medici*] [Engraved title page by William Marshall, with imprint:] Printed for Andrew Crooke. 1642.

8°. [-]¹A–M⁸ 13.2 cm.

The first unauthorized edition, with twenty-five lines to a page. Bound in red goatskin, gold tooling on cover and spine, gilt edges. The Hoe copy (with bookplate), with the signature of Robert Hoe, Jr., on the flyleaf; sold by Anderson Auction Co., New York, 25 April 1911, lot 518.

Gift of A. Conger Goodyear, 1912

Wing B 5166   Keynes 1

Browne's *Religio Medici*, 1643 (EC 18)
The title page engraved by William Marshall

BROWNE, SIR THOMAS, 1605–1682

EC 19
Religio
Medici
1642

[*Religio Medici*] [Engraved title page by William Marshall, with imprint:] Printed for Andrew Crooke. 1642.

8°. [–]¹A–K⁸   14.1 cm.

The second unauthorized edition, with twenty-six lines to a page. Bound in contemporary calf, blind tooling on the cover. Signatures of Hinery Norton and Hinery Briggs and the second flyleaf, and the inscription: "M. F. Christopher Bequeathed H. W. T. 1848."

Gift of Walter B. James, 1913.

Wing B 5167   Keynes 2

BUNYAN, JOHN, 1628–1688

EC 20
Pilgrim's
Progress
1680

The pilgrim's progress from this world to that which is to come. . . . By John Bunyan. The fourth edition, with additions. . . . London, printed for Nath. Ponder, at the Peacock in the Poultrey near the Church, 1680.

12°. A–M¹²N⁶ (lacking A₁, frontispiece)   13.9 cm.

The fourth edition, fourth issue (first, 1678). Bound by Rivière in purple goatskin, gold tooling on cover and spine, gilt edges. The Birket Foster copy, with two bookplates; sold as lot 3 in the Birket Foster sale, Sotheby's, 11 June 1894.

Given to the club in 1912.

Wing B 5560

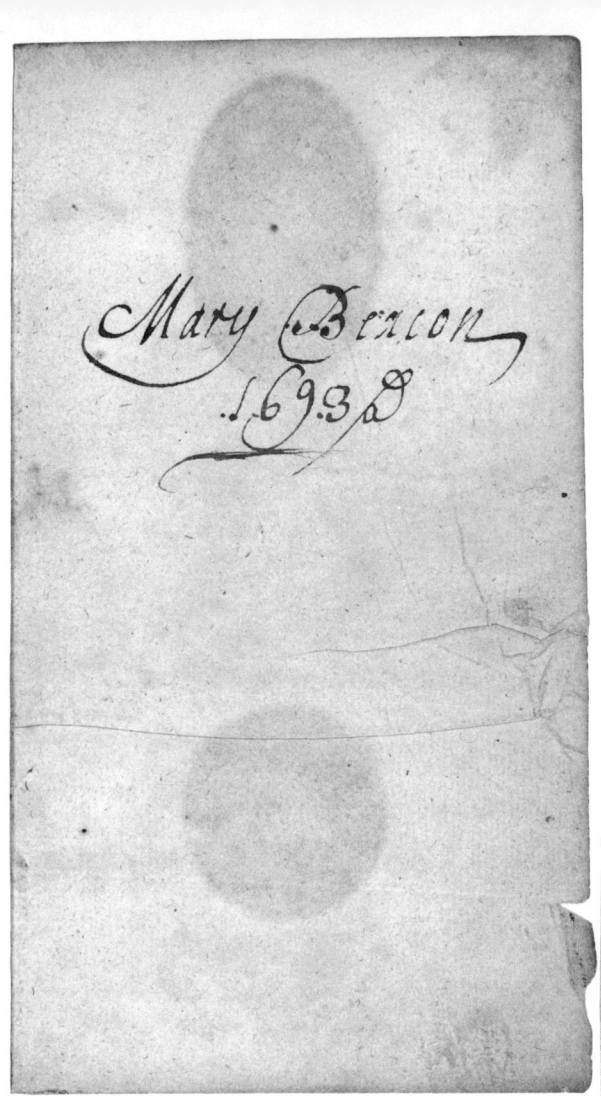

Bunyan's *Pilgrim's Progress*, 1683 (EC 21)
The ownership inscription and bookplates on the front end papers

BUNYAN, JOHN, 1628–1688

EC 21
Pilgrim's
Progress
1683

The pilgrim's progress.... By John Bunyan, the ninth edition with additions.... London, printed for Nathaniel Ponder at the Peacock in the Poultrey, near the Church, 1683.

12°. A⁶B–K¹²   13.9 cm.

Bound in contemporary sheepskin, blind tooling on cover. Signature of Mary Beacon, 1693, on the front flyleaf. Bookplates of Henry Huth (lot 1099 in the Huth sale, Sotheby's, 23 November 1911), Harold Murdock, and Chauncey Brewster Tinker.

Gift of Chauncey Brewster Tinker.

Wing B 5569

BURTON, ROBERT, 1577–1640

EC +6
Anatomy of
Melancholy
1638

[Engraved title page, without letterpress:]
The anatomy of melancholy. What it is, with all the kinds causes, symptomes, prognostickes & seuerall cures of it.... By Democritus Junior.... the fift. edition, corrected and augmented by the author. ... Oxford printed for Henry Cripps. 1638.

Fol. §⁴(§₁+χ₁)A–K⁴§²A–R⁴S⁶T–Hh⁴Ii⁶ Ll–4E⁴F²4G–5A⁴ (lacking Ll₁, cancel)   27.6 cm.

The fifth edition (first, 1621). Bound in contemporary speckled calf, blind tooling on cover and spine. Signature of John Harvey on front flyleaf, and armorial bookplate of Baron Vernon on the front endpaper.

Gift of Arthur Milliken, 1926.

STC 4163

BUTTES, HENRY, d. 1632

EC 22
Dyets Dry
Dinner
1599

Dyets dry dinner: consisting of eight seuerall courses: 1. Fruites 2. Hearbes. 3. Flesh. 4. Fish. 5. Whitmeats. 6. Spice. 7. Sauce. 8. Tabacco. . . . By Henry Buttes, Maister of Artes, . . . Printed in London by Tho. Creede, for William Wood, and are to be sold at the west end of Powles, at the signe of Tyme. 1599.

8°. $A^8 Aa^4 B–P^8$ (lacking A_1, and P_8, blanks). 13.5 cm.

The first edition. Bound in full calf. Signature of Tho. Starkey on the title page. A burn has damaged the first four leaves of sheet P, resulting in a loss of a few words on each page.

Gift of William A. White, 1912.

STC 4207

CALLIÈRES, JACQUES DE, d. 1697

EC 23
Courtier's
Calling
1675

The courtier's calling: shewing the ways of making a fortune, and the art of living at court, according to the maxims of policy & morality. . . . By a person of honour. London: printed by J. C. for Richard Tonson, at Grays-inne gate in Grays-inne Lane. 1675.

12°. $A^6 B–L^{12} M^6$ 15 cm.

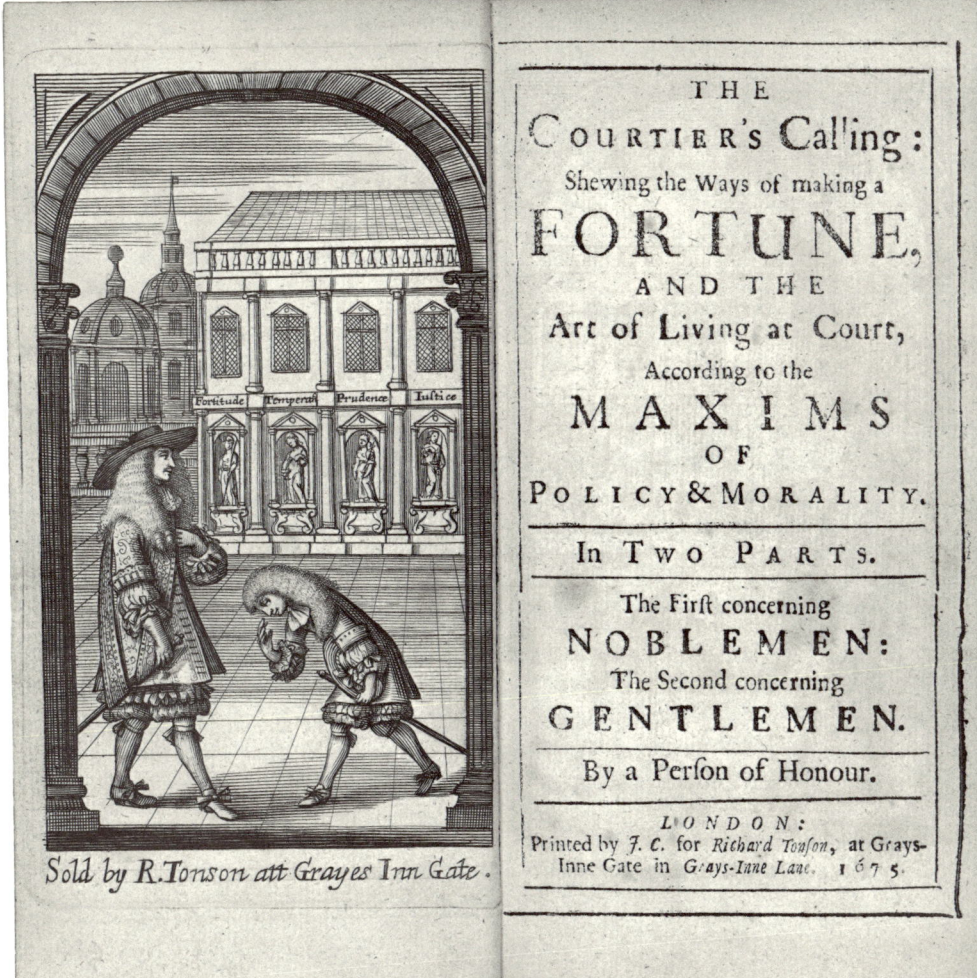

Callières' *Courtier's Calling*, 1675 (EC 23)
The frontispiece and title page

Translated by Edward Clark, and printed by James Cottrell (?). The first edition in English of *La Fortune des Gens de Qualité* (Paris, 1665). Bound by Rivière in calf, gold tooling on cover and spine, gilt edges. The first book published bearing the name of Tonson in its imprint. Bookplates of William Crampton and Henry Walker.

Gift of Alexander S. Cochran, December 1911.

Wing C 301

CALVIN, JEAN, 1509–1564

EC 24
Institutes
1577

. . . Institvtio Christianae Religionis. . . . Lavsannae, excudebat Franciscus le Preux, illustriss. dominorum Bernensium typographus. M D LXXVII

8°. ★-★★^{8}a–z^{8}A–Li^8 18.8 cm.

Bound in contemporary full vellum. This volume has an interesting association with two noted Reformed Dutch clergymen. It bears a presentation inscription to the Reverend John Frelinghuysen (d. 1754) dated 27 February 1748, from Stephen Loos; and the signature of the Reverend John Nels Abeel (d. 1812) on the title page. Presentation inscription from Louis V. Davison to Stuart W. Jackson, dated March 1908, on the front endpaper.

Gift of Stuart W. Jackson, 1940.

CAMDEN, WILLIAM, 1551–1623

EC 25
Annals
1625

[Engraved title page, without letterpress:] Annales rervm Anglicarvm, et Hibernicarvm, regnante Elizabetha, autore Gvil. Camdeno. . . . Lvg. Batavorvm ex officina Elzeviriana. M DC XXV.

8°. ★-★★⁸A–Kkk⁸ 18 cm.

The revised edition of the first part and the first edition of the second part. Bound in contemporary vellum. The first part, concerning the reign of Queen Elizabeth, had been first printed in 1615; the second part, relating to Mary Stuart, was printed in this edition for the first time, as King James had not permitted its publication in England. Signature "Cossart" on the title page and date, 8 June 1626. Ownership inscription of the Bibliotheca Abbatis Fierdepied and date, 1750, on front and rear endpapers, and bookplate of the Bibliotheca Turkheimiana.

Gift of Hollon A. Farr, March 1934.

CAMDEN, WILLIAM, 1551–1623

EC +7
Annals
1630

The historie of the most renowned and victorious Princesse Elizabeth, late queene of England. . . . Neuer heretofore so faithfully and fully published in English. London: printed for Benjamin Fisher and are to be sold at his shop in Aldersgate Street, at the signe of the Talbot. MDCXXX.

Camden's *Annals*, 1630 (EC +7)
Sir Thomas Hanmer's armorial bookplate

Fol. [-]²A⁴B²B–T⁴(Aa)-(Pp)⁴Aa–Nn⁴Nn★³Oo–Rr⁴ Ss⁶3A–4E⁴4F⁷4G³   28.1 cm.

The first edition of this translation, by Robert Norton. Bound in contemporary speckled calf, blind tooling on cover. Armorial bookplate of Sir Thomas Hanmer, dated 1707, on verso of title page.

Gift of Philip Hofer, 1933.

STC 4500

CAMPION, THOMAS, d. 1620

The Discription of a Maske, 1607. See *The Masque of Flowers.*

CAPELLA, GALEAZZO FLAVIO, 1487–1537

EC 27
Anthropologia
1533

L'Anthropologia di Galeazzo Capella secretario dell' illvstrissimo signor Dvca di Milano. ... M.D. XXXIII. [Colophon:] In Venetia nelle case delli heredi d'Aldo Romano, & d'Andrea d'Asola, nell'anno M. D. XXXIII del mese di Genaro.

8°. A–I⁸K⁴   16 cm.

Printed in Aldine Italic type throughout. Bound by R. Storr in green straight-grain goatskin, silk doublures, gold tooling on cover and spine, anchor and dolphin device stamped on both sides, gilt edges. Signature of R. le Jay on title page and manuscript notes by him throughout. Bookplates of Sir John Hayford Thorold and Syston Park (lot 411 at the Syston Park sale, Sotheby's. 13 December

1884); bookplate of Jack Randall Crawford. Binder's ticket of R. Storr, Grantham.

Gift of Jack R. Crawford, 1912.

CAREW, RICHARD, 1555–1620, *translator*

See TASSO, TORQUATO

CAREW, THOMAS, 1595?–1639?

EC 29
Coelum
Britanicum
1634

Coelum Britanicum. A masque at White-hall in the banqvetting-hovse, on Shrove-Tvesday-Night, the 18. of February, 1633. . . . London: printed for Thomas Walkley, and are to be sold at his shop neare White-hall, 1634.

4°. [A]²B–E⁴F² (lacking [A]₁, blank)   17.7 cm.

The first edition, first issue. Bound in half green straight-grain goatskin. Collation note of Bernard Quaritch, Ltd., 25 March 1909. Acquired by Mr. Cochran from Quaritch in 1909.

Gift of Alexander S. Cochran, December 1911.

STC 4618   Greg 496(a)

CARTWRIGHT, WILLIAM, 1611–1643

EC 30
Royal Slave
1639

The royall slave. A tragi-comedy. Presented to the king and queene by the students of Christ-church in Oxford. August 30. 1636. . . . Oxford, printed by William Turner for Thomas Robinson. 1639.

4°. A–H⁴I²   18.5 cm.

The first edition. Bound in imitation vellum. Bookplate of Frederick Locker (*The Rowfant Library*, pp. 11–12), and acquired by Mr. Cochran at the dispersal of that library in 1905.

Gift of Alexander S. Cochran, December 1911.

STC 4717   Greg 570(a)

CARY, ELIZABETH, Lady Falkland, 1586–1639

EC 28
Mariam
1613

The tragedie of Mariam, the faire Queene of Iewry. Written by that learned, vertuous, and truly noble ladie, E. C. London. Printed by Thomas Creede, for Richard Hawkins, and are to be solde at his shoppe in Chancery Lane, neere vnto Sargeants Inne. 1613.

4°. [-]²A–H⁴I² (lacking [-]$_1$, blank, and A$_1$)   18.2 cm.

The first edition, second issue, in which the leaf A$_1$, containing the dedicatory verses and personae, has been suppressed. Bound by Rivière in crimson goatskin, gold tooling on cover and spine, gilt edges.

Gift of Alexander S. Cochran, December 1911.

STC 4613   Greg 308(AII)

CHAMBERLIN, ROBERT, *fl.* 1640–1660

EC 31
Swaggering
Damsel
1640

The swaggering damsell. A comedy. Written by R. C. . . . London. Printed by Tho. Cotes, for Andrew Crooke; and are to be sold at his shop, at the Green Dragon, in Pauls Church-yard. 1640.

4°. A–I⁴ (lacking A$_2$) 19.3 cm.

The first edition, second issue, in which the leaf A$_2$, containing the epistle and the first commendatory verses, has been suppressed. Bound by Rivière in red goatskin, gold tooling on cover and spine. The edges of this copy are entirely uncut. Inscription "Fraues Volketon(?) her bouk" on B$_1$; signature of Robert Mellvill on flyleaf.

Gift of Alexander S. Cochran, December 1911.

STC 4946   Greg 589(AII)

CHAPMAN, GEORGE, 1559?–1634

EC 258
Alphonsus
1654

The tragedy of Alphonsus Emperour of Germany as it hath been very often acted (with great applause) at the privat house in Black-friers by his late maiesties servants. By George Chapman Gent. London, printed for Humphrey Moseley, and are to be sold at his shoppe at the Princes-arms in St. Pauls Church-yard 1654.

4°. [A]²B–L⁴ 19.2 cm.

The first edition. Bound in calf, with the Perkins arms stamped in gold on the cover; sold with the library of Frederick Perkins, by Sotheby's, 11 July 1889, lot 419. Upper margins closely trimmed, shaving page numbers and running titles. Bookplate of Nathan T. Porter, Jr.

Gift of William Kelly Simpson, in memory of Nathan Todd Porter and Kenneth Farrand Simpson, March 1984.

Wing C 1952   Greg 729(A★)

CHAPMAN, GEORGE, 1559?–1634

EC 32
Andromeda
1614

Andromeda liberata. Or the nvptials of Persevs and Andromeda. By George Chapman. . . . London, printed for Lavrence L'Isle and are to be sold at his shop in St. Paules-Church-yard, at the signe of the Tigers-head. 1614.

4°. ¶-¶¶⁴A²B–E⁴F² (lacking ¶₁, probably blank) 17.7 cm

Bound by Sangorski and Sutcliffe in blue goatskin. Outer margins trimmed, with slight loss of text and catchwords.

Gift of Andrew Keogh.

STC 4964

CHAPMAN, GEORGE, 1559?–1634

EC 34
Caesar and
Pompey
1631

Caesar and Pompey: a roman tragedy, declaring their warres. . . . By George Chapman. London: printed by Thomas Harper, and are to be sold by Godfrey Emondson, and Thomas Alchorne. M.DC.XXXI.

4°. A–I⁴K² (lacking A₁, blank).   17.4 cm.

The first edition. Bound by Rivière in red goatskin, gilt edges. Collation note signed by G. Mudie, 22 June 1896, inside back cover.

Gift of Alexander S. Cochran, December 1911.

STC 4993   Greg 444(AI★)

CHAPMAN, GEORGE, 1559?–1634

EC 35
Conspiracy of
Byron
1608

The conspiracie, and tragedie of Charles Duke of Byron, Marshall of France. Acted lately in two playes, at the Black-friers. Written by George Chapman. Printed by G. Eld for Thomas Thorppe, and are to be sold at the Tygers Head in Paules Churchyard. 1608.

4°. [A]²B–R⁴ (lacking R$_4$, blank). 16.8 cm.

The first edition, the issue in which Byron's speech on H$_2$r contains the truncated fifth line, "So long as such as he." Bound in calf, blind tooling on cover. Signature of Curtis Thos. on P$_3$r. Collation note of Bernard Quaritch, Ltd., 8 December 1904. Closely trimmed in upper and lower margins, cutting into the running titles and catchwords.

Gift of Alexander S. Cochran, December 1911.

STC 4968   Greg 274 & 275

CHAPMAN, GEORGE, 1559?–1634

EC 36
Eastward Hoe
1605

Eastward hoe. As it was playd in the Black-friers. By the Children of Her Maiesties Reuels. Made by Geo: Chapman. Ben: Ionson. Ioh: Marston. At London printed for William Aspley. 1605.

4°. A–I⁴   17.5 cm.

The first edition, second issue, in which leaves E$_3$ and E$_4$, containing a speech reflecting on the Scots, have been replaced by cancels. Bound in three-quarter olive calf. Upper margin very closely trimmed, affecting text on the title page and the running titles.

Gift of Alexander S. Cochran, December 1911.

STC 4971   Greg 217 (aII)

CHAPMAN, GEORGE, 1559?–1634

EC 37
Free and
Offenseless
Justification
1614

A free and offenceles iustification, of a lately pvblisht and most maliciously misinterpreted poeme: entitvled Andromeda liberata. . . . London, printed for Lavrence L'Isle and are to be sold at his shop in Pauls Church-yard at the signe of the Tigers-head. 1614.

4°. ★-★★^{4} 17.6 cm.

Bound by Sangorski and Sutcliffe, in blue goatskin. Closely trimmed, affecting some catchwords and marginalia.

Gift of Andrew Keogh.

STC 4977

CHAPMAN, GEORGE, 1559?–1634

EC 38
Gentleman
Usher
1606

The gentleman usher. By George Chapman. At London printed by V. S. for Thomas Thorppe. 1 6 0 6.

4°. A–I^{4}K^2 17.1 cm.

Printed by Valentine Simmes. The first edition. Bound in three-quarter blue goatskin. Bookseller's note on rear flyleaf identifying this as Thomas Corser's copy; sold as lot 485 in the sale of his books at Sotheby's, 30 July 1868. Bookplates of Thomas Jolley (lot 656 in the sale of his books at Sotheby's, 9 June 1843) and Frederick Locker (*The Rowfant Library*, p. 13) (and presumably acquired by Mr. Cochran at the dispersal of his library in 1905).

Gift of Alexander S. Cochran, December 1911.

STC 4978   Greg 226

CHAPMAN, GEORGE, 1559?–1634

EC 39
May Day
1611

May-day. A witty comedie, diuers times acted at the Blacke Fryers. Written by George Chapman. London. Printed for Iohn Browne, dwelling in Fleetstreete in Saint Dunstones Church-yard. 1611.

4°. A–K⁴   17.9 cm.

The first edition. Bound by Rivière in crimson goatskin, green silk doublures, gilt edges.

Gift of Alexander S. Cochran, December 1911.

STC 4980   Greg 297

CHAPMAN, GEORGE, 1559?–1634

EC 40
M. d'Olive
1606

Monsievr d'Olive. A comedie, as it was sundrie times acted by her maiesties children at Blacke-friers. By George Chapman. London printed by T. C. for William Holmes, and are to be sold at his shop in Saint Dun-stons Church-yard in Fleete-streete, 1606.

4°. A–H⁴ (lacking H_4, blank)   17.9 cm.

Printed by Thomas Creede. The first edition. Bound by Rivière in red goatskin, gold tooling on cover and spine, gilt edges. Illegible name and date 1695(?), on title page.

Provenance not known.

STC 4983 Greg 236

CHAPMAN, GEORGE, 1559?–1634

EC 41
Revenge of
Bussy d'Ambois
1613

The revenge of Bussy D'Ambois. A tragedie. As it hath beene often presented at the priuate play-house in the White-fryers. Written by George Chapman, Gentleman. London: printed by T. S. and are to be solde by Iohn Helme, at his shop in S. Dunstones Church-yard, in Fleetstreet. 1613.

4°. A–K⁴ (lacking A₁, blank) 17.1 cm.

Printed by Thomas Snodham. The first edition. Bound in calf; Perkins arms stamped in gold on cover. Sold with the library of Frederick Perkins at Sotheby's, 11 July 1889, lot 413. The Huth copy (with bookplate), acquired by Mr. Cochran at the Huth sale, 6 June 1912, lot 1474.

Gift of Alexander S. Cochran, December 1913.

STC 4989 Greg 307

CHAPMAN, GEORGE, 1559?–1634

EC 42
Sir Gyles
Goosecappe
1606

Sir Gyles Goosecappe Knight. A comedie presented by the Chil: of the Chappell. At London. Printed by Iohn Windet for Edward Blunt. 1606.

4°. A–I⁴L² 18 cm.

The first edition. Bound by F. Bedford in three-quarter red goatskin, top edge gilt. Initials R. B. on title page. Bookseller's stock note on rear fly, referring to the Charles Henry Craufurd sale at Sotheby's, 12 July 1876 (lot 513). Bookplate of Frederick Locker (but not located in *The Rowfant Library*), and presumably acquired by Mr. Cochran at the dispersal of that library in 1905.

Gift of Alexander S. Cochran, December 1911.

STC 12050   Greg 228(a)

CHAPMAN, GEORGE, 1559?–1634

EC 44
Widow's Tears
1612

The widdowes teares. A comedie. As it was often presented in the Blacke and White Friers. Written by Geor. Chap. London, printed for Iohn Browne, and are to be sold at his shop in Fleet-street in Saint Dunstanes Church-yard. 1612.

4°. [A]²B–K⁴L²   18 cm.

The first edition. Bound by Rivière in dark green goatskin, top edge gilt.

Gift of Alexander S. Cochran, December 1911.

STC 4994   Greg 301

CHAPMAN, GEORGE, 1559?–1634, *translator*

See HOMER

CHAPMAN, GEORGE, 1559?–1634, and James Shirley

EC 33
The Ball
1639

The ball. A comedy, as it was presented by her majesties servants, at the private house in Drury Lane. Written by George Chapman, and James

Shirley. London, printed by Tho. Cotes, for Andrew Crooke, and William Cooke. 1639.

4°. A–I⁴ 18 cm.

The first edition. Bound by Rivière in dark green goatskin, top edge gilt.

Gift of Alexander S. Cochran, December 1911.

STC 4995

CHAPMAN, GEORGE, 1559?–1634, and James Shirley

EC 43
Chabot
1639

The tragedie of Chabot Admirall of France: as it was presented by her majesties servants, at the private house in Drury Lane. Written by George Chapman, and James Shirly. London, printed by Tho. Cotes, for Andrew Crooke, and William Cooke. 1639.

4°. A–I⁴ (lacking I₄, blank)   18.2 cm.

The first edition. Bound by Rivière in crimson goatskin, green silk doublures, gilt edges.

Gift of Alexander S. Cochran, December 1911.

STC 4996   Greg 550

CHETTLE, HENRY, 1560?–1607?

EC 45
Hoffman
1631

The tragedy of Hoffman or a reuenge for a father. As it hath bin diuers times acted with great applause, at the Phenix in Druery-lane. London, printed by I. N. for Hugh Perry, and are to bee sold at his shop, at the signe of the Harrow in Brittainesburse. 1631.

4°. [A]²B–K⁴L² 18.5 cm.

Printed by John Norton. The first edition. Bound by Zaehnsdorf in brown goatskin, gold tooling on cover, gilt edges. The Hoe copy (with bookplate), sold by Anderson Auction Co., New York, 25 April 1911, lot 731.

Gift of Alexander S. Cochran, December 1911.

STC 5125   Greg 438

CHURCH OF ENGLAND. HOMILIES. 1562

EC 259
Certain
Sermons
1562

Certaine sermons appoynted by the quenes maiestie, to be declared and read, by all persons, vicars and curates, euery Sundaye and holy daye, in theyr churches: and by her graces aduise perused and ouersene, for the better understandyng of the simple people. Newely imprinted in partes, accordynge as is mencioned in the boke of common prayers. 1562. Cum priuilegio regiae maiestatis. [Colophon:] Imprinted at London in Powles Churcheyarde, by Richard Jugge, and John Cawood prynters to the quenes maiestie. Cum priuilegio regiae maiestatis.

4°. A–Aa⁴ (lacking D_3–G_3)   17.5 cm.

The thirteenth (?) edition (first, 1547). Bound in half black goatskin, paper-covered boards. Some leaves remargined, occasionally affecting text. Signature of Alf. Holmead on title page (twice) and on D_2r. Bookplate of Nathan T. Porter, Jr.

Gift of William Kelly Simpson, in memory of Nathan Todd Porter and Kenneth Farrand Simpson.

STC 13650

CHURCHYARD, THOMAS, 1520?–1604

EC 250
Misery of
Flanders
1579

The miserie of Flavnders, calamitie of Fraunce, misfortune of Portugall, unquietness of Irelande, troubles of Scotlande: and the blessed state of Englande. Written by Tho. Churchyarde Gent. 1579. Imprinted at London for Andrewe Maunsell, dwellyng in Paules Church-yard at the signe of the Parret.

4°. [-]¹A–B⁴C³D–E⁴   18.3 cm.

The first edition. Bound in green goatskin, gold tooling on cover and spine, gilt edges. The Britwell Court copy, sold at Sotheby's, 29 March 1971, lot 95.

Purchased 1979.

STC 5243

CICERO, MARCUS TULLIUS

EC 46
Cato Major
1569

The worthye booke of old age otherwyse entituled the elder Cato, contayning a learned defence and praise of age, and aged men: written in Latine by . . . Marcus Tullius Cicero, and now Englished. . . . Anno. 1569 Imprinted at London by Thomas Marshe.

8°. ‡⁸A–I⁸   13.2 cm.

Translated by Thomas Newton. The first edition of the second English translation of this work. Bound by F. Bedford in sprinkled calf, gold tooling on cover and spine. Signature of Ra: Browne on title page. Bookplate of William Edward Bools (sold at Sotheby's, 23 June 1903, lot 355).

Gift of Alexander S. Cochran, December 1911.

STC 5294

CLARK, EDWARD, *translator*

See CALLIÈRES, JACQUES DE

COMMON CONDITIONS

EC 47
Common
Conditions
[1576]

An excellent and pleasant comedie, termed after the name of the vice, Common Condicions, drawne out of the most famous historie of Galiarbus Duke of Arabia, . . . Imprinted at London by William How, for Iohn Hunter, dwellynge of London Birdge [*sic*], at the signe of the Blacke Lion. [1576]

4°. A–G^4 17 cm.

The first edition. Bound by Rivière in crimson goatskin, morocco, gold tooling on cover and spine. Edges cropped, with some loss of marginal text. The Mostyn copy, sold at Sotheby's, 1 June 1907, lot 437.

Gift of Alexander S. Cochran, December 1911.

STC 5592   Greg 69

CORNEILLE, PIERRE, 1606–1684

EC 49
Heraclius
1664

Heraclius, Emperour of the East. A tragedy. Written in French by Monsieur de Corneille. Englished by Lodowick Carlell, Esq; London, printed for John

Starkey, at the Mitre between the Middle-Temple gate and Temple-bar in Fleetstreet. 1664.

4°. A–I⁴ (lacking A₁, probably blank)   21.6 cm.

Bound by the Club Bindery in half brown goatskin. The Hoe copy (with bookplate), sold by Anderson Auction Co., New York, 25 April 1911, lot 639.

Gift of Alexander S. Cochran, December 1911.

Wing C 6310

THE COSTLY WHORE

EC 50
Costly Whore
1633

The costlie whore. A comicall historie acted by the companie of the revels. London printed by Augustine Mathewes, for William Sheares, and are to be sold at this shoppe in Brittaines Burse. 1633.

4°. A–H⁴ (lacking A₁, blank)   18.9 cm.

The first edition, with variant imprint. Bound by Rivière in red goatskin, gilt edges.

Provenance not traced.

STC 25582a   Greg 472(a+)

CURTIUS RUFUS, QUINTUS

EC 51
Curtius Rufus
1553

The historie of Qvintvs Curcius, conteyning the actes of the greate Alexander translated out of Latine into Englishe by Iohn Brende. 1553. Imprinted at London by Rycharde Tottell. . . .

4°. A⁴B–Y⁸Aa–Gg⁸Hh²   18.5 cm.

The first edition in English. Bound in limp vellum. The William Horatio Crawford copy (with bookplate), sold at Sotheby's, 23 March 1891, lot 2611.

Provenance not traced.

STC 6142

D., J.

EC 52
Knave in
Grain
1640

The knave in graine, new vampt. A witty comedy, acted at the Fortune many dayes together with great applause. Written by J. D. Gent. London: printed by J. O. and are to be sold by John Nicholson at his shop under St. Martins Church neare Ludgate. 1640.

4°. A²B–L⁴M² 18.1 cm.

Printed by John Okes. The first edition. Bound in half red goatskin. Signature erased from front flyleaf; date 1818 remains. Title page altered in ink to read "by T. D. Gent." Bookseller's collation note signed I. T. and dated 18 June 1902 on rear flyleaf.

Gift of Alexander S. Cochran, December 1911.

STC 6174 Greg 580

DALLINGTON, SIR ROBERT, 1561–1637

EC +8
Aphorisms
1613

Aphorismes civill and militarie: amplified with authorities, and exemplified with historie, out of the first quarterne of Fr. Guicciardine. . . . London, imprinted for Edward Blovnt. 1613.

Fol. A–Tt⁴Vv⁶Xx–Eee⁴ 27.5 cm.

The first edition. Bound in contemporary calf, gold tooling on cover and spine. Signatures of Joshua

Scotto, 1677/8, and Jo. Brandon, 1724, on front flyleaf, and signature of T. Davis, 8 October 1807, on page 83, repeated at the end of the text. Several signatures cut from title page, which has been re-margined. Repairs and water stains throughout.

Gift of Alfred L. Ripley, 1922.

STC 6197

DANIEL, SAMUEL, 1562–1619

EC 53
Certain
Small Poems
1605

[Certain Small Poems . . . London, 1605]

8°. A–H⁸A–F⁸ (lacking A$_1$, title; H$_8$, blank; and F$_{7,8}$, blank) 15.2 cm.

Title in manuscript facsimile. This edition, the third collected edition, contains the first edition of *Philotas* and of the short poem *Vlisses and the Syren*. Bound by Charles Smith in dark pink calf, gold tooling on cover and spine, gilt edges. The Edward Vernon Utterson copy (with bookplate), sold by Sotheby's, 21 March 1857, lot 380. Acquired by William A. White from the library of Henry F. Sewall, sold by Bangs and Co., New York, 9 November 1896, lot 971. Inscription on flyleaf from W. A. White to the Elizabethan Club, 10 November 1918.

Gift of William A. White, November 1918.

STC 6239   Greg 223(a)

D'AVENANT, SIR WILLIAM, 1606–1668

EC 54
Cruel
Brother
1630

The crvell brother. A tragedy. As it was presented, at the priuate house, in the Blacke-fryers: by his maiesties seruants. London, imprinted by A. M. for Iohn Waterson, and are to bee solde at the signe of the Crowne in Pauls Church-yard. 1630.

$4°$. A–K^4 (lacking A$_1$, blank) 19 cm.

Printed by Augustine Mathewes. The first edition. Bound by Rivière in crimson goatskin, gilt edges.

Gift of Alexander S. Cochran, December 1911.

STC 6302   Greg 427(a)

D'AVENANT, SIR WILLIAM, 1606–1668

EC 55
Platonic Lovers
1636

The platonick lovers. A tragaecomedy. Presented at the private house in the Black-fryers, by his majesties servants. The authour William D'Avenant, servant to her majestie. London, printed for Richard Meighen, next to the Middle Temple in Fleetstreet. 1636.

$4°$. A^4(–A$_4$)B–K^{4}L^1 18.9 cm.

The first edition. Bound in crimson goatskin, gilt edges.

Gift of Alexander S. Cochran, December 1911.

STC 6305   Greg 506(a)

D'AVENANT, SIR WILLIAM, 1606–1668

EC +9
Works
1673

The works of Sr William D'avenant Kt consisting of those which were formerly printed, and those which he design'd for the press: now published out of the authors originall copies. London: printed by T. N. for Henry Herringman, at the sign of the Blew Anchor in the lower walk of the New Exchange. 1673.

Fol. [-]⁴A–Ddd⁴Eee²A–Ppp⁴4A–4O⁴ 32 cm.

The first edition. Bound in contemporary mottled calf. Label of Myers & Co., booksellers, on front paste-down endpaper; unidentified armorial bookplate.

Provenance not known.

Wing D 320

EC +9
Copy 2

——Another copy, evidently a later issue. Bound in contemporary calf, rebacked. This copy lacks the portrait, has a corrected title page to *Madagascar*, and has the correct catchword on page 211 (second numbering). The name Collier is written on the title page.

Given in memory of Thomas Raynesford Lounsbury, by Mrs. Lounsbury, May 1915.

DAVENPORT, ROBERT, *fl.* 1623

EC 56
New Trick
1639

A pleasant and witty comedy: called, a new tricke to cheat the divell. Written by R. D. Gent. London: printed by Iohn Okes, for Humphrey Blunden, and are to be sold at his shop in Corne-hill, next to the Castle Taverne. 1639.

4°. A–I⁴K² 18.2 cm.

The first edition. Bound by Worsfold in sprinkled calf, gold tooling on cover and spine, gilt edges. The Hoe copy (with bookplate), sold by Anderson Auction Co., New York, 26 April 1911, lot 979. A slip laid into the volume records that when this volume was acquired at the Hoe sale by Mr. Cochran for Yale, the *Springfield Republican* commented, "We notice that Yale has paid $135 for A New trick to cheat the devil. Now let Harvard beware."

Gift of Alexander S. Cochran, December 1911.

STC 6315   Greg 561(AI)

DAVIES, JOHN, 1625–1693

See APPIANUS, of Alexandria

DAVIES, SIR JOHN, 1569–1626. *Epigrams*

See OVID

DAY, JOHN, 1574–1640?

EC 57
Blind Beggar
1659

The blind-beggar of Bednal-Green, with the merry humor of Tom Strowd the Norfolk yeoman, as it was divers times publickly acted by the princes servants. Written by John Day. London, printed for R. Pollard, and Tho. Dring, and are to be sold at the Ben Johnsons Head, behind the Exchange, and the George in Fleetstreet, near Saint Dunstans Church. 1659.

4°. A²B–K⁴L² (lacking A₁, blank)   18.5 cm.

The first edition. Bound by S. David in red goatskin, gold tooling on cover and spine, gilt edges. The Hoe copy (with bookplate), sold by Anderson Auction Co., New York, 26 April 1911, lot 1004.

Gift of Alexander S. Cochran, December 1911.

Wing D 464   Greg 801(A)

DAY, JOHN, 1574–1640?

EC 58
Isle of Gulls
1633

The ile of gvlls. As it hath been often acted in the Black Fryers, by the Children of the Revels. London, printed for William Sheares, at the Harrow in Britaines Bursse. 1633.

4°. A–H⁴   18.5 cm.

The second edition (first, 1606). Bound by Rivière in dark green goatskin, gilt edges.

Gift of Alexander S. Cochran, December 1911.

STC 6414   Greg 235(b)

A DECLARATION

EC 59
Declaration
1642

A declaration of the lords and commons assembled in parliament, for the appeasing and quietting of all unlawfull tumults and insurrections. . . . Also an ordinance of both houses, for the suppressing of stage-playes. . . . Septemb. 3. London printed for Iohn Wright. 1642.

4°. A⁴   17 cm.

The first edition. Bound by Rivière in crimson goatskin, gilt edges. This celebrated ordinance was the first of many to issue from the Long Parliament prohibiting all theatrical activity.

Gift of Alexander S. Cochran, December 1911.

Wing E 1411

DEKKER, THOMAS, 1570?–1641?

EC 62
Magnificent
Entertainment
1604

The whole magnificent entertainment: given to King James, . . . vpon the day of his majesties tryumphant passage (from the Tower) through his honorable citie . . . of London, the 15. of March. 1603. . . . Tho. Dekker. Imprinted at London by E. Allde for Tho. Man the yonger. 1604.

4°. A²B–I⁴   17.8 cm.

The second or third edition (first, 1604), the only edition having the Latin speeches translated into English. Bound by Rivière in crimson goatskin, gold tooling on cover and spine, gilt edges.

Provenance not traced.

STC 6513   Greg 202(b)

DEKKER, THOMAS, 1570?–1641?

EC 63
Whore of
Babylon
1607

The whore of Babylon. As it was acted by the princes seruants. . . . Written by Thomas Dekker London printed for Nathaniel Butter. 1607.

4°. A–K⁴L² (lacking L₂, blank)   18.3 cm.

The first edition. Bound by Rivière in red goatskin, gold tooling on cover and spine, gilt edges. The Frederick Locker copy (with bookplate; *The Rowfant Library,* p. 33), acquired by Mr. Cochran at the dispersal of that library in 1905.

Gift of Alexander S. Cochran, December 1911.

STC 6532   Greg 241(A)

DEKKER, THOMAS, 1570?–1641?, *The Witch of Edmonton*

See ROWLEY, WILLIAM, Thomas Dekker, and John Ford

DEKKER, THOMAS, 1570?–1641?, and John Webster

EC 60
Northward Hoe
1607

North-ward hoe. Sundry times acted by the Children of Paules. By Thomas Decker, and Iohn Webster. Imprinted at London by G. Eld, 1607.

4°. A–H⁴   17.9 cm.

The first edition. Bound by Clarke and Bedford in dark blue leather, gold tooling on cover and spine, gilt edges. The Huth copy (with bookplate), sold by Sotheby's, 11 June 1912, lot 2071. Acquired by Bernard Quaritch, Ltd., and listed as item 958 in their Catalog 318.

Provenance not traced.

STC 6539   Greg 250(A)

DEKKER, THOMAS, 1570?–1641?, and John Webster

EC 61
Westward Hoe
1607

West-ward hoe. As it hath beene diuers times acted by the Children of Paules. Written by Tho: Decker, and Iohn Webster. Printed at London, and to be sold by Iohn Hodgets dwelling in Paules Churchyard. 1607.

4°. A–H⁴I² 18.2 cm.

The first edition. Bound by Rivière in green goatskin, gilt edges. The Marshall Clifford Lefferts copy (with bookplate), acquired by Mr. Cochran at the dispersal of that library in 1902. This was the first of the "Hoe" plays. *Eastward Hoe* was a reply to it, as *Northward Hoe* was a reply to *Eastward Hoe*.

Gift of Alexander S. Cochran, December 1911.

STC 6540   Greg 257(A)

DEMOSTHENES

EC 64
Orations
1570

[Olynthiacae] The three orations of Demosthenes chiefe orator among the Grecians, in fauour of the Olynthians, . . . Englished out of the Greeke by Thomas Wylson Doctor of the Ciuill Lawes. . . . Imprinted at London by Henrie Denham. [Colophon:] Imprinted at London by Henrie Denham, dwelling in Pater Noster Rowe, at the signe of the Starre. . . . anno domini. 1570.

4°. [–]⁴★–★★⁴A–Y⁴ (lacking Y₄, blank)   18.2 cm.

The first edition in English. Bound in mottled calf, gilt edges. Signature of John Hull (twice) on title page. The Ashburnham copy, sold at Sotheby's,

2 July 1897, lot 1349, to Bernard Quaritch, Ltd.

Gift of Alexander S. Cochran, December 1911.

STC 6578

DOUGLAS, GAWIN, 1474?–1522, *translator*

See VIRGIL

DRYDEN, JOHN, 1631–1700

EC 65
Kind Keeper
1690

The kind keeper; or, Mr. Limberham: a comedy: as it was acted at the Duke's Theatre by his royal highnesses servants. Written by John Dryden, . . . London, printed for R. Bentley, and M. Magnes, at the the [sic] Post-House in Russel Street in Coventgarden. 1690.

4°. A–I⁴   21.9 cm.

The second edition (first, 1680). Bound in modern cloth, leather spine.

Gift of Albert Hoffman Atterbury, 1923.

Wing D 2298   MacDonald 85b

DRYDEN, JOHN, 1631–1700

EC 66
Secret Love
1679

Secret-love, or the maiden-queen: as it is acted by his majesties servants at the Theater Royal. Written by John Dryden, Esq; . . . London, printed by J. M. for Henry Herringman, at the sign of the Anchor, on the lower walk of the New-exchange, 1679.

4°. A–H⁴I² 20.2 cm.

The fourth edition (first, 1668). Bound in half brown goatskin with *The Tempest, The State of Innocence,* and *Sir Martin Marall.* Armorial bookplate of King William IV, as Duke of Clarence (apparently removed from an earlier binding).

Provenance not traced.

Wing D 2356   MacDonald 70c

DRYDEN, JOHN, 1631–1700

EC 66
Sir Martin
Marall
1678

Sr Martin Mar-all, or, the feign'd innocence. A comedy. As it was acted at his highness the Duke of York's Theater. London, printed for H. Herringman, at the sign of the Blue Anchor in the lower walk of the New Exchange. 1678.

4°. [A]²B–H⁴I² 20.2 cm.

The third edition (first, 1668). Bound in half brown goatskin with *The Tempest, The State of Innocence,* and *Secret Love.* Armorial bookplate of King William IV, as Duke of Clarence (apparently removed from an earlier binding).

Provenance not traced.

Wing D 2362   MacDonald 71c

DRYDEN, JOHN, 1631–1700

EC 66
The State of
Innocence
1678

The state of innocence, and fall of man: an opera. . . . By John Dryden, . . . London: printed by H. H. for Henry Herringman, at the Anchor in the lower walk of the New Exchange. 1678.

4°. A–H⁴   20.2 cm.

The third edition (first, 1668). Bound in half brown goatskin with *The Tempest, Sir Martin Marall,* and *Secret Love*. Armorial bookplate of King William IV, as Duke of Clarence (apparently removed from an earlier binding).

Provenance not traced.

Wing D 2374   MacDonald 81b

DRYDEN, JOHN, 1631–1700

EC 66
The Tempest
1676

The tempest, or the enchanted island. A comedy: as it is now acted at his highness the Duke of York's Theatre. London, printed by J. Macock, for Henry Herringman at the sign of the Blew Anchor in the lower walk of the New Exchange. M.DC.LXXVI.

4°. A–L⁴M² (lacking M₂, blank)   20.2 cm.

Third edition (first, 1670). Bound in half brown morocco with *The State of Innocence, Sir Martin Marall,* and *Secret Love*. Armorial bookplate of King William IV, as Duke of Clarence (apparently removed from an earlier binding).

Provenance not traced.

Wing S 2946   MacDonald 73C

The Mock Charter, 1591.

Mock
Charter
1591

ELIZABETH I, Queen of England, 1533–1603

Elizabetha Anglo[rum], id est a intore Angelo[rum] Regina fformosissima & felicissima. Too the disconsolate & retyred spryte, the hermyte of Tybolles. . . . : manuscript on vellum, written in a fine professional Chancery hand, elaborated with strapwork flourishes, signed at the end "P. Marbury" and signed on the verso by the Lord Chancellor, Sir Christopher Hatton, with the pendant second Great Seal of Elizabeth (designed and engraved by Nicholas Hilliard)
1591 May 10   ca. 26.5 cm.

This manuscript, a unique specimen of dramatic composition by Queen Elizabeth, represents the only surviving piece of stage property from the Elizabethan theater. It was passed from player to player during the great Theobalds Entertainment of 1591, and it is the only surviving original manuscript of any part of that Entertainment.

Elizabeth was entertained by her Lord High Treasurer, Lord Burghley, at his Hertfordshire house, Theobalds, between 10 and 20 May 1591. In a contemporary manuscript text of the entertainments at Theobalds (British Library, Egerton MS. 2623), there is preserved a fanciful speech by a "Hermit," delivered to the Queen on Burghley's behalf, in which, pleading for royal permission to retire from public life, he requests her to restore to him his "cell," namely, Theobalds. The present document was prepared as an answer to Burghley's request and grants the "Hermit," her "woorthely belooved Coounceloour," the right to retire to his "cave," his "own hoous," with "full & pacifik possession of all & every part thearof," and to be henceforth free from public duties if he so wishes. The text of this "charter" was printed in John Strype's *Annals of the Reformation* (1709), where it is described as having been "drawn up by the queen herself in a facetious style, to cheer the said treasurer." A highly characteristic example of Elizabethan wit, it has the form of a formal charter, certified and signed by Lord Chancellor Hatton, who is known to have taken part in a number of court entertainments. It bears the Great Seal and was no doubt read out and presented to Burghley, or to an actor representing him as a hermit. Instead of giving a simple answer to Burghley's request to retire from public life, Elizabeth evidently chose to enter into the spirit of the Hermit's request and frame her reply accordingly, having this charter drawn up by one of her chancery scribes and passed by Hatton under the Great Seal, as part of a prearranged performance for the amusement of the court on the first day of her visit to Theobalds.

The entertainment at Theobalds are described by E. K. Chambers in *The Elizabethan Stage* (II:247–248), Sir Walter Greg in the *Review of English Studies* (I[1924]:452–454), John Payne Collier in his *History of English Dramatic Poetry* (I:276), Alexander Dyce in *The Works of George Peele* (III:161–169), and John Nichols in his account of *The Progresses and Public Processions of Queen Elizabeth* (III:74).

Purchased 1985.

EVERY WOMAN IN HER HUMOR

EC 67
Every Woman in Her humor
1609

Everie woman in her humor. London printed by E. A. for Thomas Archer, and are to be solde at his shop in the Popes-head-pallace, neere the Royall Exchange. 1609.

4°. A–H⁴   18 cm.

Printed by Edward Allde. The first edition. Bound by Rivière in red goatskin, gold tooling on cover and spine, gilt edges.

Provenance not traced.

STC 25948   Greg 283(A)

FALLETTI, GIROLAMO, 1518?–1564

EC 68
De Bello Sicambrico
1557

Hieronymi Faleti de bello sicambrico libri IIII. Et eivsdem alia poemata, libri VIII. Aldus. Venetiis, M. D. LVII.

4°. A⁴a⁴B–MM⁴NN²   20.2 cm.

The first edition. Bound in vellum, label on spine. A former owner has inscribed his initial, T., on the title page.

Gift of Thomas Beer, 1913.

HIERONYMI FALETI
DE BELLO SICAMBRICO
LIBRI IIII.

ET EIVSDEM ALIA POEMATA,
LIBRI VIII.

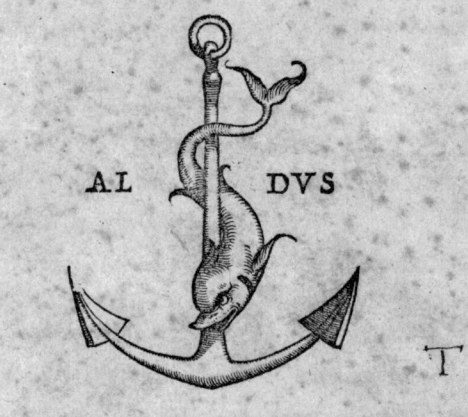

VENETIIS, M. D. LVII.

Falletti's *De Bello Sicambrico*, 1557 (EC 68)

FELICE, COSTANZO, *fl.* 1518

EC 48
Conspiracy of
Catiline
1557

The conspiracie of Catiline, written by Constancius, Felicius, Durantinus, and translated bi [*sic*] Thomas Paynell: with the historye of Jugurth, writen by the famous Romaine Salust, and translated into Englyshe by Alexander Barcklaye. [1557] [Colophon:] . . . imprinted at London in Foster Lane by Jhon Waley.

4°. A–X⁴Y⁶[-]²a–z⁴Aa–Hh⁴   18.8 cm.

The first combined edition of these two works. Bound in half calf. Collation note of Bernard Quaritch, Ltd., 13 August 1880, inside back cover.

Gift of Alexander S. Cochran, December 1911.

STC 10752

FENTON, SIR GEOFFREY, 1539?–1608, *translator*

See GUICCIARDINI, FRANCESCO

FLEMING, ABRAHAM, 1552?–1607, *translator*

See VIRGIL

FLETCHER, GILES, 1588?–1623

EC 69
Christ's
Victory
1632

Christs victorie and triumph in heaven and earth, over and after death. . . . The second edition. Cambridge: printed for Francis Green. 1632.

4°. A⁴¶⁴A–F⁴ (lacking A₁ of first gathering, and F₄, probably blank)   17.6 cm.

The second edition (first, 1610). Bound by J. Wright in calf, blind tooling on cover and spine. Indecipherable monogram (possibly B. L.) on title page. Signature of Henrietta C. Bartlett on endpaper, with note: "From: John Drinkwater London, June 17, 1923."

Gift of Henrietta C. Bartlett.

STC 11060

FLETCHER, JOHN, 1579–1625. *The Coronation*

See SHIRLEY, JAMES

FLETCHER, JOHN, 1579–1625

EC 72
Monsieur
Thomas
1639

Monsievr Thomas. A comedy. Acted at the private house in Blacke Fryers. The author, Iohn Fletcher, Gent. London, printed by Thomas Harper, for Iohn Waterson, and are to be sold at his shop in Pauls Church-yard, at the signe of the Crowne. 1639.

4°. [-]¹A²B–M⁴N²(-N₂)   18 cm.

The first edition. Bound in green goatskin, gilt edges.

Gift of Alexander S. Cochran, December 1911.

STC 11071   Greg 558(aI)

FLETCHER, JOHN, 1579–1625

EC 73
Night
Walker
1640

The night-walker, or the little theife. A comedy, as it was presented by her majesties servants, at the private house in Drury Lane. Written by John Fletcher. Gent. London, printed by Tho. Cotes, for Andrew Crooke, and William Cooke. 1640.

4°. A²B–K⁴   18.8 cm.

Revised by John Shirley. The first edition. Bound by Rivière in red goatskin, gilt edges.

Gift of Alexander S. Cochran, December 1911.

STC 11072   Greg 574(a)

FLETCHER, JOHN, 1579–1625

EC 74
Rule a Wife
1640

Rvle a wife and have a wife. A comoedy. Acted by his majesties servants. Written by John Fletcher Gent. Oxford, printed by Leonard Lichfield Printer to the University. Anno 1640.

4°. A–I⁴   18.3 cm.

The first edition. Bound in vellum, gold tooling on cover and spine. The Frederick Locker copy (with bookplate; *The Rowfant Library*, p. 43), acquired by Mr. Cochran at the dispersal of that library in 1905.

Gift of Alexander S. Cochran, December 1911.

STC 11073   Greg 598(a)

FLETCHER, JOHN, 1579–1625. *The Two Noble Kinsmen*

See SHAKESPEARE, WILLIAM, and John Fletcher

FLETCHER, JOHN, 1579–1625

EC 75
Wit without
Money
1639

Wit withovt money. A comedie, as it hath beene presented with good applause at the private house in Drurie Lane, by her majesties servants. Written by Francis Beamount, and John Fletcher. Gent. London printed by Thomas Cotes, for Andrew Crooke, and William Cooke. 1639.

4°. [A]¹B–I⁴(-I$_4$=A$_1$)   18.1 cm.

The first edition. Bound by S. David in crimson goatskin, gold tooling on cover and spine, gilt edges. This play was printed as Beaumont and Fletcher's, but it is now considered to be by Fletcher alone. The Hoe copy (with bookplate), sold by Anderson Auction Co., New York, 9 January 1912, lot 371.

Gift of Alexander S. Cochran, February 1912.

STC 1691   Greg 563(a)

FLETCHER, JOHN, 1579–1625

See also BEAUMONT, FRANCIS, and John Fletcher.

FLETCHER, JOHN, 1579–1625, and Philip Massinger

EC 71
Elder Brother
1637

The elder brother a comedie. Acted at the Blacke Friers, by his maiesties servants. . . . Written by Iohn Fletcher Gent. London, imprinted by F. K. for J. W. and J. B. 1637.

Fletcher and Massinger's *Elder Brother*, 1637
The first edition, 1637 (EC 71)

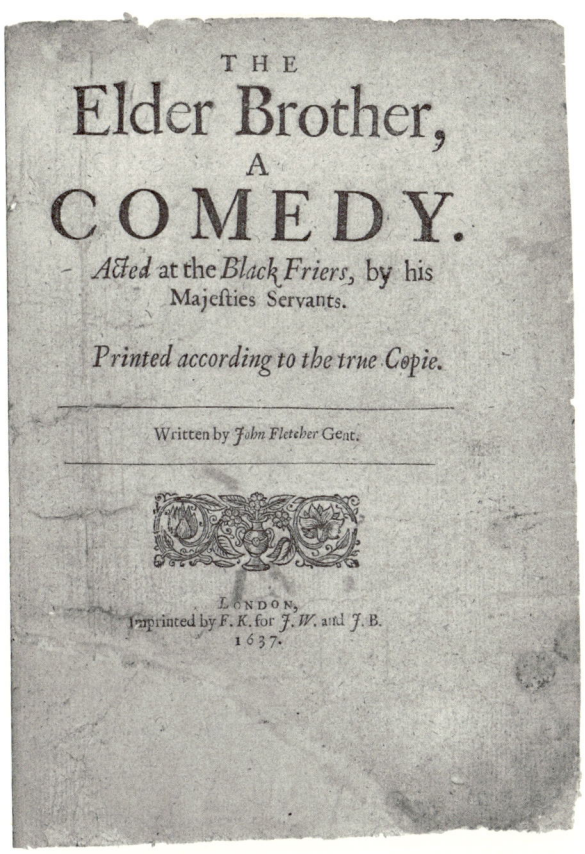

Another copy, variant b (EC 262)

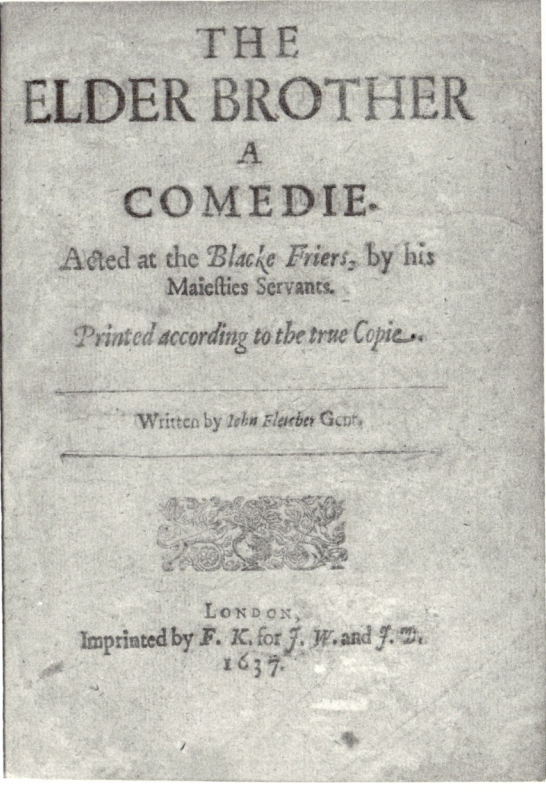

4°. [A]²B–I⁴K² 18 cm.

Printed by Felix Kingston for John Waterson and John Benson. The first edition. Bound by Rivière in green goatskin, gold tooling on cover and spine, gilt edges. Although Fletcher's name appears alone on the title page, this play is now considered to be by Fletcher and Massinger.

Gift of Alexander S. Cochran, December 1911.

STC 11066   Greg 515(a)

EC 262
Elder Brother
1637

———Another copy, 19.5 cm., edges uncut. Greg 515, variant b. According to Greg, although this edition bears the date 1637, as does variant a, this reprint was probably made several years later and comes from a different press. It is earlier than Greg 515(d), 1661, and may be later than Greg 515(c), 1651. The text is distinguished from that of variant a (EC 71, above) by the frequent use of a titling-font in place of ordinary capitals. Bound by Rivière in dark purple goatskin, gold tooling on covers and spine. Bookplate of Nathan T. Porter, Jr., and signature of W. K. Simpson, dated 1947.

Gift of William Kelly Simpson, in memory of Nathan Todd Porter and Kenneth Farrand Simpson, February 1985.

STC 11067   Greg 515(b)

FLETCHER, JOHN, 1579–1625, Phillip Massinger, and possibly others

EC 70
Bloody Brother
1639

The bloody brother. A tragedy. By B. J. F. London, printed by R. Bishop, for Thomas Allott, and Iohn Crook, and are to be sold in Pauls Churchyard, at the signe of the Greyhound 1639

4°. A⁴(-A₄=g₁)B–G⁴g¹G–I⁴ (lacking A₁, blank) 18.5 cm.

The first edition. Bound by S. David in red goatskin, gilt tooling on cover and spine, gilt edges. The Hoe copy (with bookplate), sold by Anderson Auction Co., New York, 27 April 1911, lot 1337.

Gift of Alexander S. Cochran, December 1911.

STC 11064   Greg 565(a)

FLETCHER, PHINEAS, 1582–1650

EC 76
Sicelides
1631

Sicelides a piscatory, as it hath beene acted in Kings Colledge, in Cambridge. London, printed by I. N. for William Sheares, and are to be sold at his shoppe, at the great south doore of St. Pauls Church. 1631.

4°. A²B–L⁴   18 cm.

Printed by John Norton, Jr. The first edition. Bound by Rivière in brown goatskin, gilt edges. Closely trimmed in upper margin, affecting some running heads.

Gift of Alexander S. Cochran, December 1911.

STC 11083   Greg 443(A)

THE BROKEN HEART.

A Tragedy.

ACTED
By the KINGS Majesties Seruants
at the priuate House in the
BLACK-FRIERS.

Fide Honor.

LONDON:
Printed by I. B. for HVGH BEESTON, and are to
be sold at his Shop, neere the Castle in
Corne-hill. 1633.

Ford's *Broken Heart*, 1633 (EC 77)

FLORIO, JOHN, 1553?–1625, *translator*

See MONTAIGNE, MICHEL EYQUEM DE

FORD, JOHN, 1586–1640?

EC 77
Broken Heart
1633

The broken heart. A tragedy. Acted by the kings majesties seruants at the priuate house in the Black-friers. Fide honor. London: printed by I. B. for Hvgh Beeston, and are to be sold at his shop, neere the Castle in Corne-hill. 1633.

4°. A–K⁴ (lacking A₁, blank)   19.2 cm.

Printed by John Beale. The first edition. *Fide Honor,* on the title page, is an anagram for Iohn Forde. Bound by Rivière in red goatskin, gilt edges. A few leaves are mended.

Provenance not traced.

STC 11156   Greg 480(A)

FORD, JOHN, 1586–1640?

EC 79
Fancies,
Chaste and Noble
1638

The fancies, chast and noble: Presented by the queenes maiesties servants, at the Phoenix in Drury-lane. Fide Honor. London, printed by E. P. for Henry Seile, and are to be sold at his shop, at the Tygers Head in Fleetstreet, over-against Saint Dunstans Church. 1638.

4°. A⁴(A₁ + a²)B–K⁴   18.5 cm.

Printed by Elizabeth Purslowe. The first edition. Bound by Rivière in crimson goatskin, gilt edges. Signature of J. Fleming and comment, "Pleasant," on title page.

THE LADIES TRIALL.

ACTED
By both their Majesties Servants
at the private house in
DRVRY LANE.

FIDE HONOR
John Ford

LONDON,
Printed by E. G. for *Henry Shephard*, and are to be
sold at his shop in *Chancery-lane* at the signe of
the Bible, between Sarjants Inne and Fleet-street,
neare the Kings-head Taverne. 1639.

Ford's *Lady's Trial*, 1639 (EC 80)
The title page annotated by Narcissus Luttrell

Gift of Alexander S. Cochran, December 1911.

STC 11159   Greg 532(A)

FORD, JOHN, 1586–1640?

EC 80
Lady's Trial
1639

The ladies triall. Acted by both their majesties servants at the private house in Drvry Lane. Fide Honor. London, printed by E. G. for Henry Shephard, and are to be sold at his shop in Chancery-lane at the signe of the Bible, between Sarjants Inne and Fleet-street, neare the Kings-head Taverne. 1639

4°. A–K⁴ (lacking A₁, blank)   18.8 cm.

Printed by Edward Griffin, Jr. The first edition. Bound by Rivière in red goatskin, gilt edges. Narcissus Luttrell's copy, with his record of price ("8d.") and the author's name inscribed on the title page.

Provenance not known.

STC 11161   Greg 555(A)

FORD, JOHN, 1586–1640?

EC 81
Lover's
Melancholy
1629

The lovers melancholy. Acted at the private hovse in the Black friers, and publikely at the Globe by the kings maiesties seruants. London, printed for H. Seile, and are to be sold at the Tygers Head in Saint Pauls Church-yard. 1629.

4°. A–M⁴   17.4 cm.

The first edition. Bound by Rivière in dark green goatskin, gilt edges.

Gift of Alexander S. Cochran, December 1911.

STC 11163   Greg 420(A★)

FORD, JOHN, 1586–1640?

EC 78
Perkin Warbeck
1634

The chronicle historie of Perkin Warbeck. A strange truth. Acted (some-times) by the queenes maiestie's servants at the Phenix in Drurie Lane. Fide Honor. London, printed by T. P. for Hugh Beeston, and are to be sold at his shop, neere the Castle in Cornehill. 1634.

4°. A–K⁴[L]¹   17.9 cm.

Printed by Thomas Purfoot, Jr. The first edition. Bound by Rivière in crimson goatskin, gold tooling on cover and spine, gilt edges.

Gift of Alexander S. Cochran, December 1911.

STC 11157   Greg 491(A★)

FORD, JOHN, 1586–1640?

EC 82
Sun's Darling
1656

The sun's-darling: a moral masque: as it hath been often presented at Whitehall, by their majesties servants; and after at the Cock-pit in Drury Lane, with great applause. Written by John Foard and Tho. Decker Gent. London, printed by J. Bell, for Andrew Penneycuicke, anno dom. 1656

4°. A–F⁴G²   17.7 cm.

The first edition. Bound by Rivière in red goatskin, top edge gilt.

Gift of Alexander S. Cochran, December 1911.

Wing F 1467   Greg 767(AI+)

FORD, JOHN, 1586–1640?

EC 83
'Tis Pity
She's a Whore
1633

'Tis pitty shee's a whore acted by the queenes maiesties seruants, at the Phoenix in Drury-lane. London, printed by Nicholas Okes for Richard Collins, and are to be sold at his shop in Pauls Churchyard, at the signe of the Three Kings. 1633.

4°. A²B–K⁴   16.9 cm.

The first edition. Bound by Rivière in speckled calf, gilt edges. Bridgewater Library duplicate stamp on verso of title page.

Gift of Alexander S. Cochran, December 1911.

STC 11165   Greg 486(AI)

FORD, JOHN, 1586–1640? *The Witch of Edmonton*

See ROWLEY, WILLIAM, Thomas Dekker, and John Ford

FORTUNIO, GIOVANNI FRANCESCO, *fl.* 1515

EC 84
Regole
Grammaticali
1552

Regole grammaticali della volgar lingva, di Messer Francesco Fortvnio. . . . Aldi filii M D LII.

8°. A–F⁸G⁴   15.1 cm.

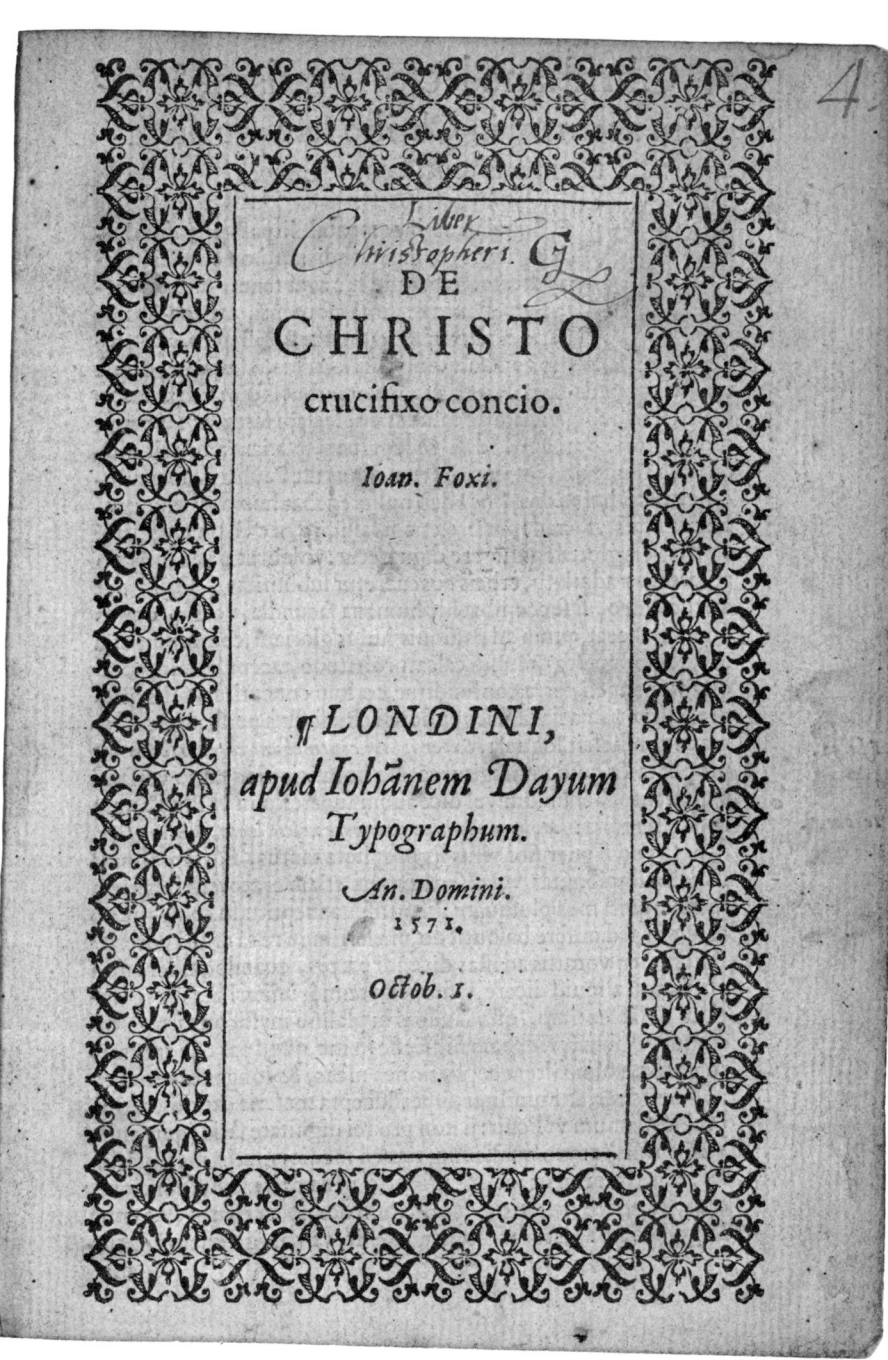

Foxe's *De Christo Crucifixo*, 1571 (EC 260)

The fifteenth edition (first, 1516). Bound in olive calf, gold tooling on cover and spine, gilt edges. Bookplates of Sir John Hayford Thorold and Syston Park (lot 807 at the Syston Park sale, Sotheby's, 16 December 1884).

Provenance not traced.

FOXE, JOHN, 1516–1587

EC 260
De Christo
Crucifixo
1571

De Christo crucifixo concio. Ioan. Foxi. Londini, apud Johānem Dayum typographum. an. domini. 1571. Octob. 1.

4°. A–Ee⁴ (lacking Ee$_4$, probably blank)   17.3 cm.

The first edition in Latin. Bound in half brown calf, marbled-paper-covered boards. This elaborate sermon was preached in English at Paul's Cross on Good Friday, 1571, on the occasion of the publication of the papal bull excommunicating Queen Elizabeth. A few marginal notes in a contemporary hand, and the inscription "Liber Christopheri G" on the title page. "Auctio Sussexiana Julii 29mo 1844" written on the front paste-down endpaper. Part I, consisting of theology, of the library of Augustus Frederick, Duke of Sussex, was sold by Evans, the sale beginning on 1 July 1844; but this volume is not individually described in the catalog for the sale of the day noted here. Bookplates of Samuel Chick and Nathan T. Porter, Jr.

Gift of William Kelly Simpson, in memory of Nathan Todd Porter, and Kenneth Farrand Simpson, March 1984.

STC 11247

FULWELL, ULPIAN, *fl.* 1590

EC 85
Like Will
to Like
1587

A pleasant enterlude, intituled, like will to like quoth the deuill to the collier. . . . Made by Vlpian Fulwel. . . . London printed by Edward Allde, and are to be solde at the long shop adioyning vnto Sainte Mildreds Church in the Pultrie. 1587.

4°. A–E⁴F² 18 cm.

The second edition (first, 1568). Bound by Rivière in red goatskin, gold tooling on cover and spine. The Mostyn copy, sold at Sotheby's, 1 June 1907, lot 448.

Gift of Alexander S. Cochran, December 1911.

STC 11474   Greg 50(c)

GARNET, HENRY, 1555–1606, *defendant*

EC 263
A True and
Perfect Relation
1606

A trve and perfect relation of the whole proceedings against the late most barbarous traitors, Garnet a Iesuite, and his confederats: contayning sundry speeches deliuered by the Lords Commissioners at their arraignments, . . . the Earle of Northamptons speech . . . and lastly all that passed at Garnets execution. Imprinted at London by Robert Barker, printer to the kings most excellent maiestie. 1606.

4°. A–Fff⁴ 19 cm.

This issue, one of three in 1606, is the variant with the imprint in four lines. Bound in contemporary limp vellum, with an early owner's initials, IS, stamped on both sides. Signature of Alexʳ Foulis

A TRVE AND PERFECT RELA-TION OF THE WHOLE
proceedings against the late most
barbarous Traitors, *Garnet* a Iesuite,
and his Confederats:

Contayning sundry Speeches deliuered
by the Lords Commissioners at their Arraign-
*ments, for the better satisfaction of those that were
hearers, as occasion was offered;*

The Earle of Northamptons Speech hauing
*bene enlarged vpon those grounds which
are set downe.*

And lastly all that passed at Garnets
Execution.

¶ IMPRINTED AT
London by ROBERT BAR-
KER, Printer to the Kings most
Excellent Maiestie. 1606.

A True and Perfect Relation, 1606 (EC 263)
The official account of the Gunpowder Plot prosecutions

on the title page, and bookplate of William Twopenny. Bookseller's collation note, 29 May 1902, on rear endpaper. This was the official account of the prosecutions occasioned by the Gunpowder Plot; Henry Garnet was tried before a special commission at the Guildhall, London, 28 March 1606, and executed on 3 May 1606.

Gift of William Kelly Simpson, in memory of Nathan Todd Porter and Kenneth Farrand Simpson, February 1985.

STC 11619a

GASCOIGNE, GEORGE, 1525?–1577

EC 86
Glass of Government
1575

The glasse of gouernement. A tragicall comedie. . . . Done by George Gascoigne Esquier. 1575. . . . Imprinted at London for C. Barker [Colophon:] Imprinted at London by H M for Christopher Barker at the signe of the Grasshopper in Paules Churchyarde, anno domini. 1575.

4°. $A^4 A-M^4 N^2$ (lacking A_1 of the first gathering, blank, and N_2, blank)   16.9 cm.

Printed by Henry Middleton. The first edition, second issue, with the errata and without the printer's name. Bound in straight-grain green goatskin, blind and gold tooling on cover and spine, gilt edges. Bookplate of Frederick Locker (*The Rowfant Library*, pp. 46–47), and acquired by Mr. Cochran at the dispersal of that library in 1905.

Gift of Alexander S. Cochran, December 1911.

STC 11643   Greg 68(AII)

GETHING, RICHARD, 1585?–1625?

EC +10
Copy Book
1616

[Engraved title page, without letterpress:] A coppie-booke of the usuall hands written: sett foorth by Richard Gething Mr. in writinge; and are to bee soulde at his house in Fetterlane, London, at the signe of the Hande and Golden Penne. Anno 1616.

28 leaves, unsigned. 18 cm.

Bound by Lloyd in sprinkled calf, gold tooling on cover and spine, gilt edges.

Given to the club in 1913.

Gething's *Copy Book*, 1616 (EC +10)

INSTRVCTION
SVR L'HERBE PETVM
DITTE EN FRANCE L'HERBE
de la Royne ou Medicée : Et sur la racine
MECHIOCAN principalement (auec
quelques autres Simples rares & exquis)
exemplaire à manier philosophique-
ment tous autres Vegetaux.

Par I. G. P.

ENVIE, D'ENVIE, EN VIE.

A PARIS.
Par Galiot du Pré, Libraire iuré: ruë S. Iaques,
à l'enseigne de la Galere d'or.
1572.

Gohory's *l'Herbe Petum*, 1572 (EC 87)
The earliest published work on tobacco

GOHORY, JACQUES, d. 1576

EC 87
l'Herbe Petum
1572

Instrvction svr lherbe petvm. . . . Et sur la racine Mechiocan. . . . Par I. G. P. . . . A Paris. Par Galiot du Pré, Libraire iuré: ruë S. Iaques, à l'enseigne de la Galere d'Or. 1572.

8°. A–B⁸A⁸ (Leaves 4 and 5 have been misbound [in the wrong order] after the first leaf of Part II.) 15.5 cm.

The first edition of the earliest published work devoted chiefly to tobacco. Bound in half calf, marbled-paper-covered boards. Signature of J. Decaisne on endpaper; presentation inscription to the Elizabethan Club from William A. White, 10 November 1918, on the flyleaf.

Gift of William A. White, November 1918.

Arents 67

GOLDING, ARTHUR, 1536–1605?, *translator*

See OVID

GREENE, THOMAS, d. 1612

EC 88
A Poet's Vision
1603

A poets vision, and a princes glorie. . . . Written by Thomas Greene Gentleman. Imprinted at London for William Leake. 1603.

4°. A–C⁴ (lacking A₁, probably blank)   17.6 cm.

The first edition. Bound in calf, blind tooling on cover. Sold at Sotheby's, 20 June 1903, lot 745 ("Property of a Lady") to Bernard Quaritch. Quaritch collation note, dated 23 June 1903, on rear endpaper.

Gift of Alexander S. Cochran, December 1911.

STC 12311

GRENEWAY, RICHARD, *translator*

See TACITUS, CORNELIUS

GUICCIARDINI, FRANCESCO, 1438–1540

EC +38
History
1618

The historie of Gvicciardin: containing the warres of Italie and other parts, continued for manie yeares under sundrie kings and princes, together with the variations and accidents of the same. . . . Reduced into English by Geffray Fenton. The third edition, diligently reuised, . . . London, imprinted by Richard Field, and are to be sold by Arthur Iohnson. 1618

Fol. A–4A^6 (lacking A$_1$, probably blank) 33.5 cm.

The third edition (first, 1579). Bound in contemporary speckled calf, rebacked. Signature of W. Bowyer on title page.

Gift of Warren H. Smith, 1976.

STC 12460

GUTENBERG, JOHANN, 1397?–1468, *printer*

See BIBLE, LATIN

HARINGTON, SIR JOHN, 1561–1616

EC 89
Epigrams
1615

Epigrams both pleasant and seriovs, written by that all-worthy knight, Sir Iohn Harrington: and neuer before printed. . . . London imprinted for Iohn Budge, and are to be sold at his shoppe at the south dore of Pauls, and at Britaines Burse. 1615.

4°. A–F^4 17.7 cm.

The first edition. Bound by Rivière in blue goatskin, gilt edges. Three engraved portraits have been inserted, two of Harington (one contemporary, the other dated 1796) and the other of William Herbert, Earl of Pembroke, the dedicatee.

Gift of Alexander S. Cochran, December 1911.

STC 12775

HAWKINS, SIR RICHARD, 1562?–1622

EC +11
Observations
1622

The observations of Sir Richard Hawkins Knight, in his voiage into the South Sea. Anno domini 1593. . . . London printed by I. D. for Iohn Iaggard, and are to be sold at his shop at the Hand and Starre in Fleete-streete, neere the Temple gate. 1622.

Fol. [-]^{3}A–Y^4 28.4 cm.

The first edition. Bound by W. Pratt in green goatskin, gold tooling on cover and spine, gilt edges. Signature of the bookseller Samuel G. Drake, 1844, on verso of title page with this inscription: "This copie of Sir R. Hawkins Observations is probably the same used by the poet Southey in writing his Naval History. I bought it when a great number of the laureat's books were sold at auction in Boston, Dec. 20th, 1844." The Huth copy (with book-plate), sold as lot 3522 in the Huth sale, 10 June 1913, and sold again with the Huth unsold and imperfect books, 27 February 1922, lot 95. At the second sale it was purchased by Bernard Quaritch and later sold to Franklin M. Crosby, Jr.

Gift of Franklin M. Crosby, Jr., March 1924.

STC 12962

HERRICK, ROBERT, 1591–1674

EC 90
Hesperides
1648

Hesperides: or, the works both humane & divine of Robert Herrick Esq. . . . London printed for John Williams, and Francis Eglesfield, and are to be sold by Tho: Hunt, book-seller in Exon. 1648.

8°. [A]^{4}B–Cc^{8}Aa–Ee^8 17 cm.

The first edition, first issue, with the Exeter imprint. Leaf C_7 is a cancel. Bound in contemporary calf, blind tooling on cover and spine. Signature of D. Travers, 1782, on [A]$_1$r.

Gift of Alexander S. Cochran, December 1911.

Wing H 1595

HEYWOOD, JOHN, 1497?–1580

EC 91
Four P's
[1555?]

The playe called the foure P a new and very mery enterlude of a palmer. A pardoner. A poticary. A pedler. Made by John Heewode. [Colophon:] Imprinted at London by Wyllyam Copland. [1555?]

4°. [A]⁴B–E⁴   17 cm.

The second edition (first, 1544?). Bound by Rivière in red goatskin, gold tooling on cover and spine. Very closely trimmed at top and bottom margins, with loss of signatures and shaving of text. The Mostyn copy, sold at Sotheby's, 1 June 1907, lot 451.

Gift of Alexander S. Cochran, December 1911.

STC 13301   Greg 21(b)

HEYWOOD, THOMAS, d. 1641

EC 92
Apology
for Actors
1612

An apology for actors. Containing three briefe treatises. 1 Their antiquity. 2 Their ancient dignity. 3 The true vse of their quality. Written by Thomas Heywood. . . . London, printed by Nicholas Okes. 1612.

4°. A⁴a⁴B–G⁴   17.5 cm.

The first edition. Bound in half olive calf. Bernard Quaritch collation note on rear endpaper, dated 13 December 1904.

Gift of Alexander S. Cochran, December 1911.

STC 13309

HEYWOOD, THOMAS, d. 1641

EC 93
English
Traveler
1633

The English traveller. As it hath beene publikely acted at the Cock-pit in Drury-lane: by her maiesties seruants. Written by Thomas Heywood. . . . London, printed by Robert Raworth: dwelling in

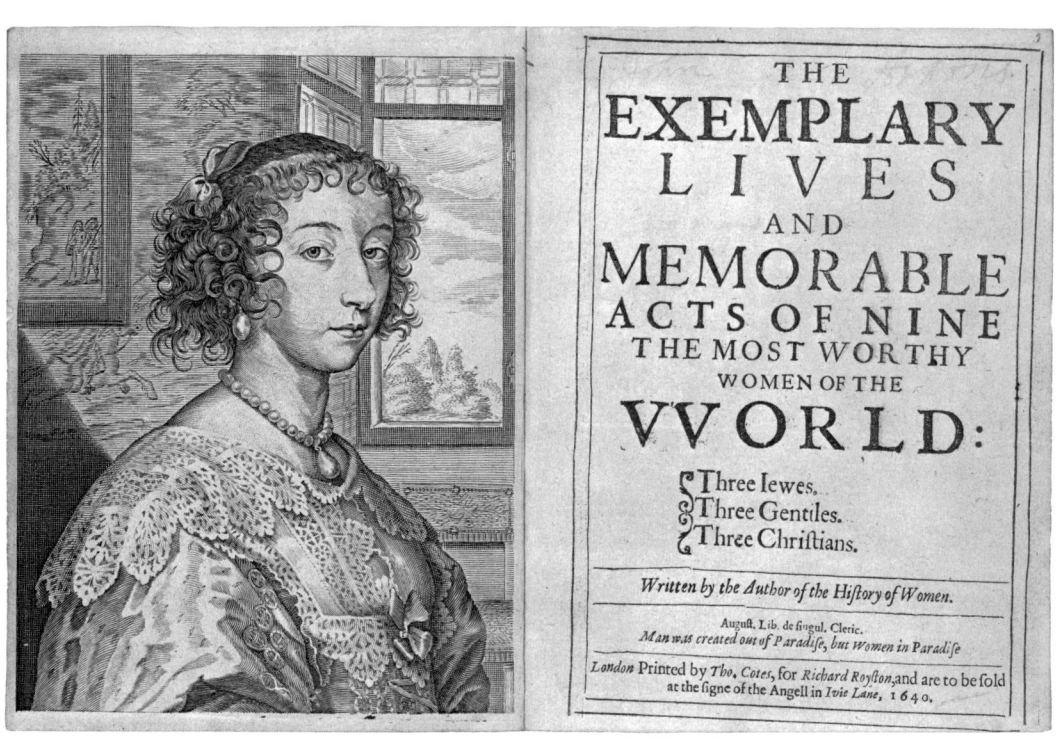

Heywood's *Exemplary Lives*, 1640 (EC 94)

Old Fish-street, neere Saint Mary Maudlins Church. 1633.

4°. A–K⁴   17.9 cm.

The first edition. Bound in half red straight-grain goatskin. Signature of John Mitford (1811) on flyleaf, and notes by Mitford on two flyleaves; sold in the Mitford sale, Sotheby's, 30 April 1860, lot 1858. Bookplate of Arthur Dalrymple; bookseller's collation note signed J. G. on front endpaper. Sold at the Adolphus F. Nichols sale, Sotheby's, 31 October 1903, lot 462, to B. F. Steevens, and sold by him to Mr. Cochran.

Gift of Alexander S. Cochran, December 1911.

STC 13315   Greg 484(A)

HEYWOOD, THOMAS, d. 1641

EC 94
Exemplary
Lives
1640

The exemplary lives and memorable acts of nine the most worthy women of the world: three Iewes. Three Gentiles. Three Christians. Written by the author of the history of women. . . . London printed by Tho. Cotes, for Richard Royston, and are to be sold at the signe of the Angell in Ivie Lane, 1640.

4°. ★–★★★⁴A–Ff⁴   18.5 cm.

The first edition. Bound in dark blue goatskin by Rivière, elaborate gold tooling on cover and spine, gilt edges. Signature of John Hibons on title page. Inscribed on flyleaf: "Oliver Burr Jennings from his Aunt Annie Burr Jennings on his being made a member of the Elizabethan Club at Yale 1917." Bookplate of Oliver Burr Jennings.

Gift of Oliver Burr Jennings.

STC 13316

HEYWOOD, THOMAS, d. 1641

EC 95
The Golden
Age
1611

The golden age. Or the liues of Jupiter and Saturne, with the defining of the heathen gods. As it hath beene sundry times acted at the Red Bull, by the queenes maiesties seruants. Written by Thomas Heywood. London, printed for William Barrenger, and are to be sold at his shop neare the great north-doore of Pauls 1611.

4°. A²B–I⁴K² 18.7 cm.

The first edition. Bound by W. Pratt in calf, gold tooling on cover and spine, gilt edges. Title and several leaves repaired, final leaf inserted from a shorter copy. The Hoe copy (with bookplate), sold by Anderson Auction Co., New York, 28 April 1911, lot 1687.

Gift of Alexander S. Cochran, December 1911.

STC 13325   Greg 294(A)

HEYWOOD, THOMAS, d. 1641

EC +12
Hierarchy
of the Angels
1635

[Engraved title page, without letterpress:] The hierarchie of the blessed angells. Their names, orders and offices. . . . Written by Tho. Heywood. . . . London printed by Adam Islop 1635.

Fol. ¶⁶A–Fff⁶Ggg⁴   27.1 cm.

The first edition. Bound in brown goatskin, gold tooling on cover and spine, signed by the unidentified binder (probably Fletcher Battershall) with a bat and the letter B. Bookplates of Fletcher and Maude Battershall and George Edward Dimock; bookseller's label of Joseph McDonough, Albany, New York. Penciled on the rear endpaper is the inscription: "11-24-1904 From J. M. D."

Gift of Samuel B. Hemingway.

STC 13327

HEYWOOD, THOMAS, d. 1641

EC 96
If you know
not me
1613

If you know not me, you know no bodie; or, the troubles of Queene Elizabeth. At London, printed for Nathaniel Butter. 1605. [*sic:* i.e., 1613]

4°. A–F⁴ (lacking A₁, probably blank)   17.7 cm.

The fifth edition (first, 1605). Title page repaired, the last letters of the imprint and date supplied (incorrectly) in facsimile. Bound by F. Bedford in green goatskin, gold tooling on cover and spine, gilt edges. The Hoe copy (with bookplate), sold by Anderson Auction Co., New York, 28 April 1911, lot 1684.

Gift of Alexander S. Cochran, December 1911.

STC 13328   Greg 215(e)

HEYWOOD, THOMAS, d. 1641

EC 97
If you know
not me, Pt. II
1606

The second part of, if you know not me, you know no bodie. . . . At London, printed for Nathaniell Butter. 1606.

4°. A–I⁴K² 18.7 cm.

The first edition. Bound by the Club Bindery, 1904, in red goatskin, red doublures. The Hoe copy (with bookplate), sold by Anderson Auction Co., New York, 28 April 1911, lot 1685.

Gift of Alexander S. Cochran, December 1911.

STC 13336 Greg 224(aI)

HEYWOOD, THOMAS, d. 1641

EC 98
Pleasant
Dialogues
1637

Pleasant dialogves and dramma's, selected ovt of Lucian, Erasmus, Textor, Ovid, &c. . . . By Tho. Heywood. . . . London, printed by R. O. for R. H. and are to be sold by Thomas Slater at the Swan in Duck-lane 1637.

8°. A–V⁸ 13.8 cm.

The first edition. Bound by W. Pratt in calf, gold tooling on cover and spine. Bookplate of William Horatio Crawford, and sold at Sotheby's, 18 March 1891, lot 1551. Collation note of Bernard Quaritch, Ltd., 19 March 1891, on rear endpaper.

Gift of Alexander S. Cochran, December 1911.

STC 13358

HEYWOOD, THOMAS, d. 1641

EC 99
Wise Woman
of Hogsdon
1638

The wise-woman of Hogsdon. A comedie. . . . Written by Tho: Heywood. . . . London, printed by M. P. for Henry Shephard, and are to be sold at his shop in Chancerie-lane, at the signe of the Bible, between Serjeants-inne and Fleete-street. 1638.

4°. A–I⁴ 17.6 cm.

Printed by Marmaduke Parsons. The first edition. Bound by Rivière in red goatskin, gold tooling on cover and spine, gilt edges.

Provenance not traced.

STC 13370   Greg 535(A)

HICKMAN, SPENCER, *translator*

See AULNOY, MARIE CATHERINE JUMELLE DE BERNEUILLE

HOLLAND, PHILEMON, 1552–1637, *translator*

See LIVY; PLINY, the younger; PLUTARCH

HOLYDAY, BARTEN, 1593–1661

EC 100
Τεχνογαμια
1618

Texnogamia [*sic*]: or the marriages of the arts. A comedie, written by Barten Holyday, Master of Arts, and Student of Christ-Church in Oxford, and acted by the students of the same house before the vniuersitie, at Shroue-tide. London printed by William Stansby for Iohn Parker, and are to be sold at his shop in Pauls church yard at the sign of the Ball. 1618.

4°. A–O⁴   18 cm.

The first edition. Bound by Rivière in dark blue goatskin, gold tooling on cover and spine, gilt edges. On O_4v is written an elaborate puzzle in the form of a rebus, dated 17 June 1618.

Gift of Alexander S. Cochran, December 1911.

STC 13617   Greg 353(a)

HOMER, *Iliad*

EC 101
Achilles'
Shield
1598

Achilles shield. Translated as the other seuen bookes of Homer, . . . By George Chapman Gent. London imprinted by Iohn Windet, and are to be sold at Paules Wharfe, at the signe of the Crosse Keyes. 1598.

4°. A–D⁴   19.2 cm.

The first edition. Bound with *Seaven Bookes of the Iliades,* 1598, *q.v.*

Gift of Alexander S. Cochran, December 1911.

STC 13635

HOMER, *Iliad*

EC 101
Iliad
1598

Seaven bookes of the Iliades of Homere, prince of poets, translated according to the Greeke, . . . by George Chapman Gent. . . . London. printed by Iohn Windet, and are to be solde at the signe of the Crosse-keyes, near Paules wharffe. 1598.

Chapman's Homer, 1598 (EC 101)
The title page, showing ownership inscriptions

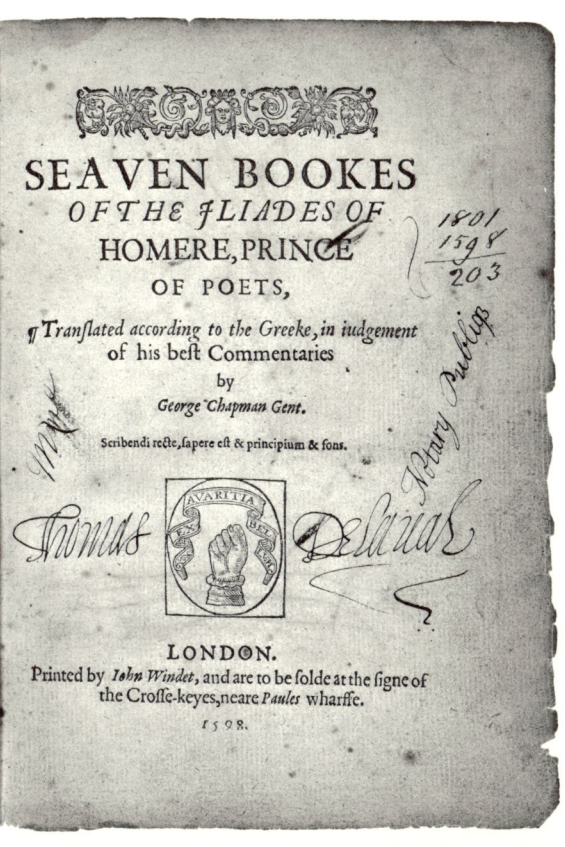

Verses on the fly leaf

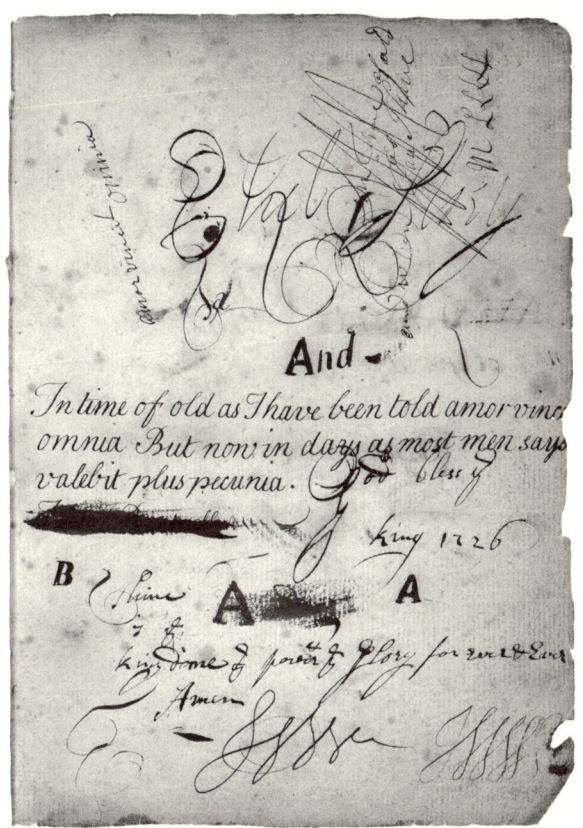

4°. A⁶B–S⁴   19.2 cm.

The first edition. Bound in contemporary vellum. Signature of Thomas Delaune on the title page, and ownership inscriptions of Eliel Story (1726) and John Dixon (22 February 1775) on front flyleaves. There is considerable scribbling on the flyleaves and title page of this copy. On the title page, a former owner has calculated its age in 1801 by subtracting 1598 from 1801, and on a flyleaf, underneath the Eliel Story inscription, another hand has written "Johannes Beadnell non est ejus liber." On another front flyleaf these lines are written:

> "In time of old as I have been told
> amor vincit omnia
> But now in days as most men says
> valebit plus pecunia."

Collation note of Bernard Quaritch, 5 November 1906, on rear endpaper. Bound with *Achilles Shield,* q.v.

Gift of Alexander S. Cochran, December 1911.

STC 13632

HORACE. *Ars Poetica*

EC 102
Art of
Poetry
1640

Q. Horatius Flaccus: his art of poetry. Englished by Ben: Jonson. . . . London: printed by J. Okes, for John Benson. 1640.

12°. A–D¹²(D₆₋₁₀ canceled) d¹²(inserted between D₅ and [D₁₁]) E¹²(E₅₋₁₁ canceled, E₁₂, blank, remaining) e¹²(inserted between E₄ and stub of [E₉])F–G¹²   14.3 cm.

The first edition. Bound in contemporary sheep, blind tooling on cover and spine. Inscribed on front flyleaf: "H. Allen. Ex dono dignissimi sui Am[ici] Francisci Bodenham Mi[noris] August 21. 1642."

Gift of Alexander S. Cochran, December 1911.

STC 13798

INGELAND, THOMAS, *fl.* 1560

EC 103
Disobedient
Child
[1569?]

A pretie and mery new enterlude: called the disobedient child. Compiled by Thomas Ingeland late student in Cambridge. Imprinted at London in Fletestrete, beneath the conduit by Thomas Colwell. [1569?]

4°. A–G^{4}H^2 18.4 cm.

The first edition. Bound by Rivière in crimson goatskin, gold tooling on cover and spine, gilt edges.

Gift of Alexander S. Cochran, December 1911.

STC 14085   Greg 54(A)

JACOB AND ESAU

EC 104
Jacob
and Esau
1568

A newe mery and wittie comedie or enterlude, newely imprinted, treating upon the historie of Iacob and Esau, . . . Imprinted at London by Henrie Bynneman, dwelling in Knightrider Streate, at the signe of the Mermayde. Anno domni. 1568.

4°. A–G^4 18.4 cm.

The first edition. Bound by Rivière in crimson goatskin, gold tooling on cover and spine, gilt edges.

Gift of Alexander S. Cochran, December 1911.

STC 14327   Greg 51(A)

JONSON, BEN, 1573?–1637

EC +16
Bartholomew
Fair
1631

Bartholmew Fayre: a comedie, acted in the yeare, 1614. By the Lady Elizabeths servants. And then dedicated to King Iames, of most blessed memorie; by the author, Ben: Iohnson. . . . London, printed by I. B. for Robert Allot, and are to be sold at the signe of the Beare, in Pauls Church-yard. 1631.

Fol. A^{6}B–M^4 (lacking A$_1$, probably blank) 28.2 cm.

Printed by John Beale. The first edition. Bound by Demander in red goatskin, with buckram sides.

Provenance not known.

STC 14753.5   Greg III, 1076–7

JONSON, BEN, 1573?–1637

EC +17
The Devil
Is an Ass
1631

The diuell is an asse: a comedie acted in the yeare, 1616. By his maiesties servants. The author Ben: Ionson. . . . London, printed by I. B. for Robert Allot, and are to be sold at the signe of the Beare, in Pauls Church-yard. 1631.

Fol. N–Y^4 29.1 cm.

Printed by John Beale. The first edition. Bound by Demander in red goatskin, with buckram sides.

Provenance not known.

STC 14753.5   Greg 457(a); III, 1076–7

JONSON, BEN, 1573?–1637

EC 107
Entertainment
of King James
1604

B. Jon: his part of King James his royall and magnificent entertainement through his honorable cittie of London, Thurseday the 15. of March. 1603. . . . Printed at London by V. S. for Edward Blount, 1604.

4°. A–E⁴F²A–B⁴   20.2 cm.

Printed by Valentine Simmes. The first edition. Bound by F. Bedford in red goatskin, gold tooling on cover and spine, top edge gilt. Bernard Quaritch collation note, dated 15 April 1905, on rear endpaper.

Gift of Alexander S. Cochran, December 1911.

STC 14756   Greg 200(a)

JONSON, BEN, 1573?–1637

EC 105
Every Man Out
of His Humor
1600

The comicall satyre of every man ovt of his hvmor. As it was first composed by the author B. I. . . . London, printed for Nicholas Linge. 1600.

4°. A–Q⁴   17.7 cm.

The third edition (first, 1600). Bound by Rivière

in red goatskin, gold tooling on cover and spine, gilt edges.

Provenance not traced.

STC 14769   Greg 163(c)

JONSON, BEN, 1573?–1637

EC 106
Fountain of
Self-love
1601

The fovntaine of selfe-love. Or Cynthias revels. As it hath beene sundry times priuately acted in the Black-friers by the Children of her maiesties Chappell. Written by Ben: Iohnson. . . . Imprinted at London for Walter Burre, and are to be solde at his shop in Paules Church-yard, at the signe of the Flower de-Luce and Crowne. 1601.

4°. A–L^{4}M^2 17.7 cm.

The first edition. Bound by Rivière in red goatskin, gold tooling on cover and spine, gilt edges.

Provenance not traced.

STC 14773   Greg 181(aI)

JONSON, BEN, 1573?–1637

EC 109
Jonsonus Virbius
1638

Ionsonvs virbivs: or, the memorie of Ben: Johnson revived by the friends of the muses. London, printed by E. P. for Henry Seile, and are to be sold at his shop, at the Tygers Head in Fleetstreet, over-against Saint Dunstans Church. 1638.

4°. A^{2}B–D^{4}d^{4}E–K^4[-]^2 20.4 cm.

Printed by Elizabeth Purslowe. The first edition. Bound by Rivière in green goatskin, gold tooling on cover and spine.

Gift of Alexander S. Cochran, December 1911.

STC 14784

JONSON, BEN, 1573?–1637

EC +18
Staple of
News
1631

The staple of newes. A comedie acted in the yeare, 1625. By his maiesties servants. The author Ben: Ionson. . . . London, printed by I. B. for Robert Allot, and are to bc sold at the signe of the Beare, in Pauls Church-yard. 1631.

Fol. Aa–Cc⁴D–H⁴I⁶   27.9 cm.

Printed by John Beale. The first edition. Bound by MacDonald in crimson goatskin, gold tooling on cover and spine, top edge gilt. Bookplate of Lansing Van der Heyden Hammond.

Gift of Lansing Van der Heyden Hammond.

STC 14753.5   Greg 456(a); III, 1076–7

JONSON, BEN, 1573?–1637

EC 108
Volpone
1607

Ben: Ionson his Volpone or the foxe. . . . Printed for Thomas Thorppe. 1607

4°. [-]²¶⁴A–N⁴O² (lacking [-]₁ and O₂, blank) 19 cm.

The first edition, first issue. Bound in half straight-grain purple goatskin.

Gift of Alexander S. Cochran, December 1911.

STC 14783   Greg 259(aI)

JONSON, BEN, 1573?–1637

EC +13
Works
1616

[Engraved title page, without letterpress:] The workes of Beniamin Jonson. . . . London printed by W. Stansby, and are to be sould by Rich. Meighen. Ano D. 1616.

Fol. ¶⁶A–4P⁶4Q⁴ (lacking ¶₁, probably blank) 29.2 cm.

The first edition, third issue (Meighen imprint). Rebound by C. Lewis, 1831, preserving portions of earlier, probably contemporary binding. Bookplate of William Gott, with a note by him that he had bought the volume at the Dent sale in 1827 and had it bound by Lewis; John Dent's books were sold by Sotheby's in two sales, 29 March and 25 April 1827, and this volume was lot 309 in the second sale. Tipped in on the front free endpaper is an autograph letter from William Gifford to Dent, 12 April 1815, thanking him for lending him this copy for use in preparing his edition of Jonson. On page 5 is a presentation inscription from Ben Jonson to Francis Young, and underneath it the initials R. G. The leaf with the presentation inscription has been remargined, and there are a few repairs elsewhere in the volume.

Gift of Alexander S. Cochran, December 1911.

STC 14751   Greg III, 1070–3

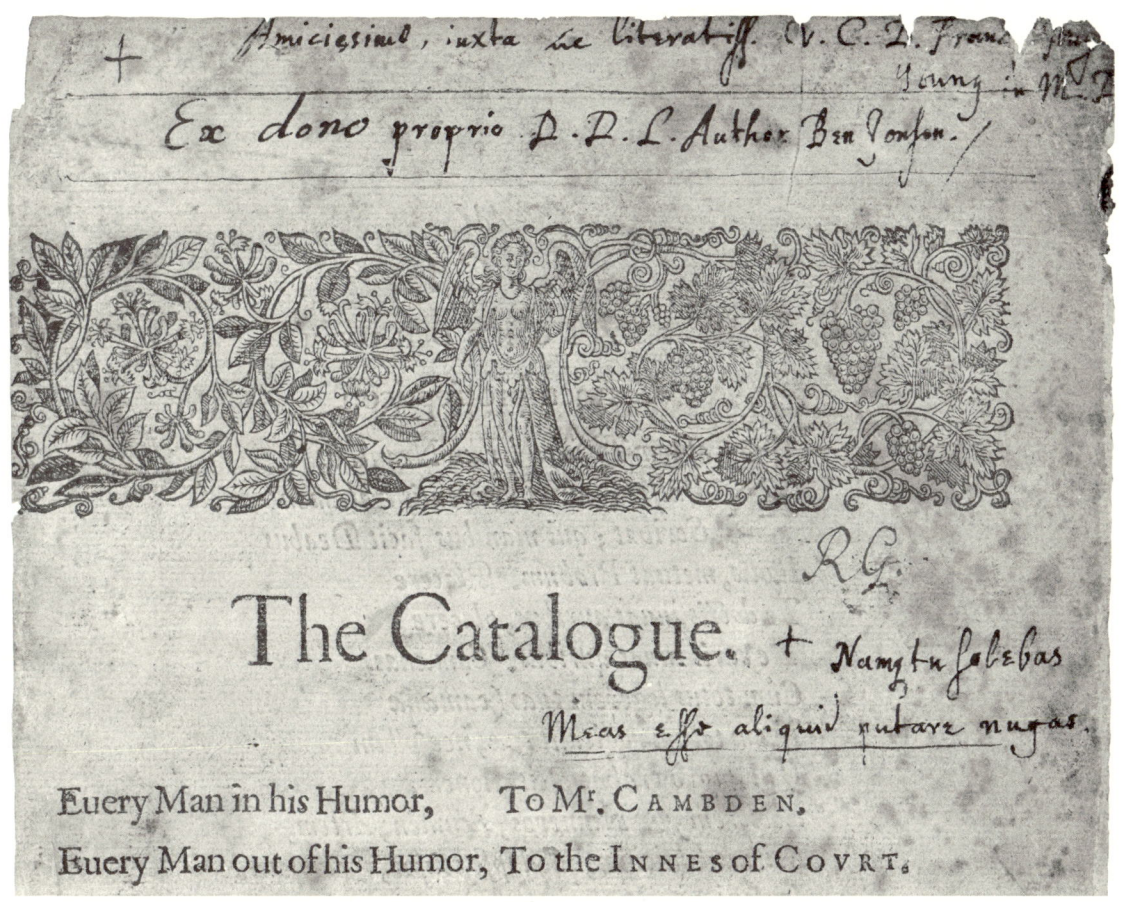

Jonson's *Works*, 1616 (EC +13)
The presentation inscription on page 5

JONSON, BEN, 1573?–1637

EC +14
Works
1640

[Engraved title page, without letterpress:] The workes of Benjamin Jonson. . . . London. Printed by Richard Bishop, and are to be sold by Andrew Crooke in St. Pauls, Church-yard. An D. 1640

Fol. A–Kkk⁶Lll⁴A–T⁶ (lacking A_1, portrait) 28.8 cm.

The second edition of the first volume. Bound in half blue goatskin, marbled-paper boards. Bookplate of Yale University Library (Edward Wells Southworth Fund), 1905.

Transferred from Yale University Library.

STC 14753   Greg III, 1073–5

JONSON, BEN, 1573?–1637

EC +15
Works
1640

The workes of Benjamin Jonson. The second volume. Containing these playes, viz. 1 Bartholomew Fayre. 2 The Staple of Newes. 2 The Divell is an Asse. London, printed for Richard Meighen, 1640.

Fol. A⁶B–M⁴Aa–Cc⁴D–H⁴I⁶N–Y⁴B–Q⁴R²S–X⁴ Y²Z⁴Aa–Oo⁴Pp²Qq⁴A–K⁴L²M–R⁴A–P⁴ Q²R–V⁴   27.4 cm.

The first edition. Bound by Demander in goatskin, gold tooling on cover and spine, gilt edges. The contents of this volume often appear in a different order from this copy. The edition includes the sheets of STC 14753.5 (EC+16, +17, +18), with additional plays and other works. Bookplate of James C. Morgan.

Gift of John Hill Morgan, 1925.

STC 14754   Greg III, 1070–7

JONSON, BEN, 1573?–1637, *translator*

See HORACE

THE KING AND QUEEN'S ENTERTAINMENT

EC 110
King and Queen's Entertainment
1636

The king and qveenes entertainement at Richmond. . . . In a masque, presented by the most illustrious prince, Prince Charles Sept. 12. 1636. . . . Oxford printed by Leonard Lichfield, M.DC.XXXVI.

4°. A–D⁴   18.2 cm.

The first edition. Bound in purple goatskin, gold tooling on cover and spine, gilt edges.

Gift of Alexander S. Cochran, December 1911.

STC 5026   Greg 512(A)

KYFFIN, MAURICE, d. 1599, *translator*

See TERENCE

LAMBARDE, WILLIAM, 1536–1601

EC 255
Duties of Constables
1599

The dveties of constables, borsholders, tythingmen, and such other lowe and lay ministers of the peace. . . . First collected by William Lambard of Lincolnes Inne Gent. 1582. and now enlarged by hime in the yeare 1599. London printed by Thomas Wight, and Bonham Norton, 1599. Cum priuilegio regiae maiestatis.

8°. A–E⁸   16.6 cm.

The ninth edition (first, 1582). Bound by Sangorksi and Sutcliffe in half red goatskin.

Gift of Henry H. Anderson, Jr., in memory of Wilmarth S. Lewis, December 1983.

STC 15152

LIVY

EC +19
Roman
History
1600

The Romane historie written by T. Livivs of Padva. . . . Translated out of Latine into English, by Philemon Holland, Doctor in Physicke. London, printed by Adam Islip. 1600.

Fol. [A]⁶B–6F⁶ (lacks A₁ and 6F₆, both blank) 32.7 cm.

The first edition in English. Bound in contemporary calf, rebacked, arms of Queen Elizabeth stamped on the cover. This was the first of Holland's translations to be published.

Gift of Alexander S. Cochran, December 1911.

STC 16613

LODGE, THOMAS, 1558–1625, *translator*

See SENECA, LUCIUS ANNAEUS

LOGGAN, DAVID, 1635–1700?

EC +03
Oxonia
Illustrata
1675

[Engraved title page, without letterpress:] Oxonia Illustrata, sive omnium celeberrimae istius universitatis collegiorum, aularum, bibliothecae Bodleianae, scholarum publicarum, theatri Sheldoniani; nec non urbis totius scenographia. Delineavit & sculpsit Dav: Loggan Univ. Oxon. Chalcographus. Oxoniae, e Theatro Sheldoniano ano. dni. M. DC. LXXV.

Fol. 5 leaves; 40 double plates.   44 cm.

Engraved throughout. Bound in contemporary speckled calf, rebacked.

Bequest of Alexander S. Van Santvoord, 1976.

Wing L2838

LYLY, JOHN, 1554?–1606

EC 111
Endymion
1591

Endimion, the man in the moone. Playd before the queenes maiestie at Greenewich on Candlemas day at night, by the Chyldren of Paules. At London, printed by I. Charlewood, for the widdowe Broome. 1591.

$4°$. A^2B-K^4 (lacking K_4, blank)   18.1 cm.

The first edition. Bound by Rivière in crimson goatskin, gold tooling on cover and spine, gilt edges.

Gift of Alexander S. Cochran, December 1911.

STC 17050   Greg 99(a)

Loggan's *Oxonia Illustrata*, 1675 (EC +03)

LYLY, JOHN, 1554?–1606

EC 112
Sappho and Phao
1591

Sapho and Phao, played beefore the queenes maiestie on Shroue-tewsday, by her maiesties Children, and the Boyes of Paules. Imprinted at London by Thomas Orwin, for William Brome. 1591

4°. A–F²–G² 18 cm.

The second edition (first, 1584). Bound by Rivière in crimson goatskin, gold tooling on cover and spine, gilt edges.

Gift of Alexander S. Cochran, December 1911.

STC 17087 Greg 82(c)

MABBE, JAMES, 1572?–1642

See ROJAS, FERANDO DE

MARLOWE, CHRISTOPHER, 1564–1593

EC 114
Hero and Leander
1622

Hero and Leander: begunne by Christopher Marloe, and finished by George Chapman. . . . London, printed by G. P. for Edward Blount: and are to be sold at his shop in Pauls Churchyard, at the signe of the Blacke Beare. 1622.

4°. A–M⁴ 18.8 cm.

Printed by George Purslowe. The tenth edition (first, 1598). Bound in brown leather, blind tooling on cover, gilt edges. The Trentham Hall copy, with the Sutherland crest stamped in gold on the cover, sold by Sotheby's, 22 November 1906, lot 1084. Bernard Quaritch collation noted on rear endpaper, dated 22 November 1906. A corner of the title page has been replaced, losing part of the ornament.

Gift of Alexander S. Cochran, December 1911.

STC 17420

MARLOWE, CHRISTOPHER, 1564–1593

EC 113
The Jew of Malta
1633

The famous tragedy of the rich Iew of Malta. As it was playd before the king and qveene, in his majesties theatre at White-hall, by her majesties servants at the Cock-pit. Written by Christopher Marlo. London; printed by I. B. for Nicholas Vavasour, and are to be sold at his shop in the Innertemple, neere the Church. 1633.

4°. A–I⁴K² (lacking, A₁, blank)   18.7 cm.

Printed by John Beale. The earliest surviving edition, not the first. Bound by Rivière in red goatskin, gold tooling on cover and spine, gilt edges.

Provenance not known.

STC 17412   Greg 475(A)

MARLOWE, CHRISTOPHER, 1564–1593, *translator*

See OVID

MARMION, SHACKERLEY, 1603–1639

EC 115
The Antiquary
1641

The antiquary. A comedy, acted by her maiesties servants at the Cock-pit. Written by Shackerly Mermion, Gent. London, printed by F. K. for I. W. and

F. E. and are to be sold at the Crane, in S. Pauls Church-yard. 1641.

4°. [A]²B–K⁴L² (lacking [A]₁, blank)   18.4 cm.

Printed by Felix Kingston for Francis Eglesfield and John Williams. The first edition. Bound in calf, gilt edges. Arms of Frederick Perkins stamped on the cover, and sold by Sotheby's, 15 July 1889, lot 1289.

Gift of Alexander S. Cochran, December 1911.

Wing M 703   Greg 601(A)

MARSTON, JOHN, 1757?–1634

EC 116
What You Will
1607

What yov will. By Iohn Marston. Imprinted at London by G. Eld, for Thoms Thorppe. 1607.

4°. A–H⁴ (lacking H₄, blank)   17 cm.

The first edition. Bound by Rivière in blue goatskin, gold tooling on cover and spine, gilt edges.

Gift of Alexander S. Cochran, December 1911.

STC 17487   Greg 252(a)

MASON, JOHN, *fl.* 1610

EC 117
The Turk
1610

The Tvrke. A worthie tragedie. As it hath bene diuers times acted by the Children of his maiesties Reuels. Written by Iohn Mason Maister of Artes. . . . London. Printed by E. A. for Iohn Busbie and are to be sold at his shop in S. Dunstons Church-yard in Fleete-streete. 1610.

4°. [A]²B–I⁴K²   17.9 cm.

Printed by Edward Allde. The first edition. Bound by Rivière in red goatskin, gold tooling on cover and spine, gilt edges.

Provenance not traced.

STC 17617   Greg 286(a)

THE MASQUE OF FLOWERS

EC 26
Masque of
Flowers
1614

The maske of flowers. Presented by the gentlemen of Graies-inne, at the Court of White-hall, in the banquetting house, vpon Twelfe night, 1613. . . . London printed by N. O. for Robert Wilson, and are to be sold at his shop at Graies-inne new gate. 1614.

4°. A–D^{4}E^2 (lacking A$_1$, blank)   17.7 cm.

Printed by Nicholas Okes. Bound in vellum-covered boards, green leather on spine. Dedication signed I. G., W. D., and T. B. Signature "Campden," probably the first or second Viscount Campden, on the title page. Bookplate of Frederick Locker (*The Rowfant Library,* pp. 10–11), and acquired by Mr. Cochran at the dispersal of that library in 1905. Bound in at the end are the last eight leaves, sheets D and E, of Thomas Campion's *Description of a Maske,* 1607 (Greg 238).

Gift of Alexander S. Cochran, December 1911.

STC 17625   Greg 320

MASSINGER, PHILIP, 1583–1640

EC 118
Emperor of
the East
1632

The Emperovr of the East. A tragae-comoedie. . . . As it hath bene diuers times acted, at the Black-friers, and Globe play-houses, by the kings maiesties seruants. Written by Philip Massinger. London, printed by Thomas Harper for Iohn Waterson, Anno 1632.

4°. A–M⁴ (lacking M₄, blank)   17.8 cm.

The first edition. Bound by S. David in red goatskin, gold tooling on cover and spine, gilt edges.

Gift of Alexander S. Cochran, December 1911.

STC 17636   Greg 459(A)

MASSINGER, PHILIP, 1583–1640

EC 120
Great Duke of
Florence
1636

The great Dvke of Florence. A comicall historie. As it hath beene often presented with good allowance by her maties servants at the Phoenix in Drurie Lane. Written by Philip Massinger. London: printed for John Marriot. 1636

4°. A⁴(-A₁=L₁)B–K⁴L¹ (A₄ is bound after L₁)
18.2 cm.

The first edition. Bound in half red goatskin. Bernard Quaritch collation note, 17 July 1907, on rear endpaper.

Gift of Alexander S. Cochran, December 1911.

STC 17637   Greg 505(A)

MASSINGER, PHILIP, 1583–1640

EC 121
Maid of Honor
1632

The maid of honovr. As it hath beene often presented with good allowance at the Phoenix in Drvrie-Lane, by the queenes majesties servants. Written by Philip Massinger. London, printed by I. B. for Robert Allot, and are to be sold at his shop at the signe of the Blacke Beare in Pauls Church-yard, 1632.

4°. [A]²B–L⁴   18 cm.

Printed by John Beale. The first edition. Bound by Rivière in crimson goatskin, gilt edges.

Gift of Alexander S. Cochran, December 1911.

STC 17638   Greg 470(AII)

MASSINGER, PHILIP, 1583–1640

EC 122
A New Way to
Pay Old Debts
1633

A new way to pay old debts a comoedie as it hath beene often acted at the Phoenix in Drury-lane, by the queenes maiesties seruants. The author. Philip Massinger. London, printed by E. P. for Henry Seyle, dwelling in S. Pauls Church-yard, at the signe of the Tygers Head. Anno. M. DC. XXXIII.

4°. A–L⁴M²   18.6 cm.

Printed by Elizabeth Purslowe. The first edition. Bound by Rivière in crimson goatskin, gilt edges.

Gift of Alexander S. Cochran, December 1911.

STC 17639   Greg 474(A)

MASSINGER, PHILIP, 1583–1640

EC 123
The Picture
1630

The pictvre. A tragecomedie, as it was often presented with good allowance, at the Globe, and Blacke-friers play-houses, by the kings maiesties seruants. Written by Philip Massinger. London. Printed by I. N. for Thomas Walkley and are to be sould at his shoppe at the Eagle and Child in Brittains Burse. 1630.

4°. A–M⁴N² 18 cm.

Printed by John Norton. The first edition. Bound by Rivière in dark blue goatskin, gilt edges.

Gift of Alexander S. Cochran, December 1911.

STC 17640   Greg 436(A★¹ + ¹)

MASSINGER, PHILIP, 1583–1640

EC 124
The Renegado
1630

The renegado, a tragaecomedie. As it hath beene often acted by the queenes maiesties seruants, at the priuate play-house in Drurye-lane. By Philip Massinger. London, printed by A. M. for Iohn Waterson, and are to be sold at the Crowne in Pauls Church-yard. 1630.

4°. A–L⁴M² 18 cm.

Printed by Augustine Mathewes. The first edition. Bound by Rivière in crimson goatskin, gilt edges.

Gift of Alexander S. Cochran, December 1911.

STC 17641   Greg 430(A)

MASSINGER, PHILIP, 1583–1640

EC 125
The Unnatural Combat
1639

The vnnatvrall combat. A tragedie. . . . Written by Philip Massinger. As it was presented by the kings majesties servants at the Globe. London, printed by E. G. for Iohn Waterson, and are to be sold at his shop at the signe of the Crowne, in S. Pauls Church-yard. 1639.

4°. A^{2}B–K^{4}L^2 17.6 cm.

Printed by Edward Griffin. The first edition. Bound in half calf. Signature of E. Gordon Duff on front endpaper.

Gift of Alexander S. Cochran, December 1911.

STC 17643   Greg 559(A)

MASSINGER, PHILIP, 1583–1640, and Nathan Field

EC 119
The Fatal Dowry
1632

The fatall dowry: a tragedy. As it hath beene often acted at the priuate house in Blackefryers, by his maiesties seruants. Written by P. M. and N. F. London, printed by Iohn Norton, for Francis Constable, and are to be sold at his shop at the Crane, in Pauls Church-yard. 1632

4°. [A]^{2}B–L^4 17.5 cm.

The first edition. Bound by F. Bedford in half brown goatskin. Collation notes of J. O. Halliwell-Phillipps and of Bernard Quaritch, 26 June 1903, on rear endpaper. Bookplate of William Edward Bools; lot 1070 at the sale of his library by Sotheby's, 25 June 1903.

Gift of Alexander S. Cochran, December 1911.

STC 17646   Greg 646(A)

MAYNE, JASPER, 1604–1672

EC 126
The Amorous War
1648

The amorovs warre. A tragi-comoedy. . . . Printed in the yeare 1648.

4°. A–L⁴ (lacking L₄, blank)   16.7 cm.

The first edition. Bound in half calf. Each leaf has been separated and interleaved between larger blank leaves. Bookplate of John Philip Kemble; sold with his books by Evans, 5 February 1821, lot 1633. Stamp of Henry W. Holland on front endpaper and flyleaf. Bookplate of Alfred E. Richards, and inscription stating that he bought the book at auction in New York in December 1905 (not traced). Inscribed by Richards to the Elizabethan Club, 27 January 1913. Closely trimmed, shaving running titles and catchwords.

Gift of Alfred E. Richards, January 1913.

Wing M 1463   Greg 67(aI)

MELISSUS, PAUL, 1539–1602

EC 163
Melissi Poetica
1586

Melissi Schediasmata poetica. Secundo edita multo auctiora. . . . Lvtetiae parisiorvm. Apud Arnoldvm Sittartvm sub scuto Coloniensi, monte divi Hilarij. Anno M D LXXXVI.

8°. 3 volumes bound in 1:
[Volume I:] á⁴é⁴A–Y⁸Aa–Oo⁸

[Volume II:] Aaa–Kkk⁸
[Volume III:] Aaaa–Xxxx⁸   17 cm.

The second edition (first, 1575). Bound in contemporary paneled calf, blind tooled on cover and spine. A collection of laudatory verses addressed to the most notable persons in Europe, including a great many addressed to Queen Elizabeth and others of her court. Ownership inscription of Martin Adelt of Smigiel on title page; ownership stamp of the Rehdiger Stadt-Bibliothek zu Breslau on verso of title page.

Gift of Walter Jennings.

MIDDLETON, THOMAS, 1570–1627

EC 127
A Game at Chess
1625

A game at chesse. As it was acted nine dayes together at the Globe on the Bank-side. . . . Printed. 1625.

4°. A²B–K⁴   17.2 cm.

The second edition, second issue (first, 1625). Bound by Rivière in crimson goatskin, gold tooling on cover and spine, gilt edges.

Gift of Alexander S. Cochran, December 1911.

STC 17885   Greg 412(bII)

MIDDLETON, THOMAS, 1570–1627

EC 128
Michaelmas Term
1607

Michaelmas terme. As it hath been svndry times acted by the Children of Paules. At London, printed for A. I. and are to be sould at the signe of the White Horse in Paules Churchyard. An. 1607.

4°. A–I⁴   17.5 cm.

The first edition. Bound by F. Bedford in green goatskin, gilt edges. Bookplate of Frederick Locker (*The Rowfant Library*, p. 78), and acquired by Mr. Cochran at the dispersal of that library in 1905.

Gift of Alexander S. Cochran, December 1911.

STC 17890   Greg 244(a)

MIDDLETON, THOMAS, 1570–1627

EC 129
No Wit / No
Help like
a Woman's
1657

No wit / no help like a womans. A comedy, by Tho. Middleton, Gent. London: printed for Humphrey Moseley, at the Prince's Arms in St. Pauls Church-yard. 1657

8°. A–G⁸H⁴ (lacking H$_4$, blank)   16.7 cm.

The first edition. Bound by Rivière in blue goatskin, gold tooling on cover and spine, gilt edges.

Gift of Alexander S. Cochran, December 1911.

Wing M 1985   Greg 778(A)

MIDDLETON, THOMAS, 1570–1627

EC 130
Two New Plays
1657

Two new playes. Viz. More dissemblers besides women. Women beware women. Written by Tho. Middleton, Gent. London, printed for Humphrey Moseley and are to be sold at his shop at the Prince's Arms in St. Pauls Churchyard. 1657.

8°. [-]¹A⁴B–N⁸O⁴a⁸b² (lacking O$_4$, probably blank) 16.6 cm.

With the portrait frontispiece and twenty-page catalog of "Books printed for Humphrey Moseley" at the end. The first edition. Bound by Rivière in purple goatskin, gold tooling on cover and spine, gilt edges.

Gift of Alexander S. Cochran, December 1911.

Wing M 1980   Greg 781(A) and 782(A)

MIDDLETON, THOMAS, 1570–1627

EC 131
Your Five
Gallants
[1608]

Your fiue gallants. As it hath beene often in action at the Black-friers. Written by T. Middleton. Imprinted at London for Richard Bonian, dwelling at the signe of the Spred-eagle, right ouer-against the great north dore of Saint Paules Church. [1608]

4°. A–I⁴   18 cm.

The first edition. Bound by Rivière in crimson goatskin, top edge gilt.

Gift of Alexander S. Cochran, December 1911.

STC 17907   Greg 266(A)

MILTON, JOHN, 1608–1674

EC 135
Comus
1637

A maske presented at Ludlow Castle, 1634: on Michaelmasse night, before the right honorable, Iohn Earle of Bridgewater, Vicount Brackly, Lord Praesident of Wales, and one of his maiesties most honorable Privie Counsell. . . . London, printed for Hvmphrey Robinson, at the signe of the Three Pidgeons in Pauls Church-yard. 1637.

A MASKE
PRESENTED
At Ludlow Castle,
1634:

On *Michaelmasse* night, before the
RIGHT HONORABLE,

IOHN Earle of *Bridgewater*, Vicount BRACKLY,
Lord President of WALES, And one of
His MAIESTIES most honorable
Privie Counsell.

Eheu quid volui misero mihi! floribus austrum
Perditus ———

LONDON,
Printed for HVMPHREY ROBINSON,
at the signe of the *Three Pidgeons* in
Pauls Church-yard. 1637.

Milton's *Comus*, 1637 (EC 135)
Inscription by Henry E. Huntington
on the fly leaf

To the Elizabethan Club
with the compliments of
HEHuntington
April 25th 1918

4°. A²B–E⁴F² 17.5 cm.

The first edition. Bound by Rivière in dark blue goatskin. Inscribed to the Elizabethan Club by Henry E. Huntington, 25 April 1918.

Gift of Henry E. Huntington, April 1918.

STC 17937 Greg 524(a)

MILTON, JOHN, 1608–1674

EC 132
ΕΙΚΟΝΟΚΛΑΣΤΗΣ
1649

[Εικονοκλαστης] in answer to a book intitl'd [Εικων Βασιλικη], the portrature of his sacred majesty in his solitudes and sufferings. The author I. M. . . . London, printed by Matthew Simmons, next dore to the Gilded Lyon in Aldersgate street. 1649.

4°. [A]²B–Ii⁴Kk² 17.5 cm.

The first edition, first issue, with pages 108 and 109 incorrectly numbered 110 and 111. Bound in half sheepskin. Numerous passages in the text are underscored, and there are a few annotations in the margins.

Gift of Frederick S. Chase, 1912.

Wing M 2112

MILTON, JOHN, 1608–1674

EC 134
Literae
1676

Literae pseudo-senatus Anglicani, Cromwelli, reliquorumque perduellium nomine ac jussu conscriptae a Joanne Miltono. Impressae anno 1676.

12°. ★²A–I¹²K⁹ 12.8 cm.

The first edition. Bound in half vellum.

Gift of George van Santvoord, 1924.

Wing M 2128

MILTON, JOHN, 1608–1674

EC 133
Lycidas
1638

Justa Edovardo King naufrago, ab amicis moerentibus, amoris & μνείας χάειν. . . . Cantabrigiae: apud Thomam Buck, & Rogerum Daniel, celeberrimae academiae typographos. 1638.

$4°$. A–D^{4}E^{6}F–G^{4}I^2 16.9 cm.

The first edition, containing the first printing of *Lycidas*. Bound in calf. Bookplate of John Bowle, with his manuscript list of authors on front flyleaves; sold at his sale by B. White, 19 January 1790. On the title page are the signatures of Izaak Walton and George Steevens; Steevens's stamp also appears on the blank verso of the last page. In the Steevens sale, by King, 19 May 1800, this book was lot 974. Manuscript notes by Thomas Caldecote, with his signature, appear on the flyleaf opposite the title page. In the Caldecote sale, at Sotheby's, 13 December 1833, this volume was lot 1222. This copy was later sold at Sotheby's, 10 August 1887, lot 991 (libraries of H. F. Hance et al., probably the property of the Reverend T. Shuttleworth Grimshawe), where it was acquired by Bernard Quaritch, who sold it to William A. White in 1892. It bears White's signature and date, 11 September 1892, on the rear flyleaf.

Gift of the heirs of William A. White, May 1929.

STC 14964

JUSTA
EDOVARDO KING
naufrago,
ab
Amicis mœrentibus,
amoris
&
μνείας χάριν.

Si rectè calculum ponas, ubique naufragium est.
Pet. Arb.

CANTABRIGIÆ:
Apud *Thomam Buck*, & *Rogerum Daniel*, celeberrimæ
Academiæ typographos. 1638.

Milton's *Lycidas* was first printed in this volume of elegaic verses for Edward King, 1638 (EC 133)
The title page bearing the signatures of Izaac Walton and George Steevens

MILTON, JOHN, 1608–1674

EC 136
Paradise
Lost
1667

Paradise lost. A poem written in ten books by John Milton. . . . London printed, and are to be sold by Peter Parker under Creed Church neer Aldgate; and by Robert Boulter at the Turks Head in Bishopsgate-street; and Matthias Walker, under St. Dunstons Church in Fleet-street, 1667.

4°. [-]²A–Tt⁴Vv² (lacking [-]₁, blank)   17.5 cm.

The first edition, with the first title page. Title page is pasted onto a stub. Bound by Rivière in black goatskin, magnificently tooled on cover in pointille, with central panel of green goatskin bearing the title and surrounded by a design of poplar, pear, and apple trees, gold tooling on spine, gilt edges.

Gift of Alexander S. Cochran, December 1911.

Wing M 2136

MILTON, JOHN, 1608–1674

EC 137
Paradise
Lost
1669

Paradise lost. A poem in ten books. The author John Milton. London, printed by S. Simmons, and are to be sold by T. Helder at the Angel in Little Brittain. 1669.

4°. A⁴a⁴A–Tt⁴Vv²   17.2 cm.

The first edition, fifth title page. In this issue the arguments and Milton's defense of blank verse are added. Bound in contemporary red goatskin, gold ornament on cover and tooling on spine. Signature of Mary Hamilton inside back cover; illegible signature on title page.

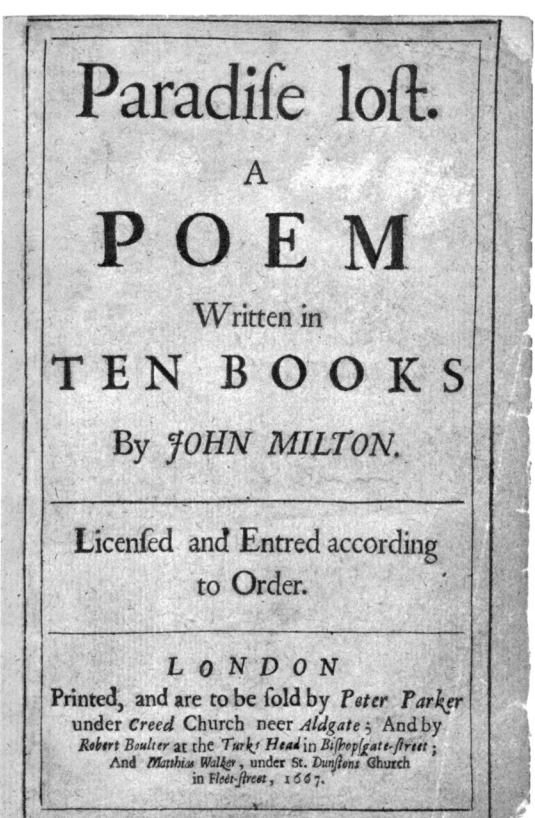

Milton's *Paradise Lost,* 1667
(EC 136)
The first edition, with the first title page

Upper cover of the binding by Rivière

Gift of Philip G. Bartlett, 1925.

Wing M 2142

MILTON, JOHN, 1608–1674

EC 138
Paradise
Regained
1671

Paradise regain'd. A poem. In IV books. To which is added Samson Agonistes. The author John Milton. London, printed by J. M. for John Starkey at the Mitre in Fleetstreet, near Temple-bar. MDCLXXI.

8°. A²B–O⁸P⁴   17.5 cm.

Printed by John Macocke. The first edition. Bound by Rivière in crimson goatskin, gold tooling on cover and spine, gilt edges.

Gift of Alexander S. Cochran, December 1911.

Wing M 2152

MILTON, JOHN, 1608–1674

EC 139
Poems
1645

Poems of Mr. John Milton, both English and Latin, compos'd at several times. . . . London, printed by Ruth Raworth for Humphrey Moseley, and are to be sold at the signe of the Princes Arms in S. Pauls Church-yard. 1645.

8°. [–]¹a⁴A–G⁸H⁴A–E⁸F⁴ (lacking a₁, blank) 14.7 cm.

The first edition. Bound by F. Bedford in red goatskin, gold tooling on cover and spine, gilt edges. Closely trimmed, shaving page numbers in upper margins.

Gift of Alexander S. Cochran, December 1912.

Wing M 2160

MONTAIGNE, MICHEL EYQUEM DE, 1533–1592

EC +20
Essays
1603

The essayes or morall, politike and millitarie discourses of Lo: Michaell de Montaigne, Knight. . . . First written by him in French. And now done into English by . . . Iohn Florio. Printed at London by Val. Sims for Edward Blount dwelling in Paules Churchyard. 1603.

Fol. $A^8 \P^2 B-Q^6 R^4 S-Pp^6 Qq^4 Rr^4 Ss-Iii^6 Kkk^4[-]^2$ 28.4 cm.

The first edition in English. Bound in contemporary calf, rebacked, with arms of Queen Elizabeth stamped on the cover. Bookplate of the Reverend Peter Gunning (1614–1684), Bishop of Ely. The Hoe copy (with bookplate), sold as lot 2357 on 2 May 1911, when it was acquired by General Brayton Ives. In the Ives sale, Anderson Auction Co., New York, 8 April 1915, it was sold as lot 718 to Mr. Cochran.

Gift of Alexander S. Cochran, 1915.

STC 18041

MORLEY, THOMAS, 1557–1604?

EC 141
Book of
Balletts
1595

Altvs. Of Thomas Morley the first booke of balletts to five voyces. In London by Thomas Este. M. D. XC. V.

Imperfect; copy severely damaged, several pages mounted and signatures bound out of order.

The first edition, *altus* part only. Bound in marbled-paper-covered boards, goatskin spine. Bookplate of Thomas Jolley, and sold as lot 1528 in the sale of his library by Sotheby's on 22 March 1844, where it was acquired by John Choules. At the Choules sale, by Leavitt, New York, 19 May 1856, it was purchased by Nicholas Brown, whose inscription recording its purchase appears on the front flyleaf. It was subsequently owned by General Rush Christopher Hawkins, and again sold by Leavitt, 23 March 1887, lot 1409, to William A. White, who inscribed his name and the date 26 March 1887 on the front flyleaf.

Gift of William A. White, April 1916.

STC 18116

NABBES, THOMAS, *fl.* 1638

EC 142
Hannibal and Scipio
1637

[Hannibal and Scipio. An historical tragedy. . . . London, . . . 1637.]

4°. A–K⁴ (lacking A$_1$, title page, and K$_4$, blank) 17.3 cm.

The first three leaves are shorter than the other leaves and were possibly inserted from another copy. A$_3$ is incorrectly bound before A$_2$. Presentation inscription to the Elizabethan Club from Alfred E. Richards on the front flyleaf.

Gift of Alfred E. Richards, 1913.

STC 18341   Greg 513(A)

NABBES, THOMAS, *fl.* 1638

EC 143
Microcosmus
1637

Microcosmus. A morall maske, presented with generall liking, at the private house in Salisbury Court, and heere set down according to the intention of the authour Thomas Nabbes. . . . London, printed by Richard Oulton for Charles Greene, and are to be sold at the White Lyon in Pauls Churchyard. 1637.

4°. [A]⁴B–C⁴ (lacking [A]₁, blank)   19.2 cm.

The first edition. Bound in imitation vellum. With the bookplate of Frederick Locker (*The Rowfant Library,* p. 84), and acquired by Mr. Cochran at the dispersal of that library in 1905.

Gift of Alexander S. Cochran, December 1911.

STC 18342   Greg 514(A)

NAPIER, JOHN, 1550–1617

EC 144
Mirifici
Logarithmorum
1614

Mirifici logarithmorum canonis descriptio, ejusque usus, in utraque trigonometria, ut etiam in omni logistica mathematica, amplissimi, facillimi, & expeditissimi explicatio. Authore ac inventore, Ioanne Nepero, Barone Merchistonii, &c. Scoto. Edinburgi, ex officina Andreae Hart bibliopola, M. DC. XIV.

4°. A–H⁴I¹a–I⁴m¹   19 cm.

The first edition, first issue. Bound in contemporary vellum. Bookplate of Christ Church, Oxford, with stamp "Sold by order of the Governing Body," 27 July 1912. Signature of Sir William Osler on rear

Napier's *Logarithms*, 1614 (EC 144)
The Christ Church duplicate bookplate

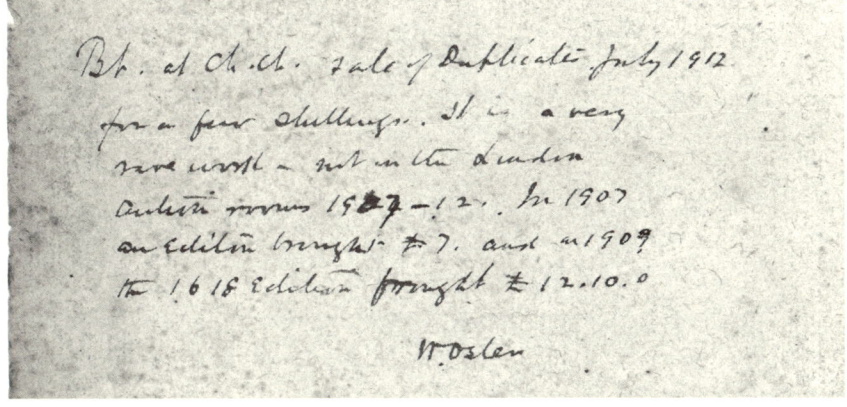

Sir William Osler's note of acquisition on the fly leaf

flyleaf, and note "Bt. at Ch. Ch. sale of Duplicates July 1912 for a few shillings. . . ."

Gift of Sir William Osler, 1913.

STC 18349

NAUNTON, SIR ROBERT, 1563–1635

EC 252
Fragmenta
Regalia
ca. 1640

Fragmenta regalia or many notable observations on Queene Eliz: her time and favorites with a short character and draught of the persons themselves their meritts & memorable achievemts: *contemporary manuscript copy*, ca. 1640.

55 leaves   18.3 cm.

Bound in speckled calf. This work was widely circulated in manuscript before it was first printed in 1641. In this manuscript the text of *Fragmenta Regalia* is followed by "The king of Morocco to ye king of England," one page, written in shorthand. Bookplate of Charles Hoare. A former owner has written on the front flyleaf: "This was bought amongst many other Books of Sir. R. Naunton in the Library of Mr. Manby formerly of Lincolns Inn. This contains more than the printed Copy."

Gift of Paul Stevens and Bennett Gilbert, 1980.

NAUNTON, SIR ROBERT, 1563–1635

EC 145 /1
Fragmenta
Regalia
1641

Fragmenta regalia, or observations on the late Queen Elizabeth, her times and favorits. Written by Sir Robert Naunton, Master of the Court of Wards. Printed, anno dom. 1641.

4°. A–E⁴F² 18.2 cm.

The first edition. Bound by Demander in goatskin, gold tooling on cover and spine, gilt edges.

Gift of the Providence Public Library, October 1927.

Wing N 249

EC 145 / 2 ——[another copy]

Bound by Bayntun in mottled calf, gold tooling on cover and spine. With the stamp of W. Musgrave on the verso of the title page (? William Musgrave, M.D., whose books were sold by Andrew Brice in 1725), the initials H. B. on the title page and final leaf, and the bookplate of Charles Tyler Prouty.

Gift of Charles T. Prouty, 1954.

NERO, Emperor of Rome

EC 146
Nero
1607

The tragedie of Claudius Tiberius Nero, Romes greatest tyrant. Truly represented out of the purest records of those times. . . . London printed for Francis Burton, dwelling in Paules Church-yard at the signe of the Flower-de-luce and Crowne. 1607.

4°. A–N⁴ (lacking A₁, blank) 18.2 cm.

The first edition. Bound by Rivière in red goatskin, gold tooling on cover and spine, gilt edges.

Provenance not traced.

STC 24063   Greg 240A★

NEW CUSTOM

EC 147
New Custom
1573

A new enterlude no lesse wittie: then pleasant, entituled new custome, deuised of late, and for diuerse causes nowe set forthe, neuer before this tyme imprinted. 1573. . . . [Colophon:] Imprinted at London in Fleetstreete by William How for Abraham Veale, dwelling in Paules Churche yarde at the signe of the Lambe.

4°. A–D⁴   18.3 cm.

The first edition. Bound by Rivière in crimson goatskin, gold tooling on cover and spine, gilt edges.

Gift of Alexander S. Cochran, December 1911.

STC 6150   Greg 59(A)

NEWTON, THOMAS, 1542–1607, *translator*

See CICERO, MARCUS TULLIUS

NICHOLAS, HENRY, 1502?–1580?

EC 148
Comoedia
[ca. 1574]

Comoedia. A worke in ryme contayning an enterlude of myndes, witnessing the mans fall from God and Christ. Set forth by HN, and by him newly perused and amended. Translated out of Base-almayne into English. [ca. 1754].

8°. A–D⁸   15 cm.

The first edition. Bound by Lortic in maroon goatskin, gold tooling on cover and spine, gilt edges. The Hoe copy (with bookplate), sold by Anderson Auction Co., New York, 17 January 1912, lot 2549.

Gift of Alexander S. Cochran, February 1912.

STC 18550   Greg 64(A)

NICOLLS, THOMAS, *fl.* 1559, *translator*

See THUCYDIDES

NORDEN, JOHN, 1548–1625?

EC 149
Speculum
Britanniae
1593

[Speculum Britanniae. . . . 1593]

Imperfect, lacking the first four leaves and the three maps. 16.8 cm.

The first edition. Bound in half red goatskin. Inscribed to the Elizabethan Club by W. A. White, 10 November 1918.

Gift of William W. White, November 1918.

STC 18635

NORTH, SIR THOMAS, 1523–1601?, *translator*

See PLUTARCH

NORTON, ROBERT, 1540?–1587?, *translator*

See CAMDEN, WILLIAM

OVERBURY, SIR THOMAS, 1581–1613

EC 150
A Wife Now the Widow
1614

A wife now the widow of Sir Thomas Overbvrye. Being a most exquisite and singular poem of the choice of a wife. . . . London printed for Lawrence Lisle, and are to bee sold at this shop in Paules Church-yard, at the signe of the Tigers Head. 1614.

4°. A–H⁴   17.5 cm.

The second edition. Bound by Aitken in mouse-colored calf, gold tooling on cover and spine, gilt edges. Two lines of verse and initials J. M. on the title page, and two six-line stanzas, also initialed J. M., on front endpaper. Thomas Corser's copy, with his mark of ownership on the front flyleaf; sold by Sotheby's as lot 604 in the Corser sale, 25 February 1870. The Corser catalog queries whether John Milton might be the author of the manuscript verses. A pencil note on Milton, signed W. F. T. 1871, is on the front endpaper. Bookplate of Thomas Jefferson McKee, and sold as lot 3083 in the McKee sale, 3 December 1901, by the Anderson Auction Co., New York.

Gift of John C. Tomlinson.

STC 18904

OVID

EC 151
Elegies
[ca. 1630]

All Ovids elegies: 3. Bookes. By C. M. Epigrams by J. D. At Middlebovrgh [ca. 1630]

8°. A–F⁸   13.5 cm.

Translated by Christopher Marlowe; epigrams by

Sir John Davies. The third edition (first, ca. 1602). Bound in brown goatskin, top edges gilt. Some catchwords trimmed.

Provenance not traced.

STC 18932

OVID

EC 152
Metamorphosis
1612

The fifteene bookes of P. Ovidivs Naso; entitvled Metamorphosis. Translated out of Latine into English meeter, by Arthur Golding Gentleman. . . . At London, printed by Thomas Purfoot. An. dom. 1612.

4°. ¶⁴A–Bb⁸Cc⁴ (lacking ¶₁, blank)   8.2 cm.

The eighth edition (first, 1567). Bound by Rivière in red goatskin, gold tooling on covers and spine, gilt edges.

Gift of Alexander S. Cochran, December 1911.

STC 18962

PALINGENIUS, MARCELLUS, STELLATUS, *fl.* 1528

EC 253
Zodiac of
Life
1565

The Zodiake of life written by the godly and zealous poet Marcellus Pallingenius stellatus, wherein are conteyned twelue bookes disclosing the haynous crymes & wicked vices of our corrupt nature: and plainlye declaring the pleasaunt and perfit pathway unto eternal lyfe, besides a number of digressions both pleasaunt & profitable, newly translated into

Englishe verse by Barnabe Googe. . . . Imprinted at London by Henry Denham, for Rafe Newberye dwelling in Fleete Streate. Anno. 1565. Aprilis. 18.

8°. ★⁸‡⁴A–2X⁸2Y⁴   13.8 cm.

The first edition in twelve books. Bound in purple goatskin, gold tooling on cover and spine, gilt edges. Title page remargined. Collation note of Bernard Quaritch, Ltd., on rear free endpaper. Bookplate of Henry Cunliffe.

Purchased 1981.

STC 19150

PATHOMACHIA

EC 153
Pathomachia
1630

Pathomachia: or, the battell of affections. Shadowed by a faigned siedge of the citie Pathopolis. Written some yeeres since, and now first published by a friend of the deceassed avthor. London, printed by Thomas and Richard Coats, for Francis Constable, and are to be sold at his shop in Pauls Church-yard at the signe of the Crane. 1630.

4°. A–G⁴ (lacking A_1 and G_4, blank)   17.7 cm.

The first edition. Bound in calf, arms of Frederick Perkins in gold stamped on cover, gilt edges. Sold as lot 1296 in the Perkins sale by Sotheby's, 15 July 1889. Bookplate of Thomas Jefferson McKee, and sold as lot 2548 by Sotheby's, 30 April 1901. Attributed to "J. Marston" in a note on the title page.

Gift of Alexander S. Cochran, December 1911.

STC 19462   Greg 434(A)

A PATTERN

EC 249
A Pattern for Princes
1680

A pattern or president for princes to rule by, and for subjects to obey by. Together with the rare example of subjects tender and singular care for the life and safety of their soveraign; . . . London, printed for William Miller at the Guilded Acorn in St. Pauls Church-yard. . . . 1680.

4°. A–E⁴   21.5 cm.

The first edition. Bound by Jane Greenfield in half calf, marbled-paper boards. This pamphlet consists of "A lively character of the most renowned Queen Elizabeth, as it was drawn by a noble, and learned pen of one that was bred under her from his youth, to her death."

Gift of Stephen Parks, in memory of Alexander S. Cochran, 1978.

Wing P 875

PEELE, GEORGE, 1558?–1597?

EC 154
Battle of Alcazar
1594

The battell of Alcazar, fovght in Barbarie, betweene Sebastian king of Portugall, and Abdelmelec king of Marocco. . . . As it was sundrie times plaid by the lord high admirall his seruants. Imprinted at London by Edward Allde for Richard Bankworth, and are to be solde at his shoppe in Pouls Church-yard at the signe of the Sunne. 1594.

4°. A–F⁴G² (lacking G₂, blank)   17.2 cm.

The first edition. Bound by Rivière in red goatskin, gold tooling on cover and spine, gilt edges.

Provenance not traced.

STC 19531   Greg 127(A)

PEELE, GEORGE, 1558?–1597?

EC 155
David and
Bathsheba
1599

The love of King David and fair Bethsabe. With the tragedie of Absalon. As it hath ben diuers times plaied on the stage. Written by George Peele. London, printed by Adam Islip. 1599

4°. [A]²B–H⁴I² (lacking [A]₁ and I₂, blank)   17 cm.

The first edition. Bound by F. Bedford in green goatskin, gold tooling on cover and spine, gilt edges. Closely trimmed, affecting some running heads. Bookplate of Frederick Locker (*The Rowfant Library,* p. 90), and acquired by Mr. Cochran at the dispersal of that library in 1905.

Gift of Alexander S. Cochran, December 1911.

STC 19540   Greg 160(A)

PHAER, THOMAS, 1510?–1560, *translator*

See VIRGIL

PHILLIP, JOHN, *fl.* 1570

EC 156
Patient Grisel
[ca. 1569]

The commodye of pacient and meeke Grissill, whearin is declared, the good example, of her patience towardes her husband: and lykewise, the due obedience of children, toward their parentes. Newly. Compiled by Iohn Phillip. . . . Imprinted at Lon-

THE COMMODYE OF
pacient and meeke Griſſill,

Whearin is declared, the good example,
of her pacience towardes her Huſ-
band: and lykewiſe, the
due obedience of Children,
toward their Parentes.
Newly.

Compiled by Iohn Phillip.

¶ Eight perſons maye eaſely play this Commody.

1. Polliticke Perſwaſion the Vice. the Epiloge. For one.
2. Preface. Marquis. For another.
3. Fidence. Indigence. The ſecond Paidge or Seruing man,
   The Sonne of Griſſill. For another.
4. Reaſon. Dilligence. Countis Mayd. Pacience.
   and the Daughter of Griſſill. For another.
5. Sobrietie. Countis of Pango. Cōmon people. Conſtancy.
6. Rumor. Iannickle.
7. Iannickells Wife. The firſt of the Pages. The Norſe.
8. Griſſill. The Midwife.

Imprinted at London,
in Fleeteſtreat beneath the Conduit,
at the ſigne of Saint Iohn Euan-
geliſt by Thomas Colwell.

Phillip's *Patient Grisel,* ca. 1569 (EC 156)
The unique surviving copy of this early play

don, in Fleetestreat beneath the Conduit, at the signe of Saint John Euangelist by Thomas Colwell. [ca. 1569].

4°. A²B–H⁴I² (lacking I$_2$, probably blank)   17 cm.

The first edition. Bound by Rivière in crimson goatskin, gold tooling on cover and spine. The Mostyn copy, sold at Sotheby's, 1 June 1907, lot 458. Some running heads trimmed. This copy is unique.

Gift of Alexander S. Cochran, December 1911.

STC 19865   Greg 52(A)

PHILOSTRATUS, FLAVIUS

EC +21
Philostratus
1680

The two first books, of Philostratus, concerning the life of Apollonius Tyaneus: written originally in Greek, and now published in English: together with philological notes upon each chapter. By Charles Blount, Gent. . . . London, printed for Nathaniel Thompson, next dore to the sign of the Cross-keys in Fetter-lane, anno domini, 1680.

Fol. A–Gg⁴Hh⁶   30.5 cm.

The first edition in English. Bound in calf, gold tooling on cover and spine. Armorial bookplace of Sir John Benn-Walsh, first Baron Ormathwaite.

Gift of Alexander S. Cochran, December 1911.

Wing P 2132

PLINY, the younger

EC +22
History
1601

The historie of the world. Commonly called, the natvrall historie of C. Plinivs Secvndvs. Translated into English by Philemon Holland Doctor in Physicke. The first tome. London, printed by Adam Islip, 1601.

Fol. [Volume I:] [-]⁶¶⁴a–b⁶A⁸B–Iii⁶Kkk⁴ (lacking [-]₁, probably blank) 31.8 cm.
[Volume II:] A–Ggg⁶Hhh⁴Iii–Ooo⁶Ppp⁸ (lacking Ppp₈, probably blank) 31.8 cm.

The first edition in English. Two volumes bound as one in contemporary calf, rebacked, blind tooling and ornamental stamp on cover.

Gift of Alexander S. Cochran, December 1911.

STC 20029

PLUTARCH

EC +23
Lives
1612

The lives of the noble Grecians and Romaines, compared together by that grave learned philosopher and historiographer Plutarke of Chaeronea: translated out of Greeke into French by Iames Amiot . . . and out of French into English, by Sir Thomas North Knight. . . . London, printed by Richard Field. 1612.

Fol. A⁸B–5O⁶5P⁸ (lacking A₁, probably blank) 32.3 cm.

The fourth edition (first, 1579). Bound in contemporary calf, blind tooling and gold ornament on cover.

Gift of Alexander S. Cochran, December 1911.

STC 20069

PLUTARCH

EC +24
Morals
1603

The philosophie, commonlie called, the morals written by the learned philosopher Plutarch of Chaeronea. Translated out of Greeke into English, and conferred with the Latine translations and the French, by Philemon Holland of Coventrie, Doctor in Physicke. . . . At London printed by Arnold Hatfield. 1603.

Fol. ¶⁴A–5X⁶5Y⁴5Z⁶6A–6E⁴6F⁶   31.6 cm.

The first edition in English. Bound in tree calf. Holland was the first to translate this entire work into English.

Gift of Alexander S. Cochran, December 1911.

STC 20063

THE QUEEN'S MAJESTIES' PASSAGE

EC 157
Queen's Majesty's
Passage
1558

The Qvenes maiesties passage through the citie of London to Westminster the daye before her coronacion. Anno. 1558. Cum priuilegio. [Colophon:] Imprinted at London in Fletestrete within Temple Barre, at the signe of the Hand and Starre, by Richard Tottill, the. xxiii. day of January.

4°. A–E⁴   18.2 cm.

The first edition. Bound by F. Bedford in red goatskin, gold tooling on cover and spine, gilt edges. This is an anonymous account of the formal coro-

The Queen's Majesty's Passage, 1559 (EC 157)
The unique surviving copy of this account of Queen Elizabeth's coronation pageant

Imprinted at London in fleteſtrete within Temple barre, at the ſigne of the hand and ſtarre, by Richard Tottill, the .xxiii. day of January.

The colophon from *The Queen's Majesty's Passage*

nation pageant of Queen Elizabeth, which took place on 14 January 1558/59. There is another edition of the work dated 1558; it is not known which is the earlier. This copy is unique.

Gift of Alexander S. Cochran, December 1911.

STC 7591

EC 157A ———[manuscript copy, of a slightly different version:] The passage of our most drad soveraigne Lady Quene Elizabeth through the Citie of London to Westminster the day before her coronation anno 1558: anonymous manuscript, in a late seventeenth-century hand.

55 pages 19 cm.

Bound by Morrell in green goatskin, gilt tooling on cover and spine. This manuscript was clearly copied from the second, and probably later, printed edition of the pamphlet (STC 7590), which bears the more flourishing title given above (as does this manuscript). This manuscript copy is incomplete, omitting the final two pages of the printed pamphlet. Bookplate of Doris Louise Benz, and sold by Christie's, 27 March 1985, lot 49, when it was purchased for the Elizabethan Club by Bernard Quaritch, Ltd.

Purchased March 1985.

RALEIGH, SIR WALTER, 1552?–1618

EC +25
History of
the World
1634

[Engraved title page without letterpress:] The history of the world [in panel below:] At London printed for Walter Bvrre. 1614 [Colophon:] London, printed for G. Lathum, and R. Young. M. DC. XXXIV.

Fol. [-]³A–B⁶C⁴a⁶b⁸A–S⁶T–V⁴Aa–Vv⁶
3A–3V⁶4A–4V⁶5A–5Z⁶(a)⁶(aa)⁶(★)⁶(★★)⁸   33.8 cm.

The fifth edition (first, 1614). Bound in contemporary calf, rebacked. First two leaves repaired; damp stains on preliminary leaves. Signature of Emeline Louise Hurd Hill, 25 December 1922, on front flyleaf.

Provenance not known

STC 20641

RANDOLPH, THOMAS, 1605–1635

EC 158
Poems
1638

Poems with the mvses looking-glasse: and Amyntas. By Thomas Randolph Master of Arts, and late Fellow of Trinity Colledge in Cambridge. Oxford, printed by Leonard Lichfield printer to the vniversity, for Francis Bowman: M. DC. XXXVIII.

4°. ★-★★★⁴A–Q⁴A–Dd⁴   17.1 cm.

The first edition. Bound by Chambolle-Duru in mauve goatskin, elaborate gold tooling on cover and spine, gilt edges. Signature of Ralph Milbanke on front flyleaf, and bookplate of Harry Vane Milbanke.

Gift of Alexander S. Cochran, December 1911.

STC 20694   Greg 548(a)

THE RETURN FROM PARNASSUS

EC 159
Return from
Parnassus
1606

The retvrne from Pernassvs: or the scourge of simony. Publiquely acted by the students in Saint Iohns Colledge in Cambridge. At London printed by G. Eld, for Iohn Wright, and are to bee sold at

Raleigh's *History of the World*, 1634 (EC +25)

his shop at Christ Church gate. 1606.

4°. A–H⁴   17.7 cm.

The first edition, second issue. Bound in brown goatskin, gold tooling on cover and spine, top edge gilt. On leaf A_3 is pasted a bookseller's advertisement slip, offering "most sorts of Plays" to be had of Thomas Dring at the White Lion. This appears not to be contemporary with the play, as Dring's shop was at the White Lion from 1668. An undated note on the front flyleaf is signed R. C. H. [Sir Richard Colt Hoare].

Gift of Alexander S. Cochran, December 1911.

STC 19310   Greg 225(b)

ROJAS, FERANDO DE, d. 1541

EC +26
The Spanish
Bawd
1631

The Spanish bawd, represented in Celestina: or, the tragicke-comedy of Calisto and Melibea. . . . London printed by J. B. and are to be sold by Robert Allot at the signe of the Beare in Pauls Churchyard. 1631.

Fol. A^8B–Bb^4Cc^6 (lacking Cc_6, blank)   27.1 cm.

Printed by John Beale. The first edition. Bound by Rivière in blue goatskin, gold tooling on cover and spine, gilt edges. Translated by John Mabbe.

Gift of Alexander S. Cochran, December 1911.

STC 4911

ROWLEY, SAMUEL, d. 1633?

EC 160
Noble Soldier
1634

The noble sovldier. Or, a contract broken, justly reveng'd. A tragedy. Written by S. R. . . . London: printed for Nicholas Vavasour, and are to be sold at his shop in the Temple, neere the Church. 1634.

4°. A–H⁴ (lacking A₁, blank)   17.7 cm.

The first edition. Bound in half brown goatskin, blind tooled on cover. Signature of C. Bohn Slingluff, Baltimore, 1870, on front flyleaf. Signature of William Henry Ireland on the title page. From the library of Thomas Jefferson McKee, and sold by Anderson Auction Co., New York, 30 April 1901, lot 2569.

Gift of Alexander S. Cochran, December 1911.

STC 21416   Greg 490(A)

ROWLEY, WILLIAM, 1585?–1642?

EC 161
A New
Wonder
1632

A new wonder, a woman never vext. A pleasant conceited comedy: sundry times acted: never before printed. Written by William Rowley, one of his maiesties servants. London, imprinted by G. P. for Francis Constable, and are to be sold at his shop at the signe of the Crane in Saint Pauls Churchyard. 1632.

4°. A–K⁴L²   18.6 cm.

Printed by George Purslowe. The first edition. Bound by Rivière in green goatskin, gold tooling on cover and spine, gilt edges.

Gift of Alexander S. Cochran, December 1911.

STC 21423   Greg 460(A)

ROWLEY, WILLIAM, 1585?–1642?, Thomas Dekker, and John Ford

EC 162
Witch of
Edmonton
1658

The witch of Edmonton: a known true story. Composed into a tragi-comedy by divers well-esteemed poets; William Rowley, Thomas Dekker, John Ford, &c. Acted by the princes servants, often at the Cock-pit in Drury-Lane, once at Court, with singular applause. Never printed till now. . . . London, printed by J. Cottrel, for Edward Blackmore, at the Angel in Paul's Church-yard. 1658.

4°. A²B–I⁴   17.3 cm.

The first edition. Bound by Rivière in red goatskin, gilt edges.

Gift of Alexander S. Cochran, December 1911.

Wing R 2097   Greg 785(A)

SAVILE, SIR HENRY, 1549–1622, *translator*

See TACITUS, CORNELIUS

SCALIGER, JOSEPH JUSTE, 1540–1609, *editor*

See VIRGIL

Rowley's *Witch of Edmonton*, 1658 (EC 162)

SECRET HISTORY

EC 256
Secret History
1695

The secret history of the most renowned Q. Elizabeth and the E. of Essex. By a person of quality. Cologne: printed for Will with the whisp, at the sign of the Moon in the Ecliptick. 1695.

12°. A–B⁶C–F¹²   14.4 cm.

The fifth edition (first, 1680). Bound by Bayntun in speckled calf, gold tooling on cover and spine. Frontispiece inlaid. Ownership inscription of Rebecca Hargood on verso of last leaf.

Gift of Henry H. Anderson, Jr., in memory of Wilmarth S. Lewis, December 1983.

Wing S 2345

SELDEN, JOHN, 1584–1654

EC 164
History of
Tithes
1618

The historie of tithes that is, the practice of payment of them. The positiue laws made for them. The opinions touching the right of them. . . . By, I. Selden. . . . M. DC. XVIII.

4°. a–e⁴A–Kkk⁴a–f⁴   18.2 cm.

The first edition. Bound by Demander in goatskin, gold tooling on cover. Signature of Jo. Cotes on title page and of Thomas Menzies on p. 1. Tipped in is a letter from Adeline Selden Coffin, 4 May 1921, to Andrew Keogh, presenting the volume to the club. She states that this copy had been obtained by her father, Samuel Hart Selden, from a priest in Wisconsin. There are pencil annotations throughout, and a few pages are torn, but not affecting the text.

Gift of the daughters of Samuel Hart Selden, May 1922.

STC 22172.7

SENECA, LUCIUS ANNAEUS

EC 165
Tragedies
1581

Seneca his tenne tragedies, translated into Englysh. . . . Imprinted at London in Fleetstreete neere vnto Saincte Dunstans Church by Thomas Marsh. 1581

4°. A^{4}B–Ee^{8}Ff^4 (lacking A$_1$ and Ff$_4$, blank) 18 cm.

The first edition of this collection of all Seneca's tragedies, translated by various hands. Of the ten, five had earlier separate editions. Bound by Rivière in blue goatskin, gold tooling cover and spine, gilt edges.

Gift of Alexander S. Cochran, December 1911.

STC 22221

SENECA, LUCIUS ANNAEUS

EC +27
Works
1614

The workes of Lvcius Annaevs Seneca, both morall and naturall. . . . Translated by Tho. Lodge, D. in Physicke. London printed by William Stansby. 1614.

Fol. [–]^{6}b–d^{6}B–4I^{6}4K^4 (lacks [–]$_1$, blank; b$_{1-3,6}$ supplied in photo-facsimile) 32.8 cm.

The first edition in English. Bound in contemporary calf, blind tooling and gold ornament on cover. Signature of James Davis, 1755, on the title page, and occasional annotations in the text, probably in his hand.

Gift of Alexander S. Cochran, December 1911.

STC 22213

SHADWELL, THOMAS, 1642?–1692

EC 167
The Humorists
1691

The humorists; a comedy. Acted by their majesties servants. Written by Tho. Shadwell, Poet-Laureat, and Historiographer-Royal. . . . London, printed for Henry Herringman, and are to be sold by Francis Saunders at the Blew Anchor in the lower walk of the New Exchange, and James Knapton at the Crown in St. Pauls Church-yard. 1691.

4°. A–I^4 21 cm.

The second edition (first, 1671). Bound in modern half brown goatskin. Bookplate of Alfred E. Richards and date, 30 August 1906; presentation inscription from Richards to the club dated 27 January 1913.

Gift of Alfred E. Richards, January 1913.

Wing S 2852

SHADWELL, THOMAS, 1642?–1692

EC 166
Timon of
Athens
1688

The history of Timon of Athens, the man-hater. As it is acted at the Duke's Theatre. Made into a play. By Tho. Shadwell. . . . London, printed by J. M. for Henry Herringman, and are to be sold by Jos.

Knight and F. Saunders at the Blue Anchor in the lower walk of the New Exchange, 1688.

A–K⁴ 21.4 cm.

Printed by John Maycocke. The third edition (first, 1678). Bound by Demander in maroon goatskin, gold tooling on cover and spine.

Provenance not known.

Wing S 2847

SHAKESPEARE, WILLIAM, 1564–1616

I. THE FOLIOS
EC +28
First Folio
1623

Mr. William Shakespeares comedies, histories, & tragedies. Published according to the true originall copies. London printed by Isaac Iaggard, and Ed. Blount. 1623. [Colophon:] Printed at the Charges of W. Jaggard, Ed. Blount, I. Smithweeke, and W. Aspley, 1623.

Fol. A⁶(A₁+₁)[B]²A–Bb⁶Cc²a–g⁶gg⁸h–v⁶ x⁴[-]²¶–¶¶⁶¶¶¶¹aa–ff⁶gg²Gg⁶hh⁶ kk–bbb⁶ 31.5 cm.

The first edition. Bound in red leather, gold tooling on cover and spine. This copy was purchased about 1790 by Henry Constantine Jennings from the bookseller Thomas Payne; acquired about 1820 by George Hibbert, at whose sale, 30 May 1829 (lot 7564, Sotheby's), it was bought by John Wilks, M.P. Purchased at the Wilks sale, 22 March 1847 (lot 2135, Sotheby's), by John Dunn Gardner, and at the Gardner sale, 15 July 1854 (lot 2058, Sotheby's), by Henry Huth. In the Gardner catalog, this folio was described in the following manner:

Shakespeare's *Works*, 1623 (EC +28)   The First Folio

"This copy, from the Libraries of Mr. Hibbert and Mr. Wilks, is ONE OF THE FINEST COPIES KNOWN, and without doubt, THE FINEST that has ever been sold by public auction. It may, though bound in russia, with border of gold, in the quiet good taste of Montague, be called in its *original state,* and may be fairly stated, as far as a book can be so designated, AN IMMACULATE COPY." The Huth copy (with bookplate) acquired by Mr. Cochran in November 1911 prior to the public sale.

Gift of Alexander S. Cochran, December 1911.

STC 22273   Greg III, 1109–1113

SHAKESPEARE, WILLIAM, 1564–1616

EC +29
Second Folio
1632

Mr. William Shakespeares comedies, histories, and tragedies. Published according to the true originall copies. The second impression. London, printed by Tho. Cotes, for Robert Allot, and are to be sold at the signe of the Blacke Beare in Pauls Church-yard. 1632. [Colophon:] Printed at London by Thomas Cotes, for John Smethwick, William Aspley, Richard Hawkins, Richard Meighen, and Robert Allot, 1632.

Fol. $A^6{\star}^4 A-Bb^6 Cc^2 a-y^6 aa-ccc^6 ddd^4$ 33.6 cm.

The second edition (first, 1623). Bound by F. Bedford in red goatskin, gold tooling on cover and spine, gilt edges. The Huth copy (with bookplate) acquired by Mr. Cochran in November 1911 prior to the public sale.

Gift of Alexander S. Cochran, December 1911.

STC 22274   Greg III, 1113–1115

EC +29
Copy 2

———Another Copy

Fragment only, consisting of *Troilus and Cressida, Coriolanus, Titus Andronicus,* and one page of *Romeo and Juliet.*

Bound in tan goatskin, gold tooling on cover and spine, gilt edges. Bookplate of Monty Woolley.

Bequest of Monty Woolley, 1963.

SHAKESPEARE, WILLIAM, 1564–1616

EC +30
Third Folio,
First Issue
1663

Mr. William Shakespeares comedies, histories, and tragedies. Published according to the true original copies. The third impression. London, printed for Philip Chetwinde, 1663.

Fol. $A^4b^6A–Aa^6Bb^8Cc–4D^64E^4$ 32.4 cm.

The third edition, first issue. Leaf A_1 has been supplied from another, smaller, copy. Bound in red russia leather, gold tooling on cover and spine, gilt edges. Unidentified signature, heavily overscored, on title page. The Huth copy (with bookplate) acquired by Mr. Cochran in November 1911 prior to the public sale.

Gift of Alexander S. Cochran, December 1911.

Wing S 2913   Greg III, 1116–1117

SHAKESPEARE, WILLIAM, 1564–1616

EC +31
Third Folio,
Second Issue
1664

Mr. William Shakespear's comedies, histories, and tragedies. Published according to the true original copies. The third impression. And unto this impression is added seven playes, never before printed in folio. viz. Pericles Prince of Tyre. The London Prodigall. The History of Thomas Ld. Cromwell. Sir John Oldcastle Lord Cobham. The Puritan Widow. A Yorkshire Tragedy. The Tragedy of Locrine. London, printed for P. C. 1664

Fol. A⁴[A₁₋₂ cancellans]b⁶A–Aa⁶Bb⁸Cc–4D⁶4E⁴
a⁶b⁴★–4★⁴¶A–¶B⁶¶C–¶F⁴¶G⁶   32.6 cm.

The third edition, second issue (first, 1623). Bound in brown goatskin, gold tooling on cover and spine, gilt edges. Bookplate of Edward Craven Hawtrey, D. D., Provost of Eton (but not in the catalog of the sale of his books by Sotheby's, 30 June 1862). The Huth copy (with bookplate) acquired by Mr. Cochran in November 1911 prior to the public sale.

Gift of Alexander S. Cochran, December 1911.

Wing S 2914   Greg III, 1118

SHAKESPEARE, WILLIAM, 1564–1616

EC +32
Fourth Folio
1685

Mr. William Shakespear's comedies, histories, and tragedies. Published according to the true original copies. Unto which is added, seven plays, never before printed in folio: viz. Pericles Prince of Tyre. The London Prodigal. The History of Thomas

Lord Cromwel. Sir John Oldcastle Lord Cobham. The Puritan Widow. A Yorkshire Tragedy. The Tragedy of Locrine. The fourth edition. London, printed for H. Herringman, E. Brewster, and R. Bentley, at the Anchor in the New Exchange, the Crane in St. Pauls Church-yard, and in Russel-street Covent-garden. 1685.

Fol. [-]²A⁴A–Y⁶Z⁴Bb–Zz⁶★3A–★3D⁶★3E⁸ 3A–4B⁶4C² 35.6 cm.

The fourth edition (first, 1623). In this copy, $A_{2,3}$ are bound after Zz_4. Bound in brown leather, blind tooling on cover and spine, gilt edges. The Huth copy (with bookplate) acquired by Mr. Cochran in November 1911 prior to the public sale.

Gift of Alexander S. Cochran, December 1911.

Wing S 2915   Greg III, 1119–1121

Copy 2   ———Another Copy

Bound by Rivière in maroon goatskin, gold tooling on cover and spine, gilt edges. A number of leaves have been skillfully remargined.

Provenance not traced.

SHAKESPEARE, WILLIAM, 1564–1616

II. INDIVIDUAL
WORKS
EC 168
Hamlet
1604

The tragicall historie of Hamlet, Prince of Denmarke. By William Shakespeare. Newly imprinted and enlarged to almost as much againe as it was, according to the true and perfect coppie. At London, printed by I. R. for N. L. and are to be sold at his shoppe vnder Saint Dunstons Church in Fleetstreet. 1604.

4°. [A]²B–N⁴O² (lacking [A]₁, probably blank) 18.5 cm.

Printed by James Roberts for Nicholas Ling. The second edition (first, 1603). This is the first authoritative edition of the play, the first quarto of 1603 being a shortened version of the text, different in many ways, and possibly a surreptitious publication. Bound in straight-grain red goatskin, gold tooling on cover and spine, gilt edges. Signature of Jacobus Cummyng P. H. on B₁r. Bookplate of Plummer of Middlestead. The Huth copy (with bookplate) acquired by Mr. Cochran in November 1911 prior to the public sale.

Gift of Alexander S. Cochran, December 1911.

STC 22276   Greg 197(b)

SHAKESPEARE, WILLIAM, 1564–1616

EC 169
Hamlet
1611

The tragedy of Hamlet Prince of Denmarke. By William Shakespeare. Newly imprinted and enlarged to almost as much againe as it was, according to the true and perfect coppy. At London, printed for Iohn Smethwicke, and are to be sold at his shoppe in Saint Dunstons Church yeard in Fleetstreet. Vnder the Diall. 1611.

4°. A²B–N⁴O² (lacking A₁, blank)   17.9 cm.

The third edition (first, 1603). Bound in brown

leather, blind and gold tooling on cover and spine. On the title page is written, in a seventeenth-century hand, "for Marc Stapfer." This copy was owned by Bulkeley Bandinel, Bodley's Librarian, and it was sold with his library by Sotheby's, 16 August 1861, lot 264. The catalog noted the title page inscription and queried: "?in the hand of the poet!" The Huth copy (with bookplate) acquired by Mr. Cochran in November 1911 prior to the public sale.

Gift of Alexander S. Cochran, December 1911.

STC 22277   Greg 197(c)

SHAKESPEARE, WILLIAM, 1564–1616

EC 170
Hamlet
N.D.

The tragedy of Hamlet Prince of Denmarke. Newly imprinted and inlarged, according to the true and perfect copy lastly printed. By William Shakespeare. London, printed by W. S. for Iohn Smethwicke, and are to be sold at his shop in Saint Dunstans Churchyard in Fleetstreet: vnder the Diall, [n.d.]

4°. A–N^4 (lacking N$_4$, blank)   17.9 cm.

Printed by William Stansby. The fourth edition (first, 1603). Bound by F. Bedford in red goatskin, gold tooling on cover and spine, gilt edges. The Huth copy (with bookplate), acquired by Mr. Cochran in November 1911, prior to the public sale.

Gift of Alexander S. Cochran, December 1911.

STC 22278   Greg 197(d)

SHAKESPEARE, WILLIAM, 1564–1616

EC 172
Henry IV,
Part I
1599

The history of Henrie the Fovrth; with the battell at Shrewsburie, betweene the king and Lord Henry Percy, surnamed Henry Hotspur of the north. With the humorous conceits of Sir Iohn Falstalffe. Newly corrected by W. Shake-speare. At London, printed by S. S. for Andrew Wise, dwelling in Paules Churchyard, at the signe of the Angell. 1599.

4°. A–K⁴ 19.2 cm.

Printed by Simon Stafford. The second edition (first, 1598). Bound by F. Bedford in red goatskin, gold tooling on cover and spine, top edge gilt. Individual leaves in sheets I and K have been remargined; headings and catchwords shaved. Corners mended throughout. The James Orchard Halliwell copy, sold by Sotheby's, 21 May 1857, lot 875. The Huth copy (with bookplate) acquired by Mr. Cochran in November 1911 prior to the public sale.

Gift of Alexander S. Cochran, December 1911.

STC 22281   Greg 145(c)

SHAKESPEARE, WILLIAM, 1564–1616

EC 173
Henry IV,
Part I
1613

The history of Henrie the fourth, with the battell at Shrewseburie, betweene the king, and Lord Henrie Percy, surnamed Henrie Hotspur of the north. With the humorous conceites of Sir Iohn Falstaffe. Newly corrected by W. Shake-speare. London, printed by W. W. for Mathew Law, and are to be sold at his shop in Paules Churchyard, neere vnto S. Augustines gate, at the signe of the Foxe. 1613.

4°. A–K⁴ 17.9 cm.

Printed by William White. The fifth edition (first, 1598). Bound by Hayday in red goatskin, gold tooling on cover and spine, gilt edges. Collation note of James Orchard Halliwell on rear endpaper, and on the front endpaper his inscription: "This copy belonged to the late Mr. Windus & was purchased at his sale, March, 1868, by Lilly for [erased]. I obtained it in April, 1870, by exchange with Wm. Harrison Esq. of Sambsbury Hall, J. O. H." The Huth copy (with bookplate) acquired by Mr. Cochran in November 1911 prior to the public sale.

Gift of Alexander S. Cochran, December 1911.

STC 22284   Greg 145(f)

SHAKESPEARE, WILLIAM, 1564–1616

EC 174
Henry IV,
Part II
1600

The second part of Henrie the fourth, continuing to his death, and coronation of Henrie the fift. With the humours of Sir Iohn Falstaffe, and swaggering Pistoll. As it hath been sundrie times publikely acted by the right honourable, the lord chamberlaine his seruants. Written by William Shakespeare. London printed by V. S. for Andrew Wise, and William Aspley. 1600.

4°. A–D⁴E⁶F–K⁴L² 17 cm.

Printed by Valentine Simmes. The first edition, second issue, in which leaves $E_{3,4}$ have been canceled, and replaced by a complete sheet of four leaves, of which the first three are signed E_3, E_4, and E_5. Bound by F. Bedford in red goatskin, gold tooling on cover and spine, gilt edges. A few leaves remargined, but without loss of text. The James Orchard Halliwell copy, sold by Sotheby's, 21 May 1857, lot 872. The Huth copy (with bookplate) acquired by Mr. Cochran in November 1911 prior to the public sale.

Gift of Alexander S. Cochran, December 1911.

STC 22288a   Greg 167(aII)

SHAKESPEARE, WILLIAM, 1564–1616

EC 175
Henry V
1600

The cronicle history of Henry the fift, with his battell fought at Agin Court in France. Together with auntient Pistoll. As it hath bene sundry times playd by the right honorable the lord chamberlaine his seruants. London printed by Thomas Creede, for Tho. Millington, and Iohn Busby. And are to be sold at his house in Carter Lane, next the Powle head. 1600.

4°. A–G⁴   18 cm.

The first edition. Bound in vellum. Manuscript note by Richard Heber on front endpaper, and Bibliotheca Heberiana stamp; sold as lot 5461 in the Heber sale by Sotheby's, 28 June 1834. Sold as lot 1431 in the George Daniel sale by Sotheby's, 26 July 1864. The Huth copy (with bookplate) acquired by Mr. Cochran in November 1911 prior to the public sale.

Gift of Alexander S. Cochran, December 1911.

STC 22289   Greg 165(a)

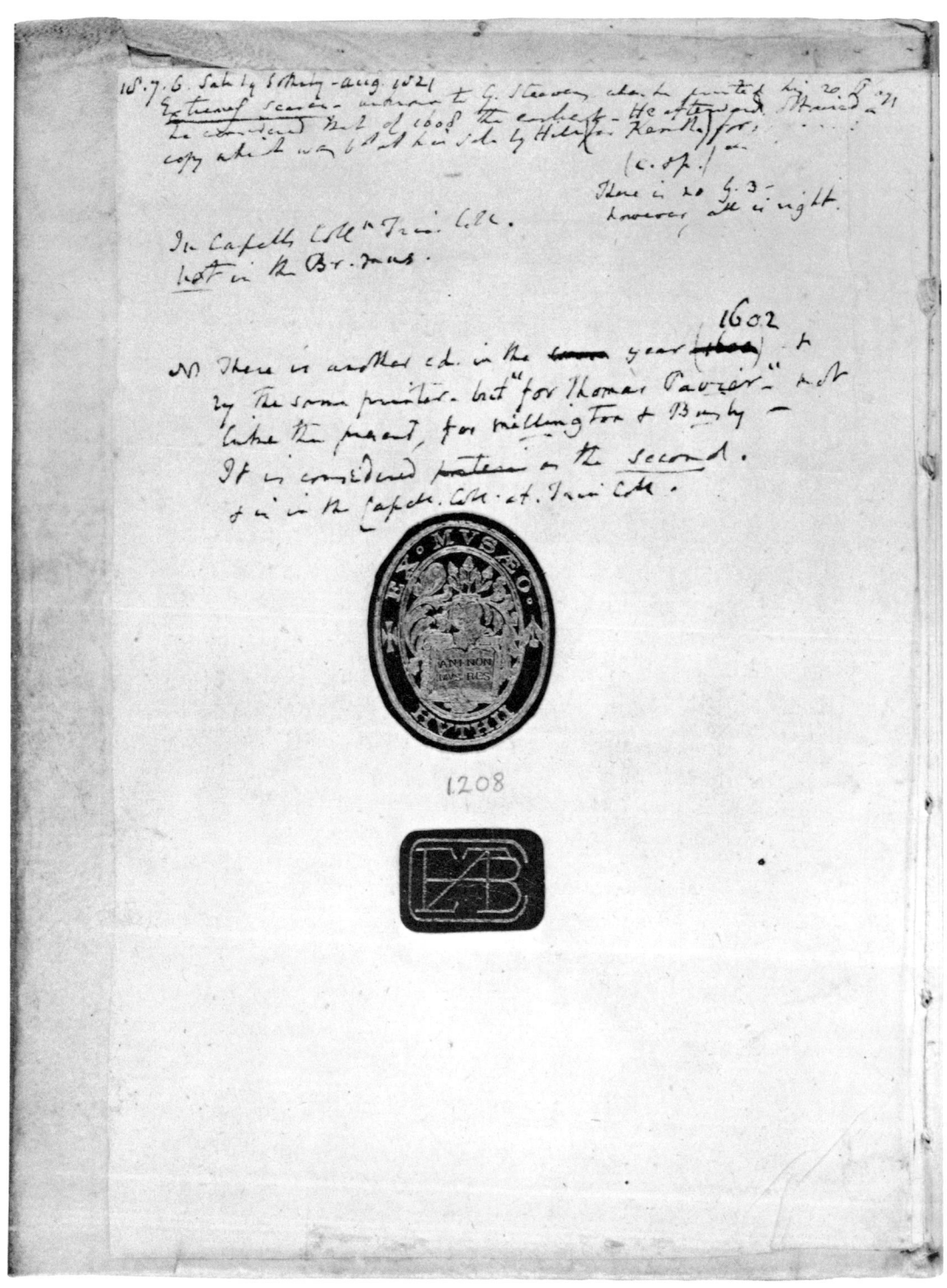

Shakespeare's *Henry V*, 1600 (EC 175)
Richard Heber's notes, and Henry Huth's bookplate, on the front end paper

SHAKESPEARE, WILLIAM, 1564–1616

EC 176
Henry V
[1619]

The chronicle history of Henry the fift, with his battell fought at Agin Court in France. Together with ancient Pistoll. As it hath bene sundry times playd by the right honourable the lord chamberlaine his seruants. Printed for T. P. 1608. [*recte* 1619]

4°. A–G⁴   18.8 cm.

The third edition (first, 1600). Bound by F. Bedford in red goatskin, gold tooling on cover and spine, gilt edges. This is one of ten plays reprinted by William Jaggard in 1619, possibly as part of a collection for which a general title page was never printed. All ten of these quartos are in the club's collection. The Huth copy (with bookplate) acquired by Mr. Cochran in November 1911 prior to the public sale.

Gift of Alexander S. Cochran, December 1911.

STC 22291   Greg 165(c)

SHAKESPEARE, WILLIAM, 1564–1616

EC 200
Henry VI, Parts II and III
[1619]

The whole contention betweene the two famous houses, Lancaster and Yorke. With the tragicall ends of the good Duke Humfrey, Richard Duke of Yorke, and King Henrie the sixt. Diuided into two parts: and newly corrected and enlarged. Written by William Shakespeare, Gent. printed at London, for T. P. [1619]

4°. A–Q⁴   18 cm.

The third, bad quarto, edition (first, 1594). Bound

in olive green goatskin, gold tooling with acorns on the cover. This is a style of binding made for John Bellingham Inglis about 1825 (Seymour De Ricci, *English Collectors of Books and Manuscripts,* pp. 97–98; this copy was lot 94 in the Inglis sale, Sotheby's, 12 April 1826). These plays are "bad quarto" versions of 2 and 3 Henry VI. These are two of ten plays reprinted by William Jaggard in 1619, possibly as part of a collection for which a general title page was never issued. The Huth copy (with bookplate) acquired by Mr. Cochran in November 1911 prior to the public sale.

Gift of Alexander S. Cochran, December 1911.

Wing S 2923

SHAKESPEARE, WILLIAM, 1564–1616

EC 171
Julius Caesar
[after 1691]

Julius Caesar. A tragedy. As it is now acted at the Theatre Royal. Written by William Shakespeare. London, printed by H. H. Jun. for Hen Herringman and R Bentley in Russel-street in Covent Garden, and sold by Joseph Knight and Francis Saunders at the Blew Anchor in the lower walk of the New-exchange in the Strand. [after 1691]

4°. A–H^4 21.7 cm.

Printed by Henry Hills, Jr. The third quarto edition (first, 1684). Bound by F. Bedford in red goatskin, gold tooling on cover and spine, gilt edges. The Huth copy (with bookplate) acquired by Mr. Cochran in November 1911 prior to the public sale.

Gift of Alexander S. Cochran, December 1911.

Wing S 2923

EC 177
King Lear
[1619]

SHAKESPEARE, WILLIAM, 1564–1616

M. William Shake-speare, his true chronicle history of the life and death of King Lear, and his three daughters. With the unfortunate life of Edgar, sonne and heire to the Earle of Glocester, and his sullen and assumed humour of Tom of Bedlam. As it was plaid before the kings maiesty at White-hall, uppon S. Stephens night, in Christmas hollidaies. By his maiesties seruants, playing vsually at the Globe on the Banck-side. Printed for Nathaniel Butter. 1608. [*recte* 1619]

4°. A–L⁴   18.2 cm.

The second edition (first, 1608). Bound by Lewis in blue goatskin, gold tooling on cover and spine, gilt edges. This is one of the ten plays reprinted by William Jaggard in 1619, possibly as part of a collection for which a general title page was never printed. The James Orchard Halliwell copy, sold by Sotheby's, 23 May 1856, lot 344; the catalog note states that "This volume was bought for the low price of £12 12s. many years ago, of the late Mr. Thorpe, whose taste and judgment are only now beginning to be fully appreciated, nearly all the rarities collected by him realizing far beyond his price." The Halliwell copy brought £22.10s. The Huth copy (with bookplate) acquired by Mr. Cochran in November 1911 prior to the public sale.

Gift of Alexander S. Cochran, December 1911.

STC 22293   Greg 265(b)

SHAKESPEARE, WILLIAM, 1564–1616

EC 179
Lucrece
1594

Lvcrece. London. Printed by Richard Field, for Iohn Harrison, and are to be sold at the signe of the White Greyhound in Paules Church-yard. 1594.

4°. A²B–M⁴N² (lacking N₂, blank)   18.2 cm.

The first edition. Bound in brown goatskin, gilt edges. George Daniel's copy, with a manuscript note, signed, on a front flyleaf; sold as lot 1451 in the Daniel sale, Sotheby's, 26 July 1864. The Huth copy (with bookplate) acquired by Mr. Cochran in November 1911 prior to the public sale.

Gift of Alexander S. Cochran, December 1911.

STC 22345

SHAKESPEARE, WILLIAM, 1564–1616

EC 180
Merchant
of Venice
1600

The most excellent historie of the merchant of Venice. With the extreame crueltie of Shylocke the Iewe towards the sayd merchant, in cutting a iust pound of his flesh: and the obtayning of Portia by the choyse of three chests. As it hath beene diuers times acted by the lord chamberlaine his seruants. Written by William Shakespeare. At London, printed by I. R. for Thomas Heyes, and are to be sold in Paules Church-yard, at the signe of the Greene Dragon. 1600.

4°. A–I⁴K²   177 cm.

Printed by James Roberts. The first edition. Bound by C. Murton in straight-grain brown goatskin, gold tooling on cover and spine, gilt edges. Manu-

Lucrece.

London.
Printed by Richard Field, for John Harrison,
and are to be sold at the Signe of the New
white Greyhound in Paules Church-yard. 1594.

4to.

First Edition. Beautiful copy,
and
Quite Perfect.

This volume is of most extraordinary rarity.
Only two other perfect copies are known
to exist. One is in the Malone Collection
at Oxford.* An indifferent copy, wanting
the last Leaf, was sold by Mr. Evans (Lot
1584, Combes's Library) Dec.r 9: 1837.
for   . The purchasers were Messrs Payne
& Foss, for the Honble Thomas Grenville.

George Daniel,
Islington.

† The other copy is also at Oxford — it was
bequeathed to the Bodleian Library by the
late Mr. Caldecott.

Since writing the foregoing, one other copy has been discovered, a very indifferent one, but perfect with
the following exceptions; viz.— "Paules Church-yard," in the title, almost entirely torn away — front of the
broken in sheet B; and "This said," &c. & "publisht" in the last page, also ten ff. It is in Mr. Rodd's
catalogue for 1840. № 3108. The price Mr Rodd obtained for it was

Shakespeare's *Lucrece*, 1594 (EC 179)
George Daniel's notes on the front fly leaf

The most excellent Historie of the *Merchant of Venice*.

VVith the extreame crueltie of *Shylocke* the Iewe towards the sayd Merchant, in cutting a iust pound of his flesh: and the obtayning of *Portia* by the choyse of three chests.

As it hath beene diuers times acted by the Lord Chamberlaine his Seruants.

Written by William Shakespeare.

AT LONDON,
Printed by *I. R.* for Thomas Heyes,
and are to be sold in Paules Church-yard, at the signe of the Greene Dragon.
1600.

Shakespeare's *Merchant of Venice*, 1600 (EC 180)
The first edition

script note, probably by Henry Huth, on the front flyleaf. The Huth copy (with bookplate) acquired by Mr. Cochran in November 1911 prior to the public sale.

Gift of Alexander S. Cochran, December 1911.

STC 22296   Greg 172(a)

SHAKESPEARE, WILLIAM, 1564–1616

EC 181
Merchant
of Venice
[1619]

The excellent history of the merchant of Venice. With the extreme cruelty of Shylocke the Iew towards the saide merchant, in cutting a iust pound of his flesh. And the obtaining of Portia, by the choyse of three caskets. Written by W. Shakespeare. Printed by J. Roberts, 1600. [*recte,* 1619]

4°. A–K⁴   17.6 cm.

The second edition (first, 1600). Bound by F. Bedford in crimson goatskin, gold tooling on cover and spine, gilt edges. This is one of the ten plays reprinted by William Jaggard in 1619, possibly as part of a collection for which a general title page was never printed. The Huth copy (with bookplate) acquired by Mr. Cochran in November 1911 prior to the public sale.

Gift of Alexander S. Cochran, December 1911.

STC 22297   Greg 172(b)

SHAKESPEARE, WILLIAM, 1564–1616

EC 182
Merry Wives
1619

A most pleasant and excellent conceited comedy, of Sir Iohn Falstaffe, and the merry wives of Windsor. With the swaggering vaine of ancient Pistoll, and

Corporall Nym. Written by W. Shakespeare. Printed for Arthur Johnson, 1619.

4°. A–G⁴ 17.5 cm.

The second edition (first, 1602). Bound in red straight-grain goatskin, gold tooling on cover and spine, gilt edges. This is one of the ten plays reprinted by William Jaggard in 1619, possibly as part of a collection for which a general title page was never printed. The Huth copy (with bookplate) acquired by Mr. Cochran in November 1911 prior to the public sale.

Gift of Alexander S. Cochran, December 1911.

STC 22300   Greg 187(b)

SHAKESPEARE, WILLIAM, 1564–1616

EC 183
Midsummer
Night's Dream
1600

A midsommer nights dreame. As it hath beene sundry times publickely acted, by the right honourable, the lord chamberlaine his seruants. Written by William Shakespeare. Imprinted at London, for Thomas Fisher, and are to be soulde at his shoppe, at the signe of the White Hart, in Fleetestreete. 1600.

4°. A–H⁴ 19.4 cm.

The first edition. Bound in marbled-paper wrappers. Bibliotheca Heberiana stamp on endpaper; lot 5442 in the Heber sale, Sotheby's, 28 June 1834; on the endpaper is a note, probably by Heber, stating that this copy had come from "Bindleys Sale Pt. III 2040—Feb. 1819." This copy was also owned by George Daniel, and it was sold with his books, by Sotheby's, on 26 July 1864, lot 1425. The Huth copy (with bookplate) acquired by Mr. Cochran in November 1911 prior to the public sale.

Gift of Alexander S. Cochran, December 1911.

STC 22302   Greg 170(a)

SHAKESPEARE, WILLIAM, 1564–1616

EC 184
Midsummer Night's Dream
[1619]

A midsommer nights dreame. As it hath beene sundry times publickely acted, by the right honourable, the lord chamberlaine his seruants. Written by William Shakespeare. Printed by Iames Roberts, 1600. [*recte*, 1619]

4°. A–H⁴   17.8 cm.

The second edition (first, 1600). Bound by Rivière in dark green goatskin, gilt edges. This is one of ten plays reprinted by William Jaggard in 1619, possibly as part of a collection for which a general title page was never printed.

Gift of Alexander S. Cochran, December 1911.

STC 22203   Greg 170(b)

SHAKESPEARE, WILLIAM, 1564–1616

EC 185
Much Ado about Nothing
1600

Much adoe about nothing. As it hath been sundrie times publikely acted by the right honourable, the lord chamberlaine his seruants. Written by William Shakespeare. London printed by V. S. for Andrew Wise, and William Aspley. 1600.

4°. A–I⁴   17.5 cm.

Printed by Valentine Simmes. The first edition. Bound by F. Bedford in brown goatskin, gold tooling on cover and spine, gilt edges. The Huth copy (with bookplate) acquired by Mr. Cochran in November 1911 prior to the public sale.

Gift of Alexander S. Cochran, December 1911.

STC 22304   Greg 168(a)

SHAKESPEARE, WILLIAM, 1564–1616

EC 186
Othello
1622

The tragoedy of Othello, the Moore of Venice. As it hath been diuerse times acted at the Globe, and at the Black-Friers, by his maiesties seruants. Written by William Shakespeare. London, printed by N. O. for Thomas Walkley, and are to be sold at his shop, at the Eagle and Child, in Brittans Bursse. 1622.

$4°$. $A^2B-M^4N^2$ 17.9 cm.

Printed by Nicholas Okes. The first edition. Bound in straight-grain blue goatskin, elaborate gold tooling on cover and spine, initials of George Daniel on the upper side of the cover, gilt edges. Sold with Daniel's books, by Sotheby's, 26 July 1864, lot 1439. The Huth copy (with bookplate) acquired by Mr. Cochran in November 1911 prior to the public sale.

Gift of Alexander S. Cochran, December 1911.

STC 22305   Greg 379(a)

Shakespeare's *Othello*, 1622 (EC 186)
The first edition

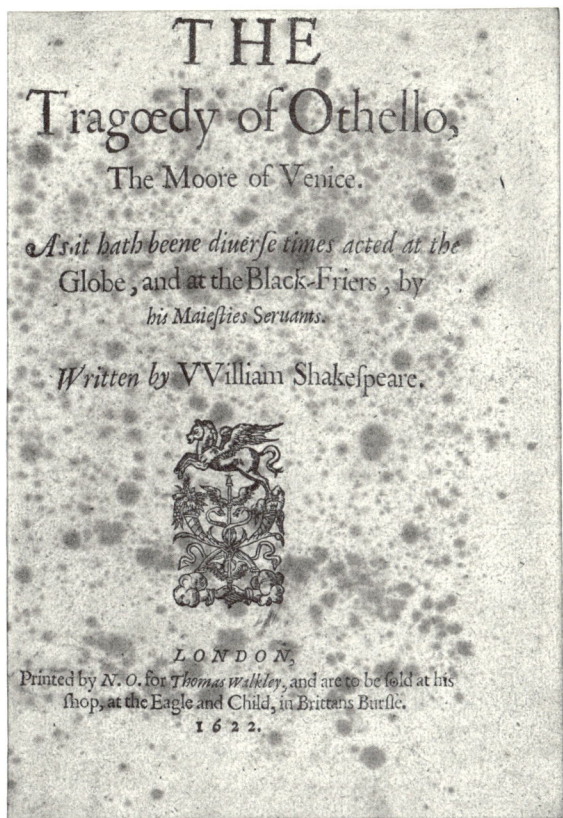

George Daniel's initials on the upper cover

Shakespeare's *Othello*, 1630 (EC 187)
The upper cover of the binding, done for J. B. Inglis about 1825

SHAKESPEARE, WILLIAM, 1564–1616

EC 187
Othello
1630

The tragoedy of Othello, the Moore of Venice. As it hath beene diuerse times acted at the Globe, and at the Black-Friers, by his maiesties seruants. Written by William Shakespeare. London, printed by A. M. for Richard Hawkins, and are to be sold at his shoppe in Chancery-lane, neere Sergeants-inne. 1630.

4°. A–M⁴ 18.4 cm.

Printed by Augustine Mathewes. The second edition (first, 1622). Title page mended. Bound in straight-grain green goatskin, gold tooling with acorns on the cover. This is a style of binding made for J. B. Inglis about 1825 (Seymour de Ricci, *English Collectors of Books and Manuscripts,* pp. 97–98). This copy was lot 104 in the Inglis sale by Sotheby's, 12 April 1826. The Huth copy (with bookplate) acquired by Mr. Cochran in November 1911 prior to the public sale.

Gift of Alexander S. Cochran, December 1911.

STC 22306   Greg 379(c)

SHAKESPEARE, WILLIAM, 1564–1616

EC 188
Pericles
1609

The late, and much admired play, called Pericles, Prince of Tyre. With the true relation of the whole historie, aduentures, and fortunes of the said prince: as also, the no lesse strange, and worthy accidents, in the birth and life, of his daughter Mariana. As it hath been dieuers and sundry times acted by his

THE LATE, *Scipio Squyer. 5. May. 160*

And much admired Play,

Called

Pericles, Prince
of Tyre.

With the true Relation of the whole Historie,
aduentures, and fortunes of the said Prince:

As also,

The no lesse strange, and worthy accidents,
in the Birth and Life, of his Daughter
MARIANA.

As it hath been diuers and sundry times acted by
his Maiesties Seruants, at the Globe on
the Banck-side.

By William Shakespeare.

Imprinted at London for *Henry Gosson,* and are
to be sold at the signe of the Sunne in
Pater-noster row, &c.
1609.

Shakespeare's *Pericles,* 1609 (EC 188)

maiesties seruants, at the Globe on the Banck-side. By William Shakespeare. Imprinted at London for Henry Gosson, and are to be sold at the signe of the Sunne in Pater-noster Row, &c. 1609.

4°. A–I⁴   18 cm.

The first edition. Bound by Lewis in brown goatskin, gold tooling on cover and spine, gilt edges; initials of George Daniel on upper side of the cover. Sold with Daniel's books by Sotheby's, 26 July 1864, lot 1438. Signature of Scipio Squyer, and dated 5 May 160[9] on the title page. The Huth copy (with bookplate) acquired by Mr. Cochran in November 1911 prior to the public sale.

Gift of Alexander S. Cochran, December 1911.

STC 22334   Greg 284(a)

SHAKESPEARE, WILLIAM, 1564–1616

EC 189
Pericles
1619

The late, and much admired play, called, Pericles, Prince of Tyre. With the true relation of the whole history, aduentures, and fortunes of the saide prince. Written by W. Shakespeare. Printed for T. P. 1619.

4°. [-]¹R–Z⁴Aa⁴Bb¹   18 cm.

Printed by William Jaggard for Thomas Pavier. The fourth edition (first, 1609). The signatures show that it was intended to follow *The Whole Contention* in the collection Jaggard was apparently preparing to issue in 1619. Bound in vellum, gold tooling on cover and spine, gilt edges. The Huth copy (with bookplate) acquired by Mr. Cochran in November 1911 prior to the public sale.

Gift of Alexander S. Cochran, December 1911.

STC 26101   Greg 284(d)

SHAKESPEARE, WILLIAM, 1564–1616

EC 190
Poems
1640

Poems: written by Wil. Shake-speare. Gent. Printed at London by Tho. Cotes, and are to be sold by Iohn Benson, dwelling in St. Dunstans Church-yard. 1640.

$8°$. $[-]^1 \star^4 A–L^8 M^4$ 13.8 cm.

The first edition. Bound in contemporary calf, blind tooling on cover.

Gift of Alexander S. Cochran, December 1911.

STC 22344

SHAKESPEARE, WILLIAM, 1564–1616

EC 178
Richard II
1608

The tragedie of King Richard the second. As it hath been publikely acted by the right honourable the lord chamberlaine his seruants. By William Shake-speare. London, printed by W. W. for Mathew Law, and are to be sold at his shop in Paules Church-yard, at the signe of the Foxe. 1608.

$4°$. $A–K^4$ 17.5 cm.

Printed by William White. The fourth edition (first, 1597). Bound by F. Bedford in crimson goatskin, gold tooling on cover and spine, gilt edges. The Huth copy (with bookplate) acquired by Mr. Cochran in November 1911 prior to the public sale.

Gift of Alexander S. Cochran, December 1911.

STC 22310   Greg 141(d★)

SHAKESPEARE, WILLIAM, 1564–1616

EC +33
Richard III
[1597]

[The tragedy of King Richard the third. . . . 1597]

4°. C–D⁴ [a fragment]

A fragment only, consisting of four half sheets, uncut and unsewn, as issued, measuring 19.7 by 28.2 cm. Mounted in an album bound in red goatskin, gold tooling on cover and spine. Each leaf bears the British Museum duplicate stamp.

Acquired by exchange with the British Museum, for the Huth copy, which was complete, November 1911.

SCT 22314   Greg 142(a)

SHAKESPEARE, WILLIAM, 1564–1616

EC 191
Romeo and
Juliet
1599

The most excellent and lamentable tragedie, of Romeo and Iuliet. Newly corrected, augmented, and amended: as it hath bene sundry times publiquely acted, by the right honourable the lord chamberlaine his seruants. London, printed by Thomas Creede, for Cuthbert Burby, and are to be sold at his shop neare the Exchange. 1599.

4°. A–L⁴M²   16.7 cm.

The second edition (first, 1597). The text of this and later editions represents a different version of

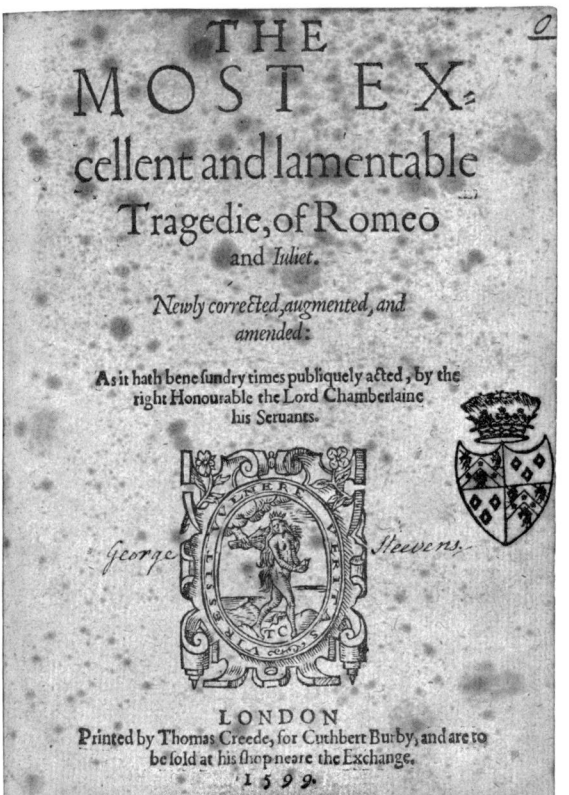

Shakespeare's *Romeo and Juliet*, 1599 (EC 191) The second edition, but a different version from that of the first edition of 1597

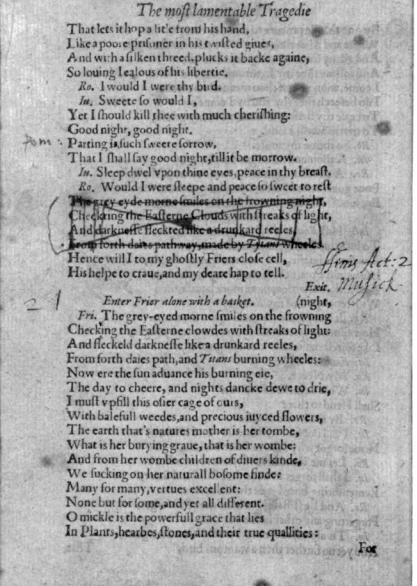

Anagram on f. H₃v   Performance notes on f. D₄v

the play, fuller than that previously published in the first quarto of 1597. Bound in red goatskin, gold tooling on cover and spine, gilt edges; initials of George Daniel on upper side of cover, On H_3v is written in a seventeenth-century hand, "Anagr. Elisabeth Rotton Her Lot is to b neat." There are annotations for performance throughout in a seventeenth-century hand. Signature of George Steevens on the title page, and a few notes by him in the text; this copy was possibly lot 1299 in the Steevens sale by King, 21 May 1800. Bookstamp of the Duke of Roxburghe on the title page; sold as lot 3860 in the Roxburghe sale by Evans, 6 June 1812. This copy was later owned by the Marquis of Blandford, and in his sale (White Knights library) by Evans, 30 June 1819, it was lot 3957. This copy also appears, as an anonymous property, in a sale by Evans, 25–29 January 1830, lot 796. It was then owned by George Daniel, whose monogram is stamped on the cover; in his sale by Sotheby's, 26 July 1864, it was lot 1430. The Huth copy (with bookplate) acquired by Mr. Cochran in November 1911 prior to the public sale.

Gift of Alexander S. Cochran, December 1911.

STC 22323   Greg 143(b)

SHAKESPEARE, WILLIAM, 1564–1616

EC 192
Romeo and
Juliet
[1622]

The most excellent and lamentable tragedie, of Romeo and Ivliet. As it hath beene sundrie times publikely acted, by the kings maiesties seruants at the Globe. Written by W. Shake-speare. Newly corrected, augmented, and amended. London, printed for Iohn Smethwicke, and are to bee sold at his shop in Saint Dunstanes Church-yard, in Fleetestreete vnder the Dyall. [1622]

4°. A–L⁴   17.7 cm.

The fourth edition (first, 1597), second issue. Bound by F. Bedford in red goatskin, gold tooling on cover and spine, gilt edges. The Huth copy (with bookplate) acquired by Mr. Cochran in November 1911 prior to the public sale.

Gift of Alexander S. Cochran, December 1911.

STC 22325a   Greg 143(e+)

SHAKESPEARE, WILLIAM, 1564–1616

EC 193
Romeo and
Juliet
1637

The most excellent and lamentable tragedie of Romeo and Juliet. As it hath been sundry times publikely acted by the kings majesties servants at the Globe. Written by W. Shake-speare. Newly corrected, augmented, and amended. London, printed by R. Young for John Smethwicke, and are to be sold at his shop in St. Dunstans Church-yard in Fleetstreet, under the Dyall. 1637.

4°. A–L⁴   19 cm.

The fifth edition (first, 1597). Bound by F. Bedford in red goatskin, gold tooling on cover and spine. The Thomas Corser copy, with his collation mark on the front endpaper; sold as lot 416 in the Corser sale by Sotheby's, 14 February 1871. The Huth copy (with bookplate) acquired by Mr. Cochran in November 1911 prior to the public sale.

Gift of Alexander S. Cochran, December 1911.

STC 22326   Greg 143(g)

SHAKESPEARE, WILLIAM, 1564–1616

EC 194
Sonnets
1609

Shake-Speares sonnets. Neuer before imprinted. At London by G. Eld for T. T. and are to be solde by Iohn Wright, dwelling at Christ Church gate. 1609.

4°. [A]²B–L⁴M²   17.5 cm.

The first edition. Bound by F. Bedford in straight-grain green goatskin, gold tooling on cover and spine, gilt edges. The Huth copy (with bookplate) acquired by Mr. Cochran in November 1911 prior to the public sale.

Gift of Alexander S. Cochran, December 1911.

STC 22353a

SHAKESPEARE, WILLIAM, 1564–1616

EC 195
Taming of the Shrew
1631

A wittie and pleasant comedie called the taming of the shrew. As it was acted by his maiesties seruants at the Blacke Friers and the Globe. Written by Will. Shakespeare. London, printed by W. S. for Iohn Smethwicke, and are to be sold at his shop in Saint Dunstones Church-yard vnder the Diall. 1631.

4°. A–I⁴   18.5 cm.

Printed by William Stansby. The first separate edition. Bound by F. Bedford in rust goatskin, gold tooling on cover and spine, gilt edges.

Gift of Alexander S. Cochran, December 1911.

STC 22327   Greg 140(e)

SHAKESPEARE, WILLIAM, 1564–1616

EC 196
Titus
Andronicus
1611

The most lamentable tragedie of Titus Andronicus. As it hath svndry times beene plaide by the kings maiesties seruants. London, printed for Eedward [sic] White, and are to be solde at his shoppe, nere the little north dore of Pauls, at the signe of the Gun. 1611.

4°. A–K⁴   17 cm.

The third edition (first, 1594). Bound by Lewis in green goatskin, gold tooling on cover and spine, gilt edges. The Huth copy (with bookplate) acquired by Mr. Cochran in November 1911 prior to the public sale.

Gift of Alexander S. Cochran, December 1911.

STC 22330   Greg 117(c)

SHAKESPEARE, WILLIAM, 1564–1616

EC 197
Troilus and
Cressida
1609

The famous historie of Troylus and Cresseid. Excellently expressing the beginning of their loues, with the conceited wooing of Pandarus Prince of Licia. Written by William Shakespeare. London imprinted by G. Eld for R. Bonian and H. Walley, and are to be sold at the spred Eagle in Paules Churchyard, ouer against the great north doore. 1609.

4°. ¶²A–L⁴M²   18.1 cm.

The first edition, first issue, with the title and pro-

THE
Famous Historie of
Troylus *and* Cresseid.

Excellently expressing the beginning
of their loues, with the conceited wooing
of *Pandarus* Prince of *Licia*.

Written by William Shakespeare.

LONDON
Imprinted by *G. Eld* for *R. Bonian* and *H. Walley*, and
are to be sold at the spred Eagle in Paules
Church-yeard, ouer against the
great North doore.
1609.

Shakespeare's *Troilus and Cressida*, 1609 (EC 197)
The title page on ¶¹

logue of the second issue inserted before the first title. Bound by Lewis in brown goatskin, gold tooling on cover and spine, gilt edges; initials of George Daniel on upper side of cover. Sold with Daniel's books by Sotheby's, 26 July 1864, lot 1439. The Huth copy (with bookplate) acquired by Mr. Cochran in November 1911 prior to the public sale.

Gift of Alexander S. Cochran, December 1911.

STC 22331   Greg 279(aII)

SHAKESPEARE, WILLIAM, 1564–1616

EC 199
Venus and Adonis
1594

Venvs and Adonis. . . . London. Imprinted by Richard Field, and are to be sold at the signe of the White Greyhound in Paules Church-yard. 1594.

4°. [A]^{2}B–G^{4}H^2 18.4 cm.

The second edition (first, 1593). Bound by Hayday in red leather, gold tooling on cover and spine, gilt edges. A few leaves have been remargined. George Daniel's copy, and sold as lot 1453 in his sale by Sotheby's, 26 July 1864, in which the catalog notes: "This is a taller copy than Jolley's, a poor one, bought by Mr. Grenville for £106 at these rooms in 1844. The Bodleian copy is a wretched one, perfect as to leaves, but with several slight defects. The present cannot be called a fine copy, yet still it may be considered the finest known. We are not aware that more than three copies exist." The Huth copy (with bookplate) acquired by Mr. Cochran in November 1911 prior to the public sale.

Gift of Alexander S. Cochran, December 1911.

STC 22355

SHAKESPEARE, WILLIAM, 1564–1616, *apocrypha*

EC 201
Fair Em
1631

A pleasant comedie of Faire Em, the millers daughter of Manchester: with the loue of William the Conqueror. As it was sundty [*sic*] times publiquely acted in the honourable citie of London, by the right honourable the Lord Strange his seruants. London, printed for Iohn Wright, and ar to be sold at his shop at the signe of the Bible in Guilt-spur street without New-gate. 1631.

4°. A–F⁴ (lacking F$_4$, blank)   17.3 cm.

The second edition (first, ?1593). Bound by Rivière in crimson goatskin, gold tooling on cover and spine. Many leaves have been remargined or mended.

Gift of Alexander S. Cochran, December 1911.

STC 7676   Greg 113(b)

SHAKESPEARE, WILLIAM, 1564–1616, *apocrypha*

EC 202
London Prodigal
1605

The London prodigall. As it was plaide by the kings maiesties seruants. By William Shakespeare, London. Printed by T. C. for Nathaniel Butter, and are to be sold neere S. Austins gate, at the signe of the Pyde Bull. 1605.

4°. A–G⁴   17.8 cm.

Printed by Thomas Creede. The first edition. Bound by Lewis in dark blue goatskin, gold tooling on cover, gilt edges; initials of George Daniel on upper side of cover. Sold with Daniel's books by Sotheby's, 26 July 1864, lot 1462. The Huth copy (with bookplate) acquired by Mr. Cochran in November 1911 prior to the public sale.

Gift of Alexander S. Cochran, December 1911.

STC 22333   Greg 222(a)

SHAKESPEARE, WILLIAM, 1564–1616, *apocrypha*

EC 203
Puritan Widow
1607

The pvritaine or the widdow of Watling-streete. Acted by the children of Paules. Written by W. S. Imprinted at London by G. Eld. 1607.

4° A–H⁴ (lacking A_1, probably blank)   17.7 cm.

The first edition. Bound in purple goatskin, gold tooling on cover and spine, gilt edges; initials of George Daniel on upper side of cover. Sold with Daniel's books by Sotheby's, 26 July 1864, lot 1463. The Huth copy (with bookplate) acquired by Mr. Cochran in November 1911 prior to the public sale.

Gift of Alexander S. Cochran, December 1911.

STC 21531   Greg 251(a)

SHAKESPEARE, WILLIAM, 1564–1616, *apocrypha*

EC 204
Sir John
Oldcaste
[1619]

The first part of the true & honorable history, of the life of Sir Iohn Old-castle, the good Lord Cobham. As it hath bene lately acted by the right honorable the Earle of Notingham Lord High Admirall of England, his seruants. Written by William Shakespeare. London printed for T. P. 1600. [*recte* 1619]

4°. A–K⁴   18.8 cm.

The second edition (first, 1600). Printed by William Jaggard for Thomas Pavier; in this instance, Jaggard retained the date of the original first edition. This is one of the ten plays reprinted by William Jaggard in 1619, possibly as part of a collection for which a general title page was never printed. Bound by F. Bedford in brown goatskin, gold tooling on cover and spine, gilt edges. The attribution to Shakespeare appears for the first time on this title page; the true authors were Anthony Munday, Michael Drayton, Robert Wilson, and Richard Hathway. The Huth copy (with bookplate) acquired by Mr. Cochran in November 1911 prior to the public sale.

Gift of Alexander S. Cochran, December 1911.

STC 18796   Greg 166(b)

SHAKESPEARE, WILLIAM, 1564–1616, *apocrypha*

EC 205
Thomas Lord
Cromwell
1613

The true chronicle historie of the whole life and death of Thomas Lord Cromwell. As it hath beene sundry times publikely acted by the kings maiesties

The first part

Of the true & honorable history, of the Life of Sir Iohn Old-castle, the good Lord Cobham.

As it hath bene lately acted by the Right honorable the Earle of Notingham Lord High Admirall of England, his Seruants.

Written by William Shakespeare.

London printed for T. P.
1600.

Sir John Oldcastle, 1619 (EC 204)
The second edition, bearing the date of the first, and showing Shakespeare's name on a title page for the first time

seruants. Written by W. S. London: printed by Thomas Snodham. 1613.

4°. A–G⁴ 17.5 cm.

The second edition (first, 1602). Bound by F. Bedford in crimson goatskin, gold tooling on cover and spine, gilt edges. The first attribution to Shakespeare of this play occurs in the catalog found at the end of *The Old Law,* by Massinger, Middleton, and Rowley, 1656. Many names have been proposed for "W. S.," but none with any certainty. The Huth copy (with bookplate) acquired by Mr. Cochran in November 1911 prior to the public sale.

Gift of Alexander S. Cochran, December 1911.

STC 21532   Greg 189(b)

SHAKESPEARE, WILLIAM, 1564–1616, *apocrypha*

EC 206
Troublesome
Reign Of
King John
1622

The first and second part of the troublesome raigne of Iohn King of England. . . . As they were (sundry times) lately acted. Written by W. Shakespeare. London, printed by Aug: Mathewes for Thomas Dewe, and are to be sold at his shop in St. Dunstones Church-yard in Fleet-street, 1622.

4°. A–L⁴M² 18.1 cm.

The second edition (first, 1611). Bound in calf, blind and gold tooling on cover and spine. The two parts were first published separately in 1591. Dogmersfield library bookplace of Sir Henry St. John

Mildmay, and sold as lot 475 in the Mildmay sale by Sotheby's, 20 April 1907. Collation note of Bernard Quaritch on rear endpaper.

Gift of Alexander S. Cochran, December 1911.

STC 14647   Greg 101/102(c)

SHAKESPEARE, WILLIAM, 1564–1616, *apocrypha*

EC 207
A Yorkshire Tragedy
1619

A Yorkshire tragedie. Not so new, as lamentable and true. Written by W. Shakespeare. Printed for T. P. 1619:

4°. [-]¹A–D⁴(-D$_4$, title)   17.9 cm.

Printed by William Jaggard for Thomas Pavier. The second edition (first, 1608). The title was printed on D$_4$, and the leaf was transferred to the beginning. This is one of ten plays reprinted by Jaggard in 1619, possible as part of a collection for which a general title page was never printed. The attribution to Shakespeare occurs both in the Stationer's Register entry and on the title page to the first edition. Bound in straight-grain green goatskin, gold tooling with acorns on the cover. This is a type of binding made for J. B. Inglis about 1825 (Seymour de Ricci, *English Collectors of Books and Manuscripts*, pp. 97–98). This copy was sold as lot 100 in the Inglis sale by Sotheby's, 12 April 1826. The Huth copy (with bookplate) acquired by Mr. Cochran in November 1911 prior to the public sale.

Gift of Alexander S. Cochran, December 1911.

STC 22341   Greg 272(b)

SHAKESPEARE, WILLIAM, 1564–1616, and John Fletcher

EC 198
Two Noble
Kinsmen
1634

The two noble kinsmen: presented at the Blackfriers by the kings maiesties servants, with great applause: Written by the memorable worthies of their time; Mr. John Fletcher, and Mr. William Shakespeare. Gent. printed at London by Tho. Cotes, for Iohn Waterson: and are to be sold at the signe of the Crowne in Pauls Church-yard. 1634.

4°. [A]¹B–M⁴N¹   18.1 cm.

The first edition. Bound in brown goatskin, gold tooling on cover and spine, gilt edges.

Gift of Alexander S. Cochran, December 1911.

STC 11075   Greg 492(a)

SHIRLEY, JAMES, 1596–1666

EC 208
Constant Maid
1640

The constant maid. A comedy. Written by James Shirley. London, printed by J. Raworth, for R. Whitaker. 1640.

4°. A–I⁴ (lacks I₄, blank)   17.8 cm.

The first edition. Bound in mottled calf, gold tooling on cover and spine, gilt edges.

Gift of Alexander S. Cochran, December 1911.

STC 22438   Greg 592(a)

SHIRLEY, JAMES, 1596–1666

EC 209
The Coronation
1640

The coronation a comedy. As it was presented by her majesties servants at the private house in Drury Lane. Written by John Fletcher. Gent. London, printed by Tho. Cotes, for Andrew Crooke, and William Cooke and are to be sold at the signe of the Greene Dragon, in Pauls Chruch-yard, 1640.

4°. A²B–I⁴K² 18.7 cm.

The first edition. Bound in blue cloth. This play was printed as Fletcher's, but Shirley claimed it in a catalog of his plays appended to *The Cardinal* in the collection *Six New Plays* (1653). Bookplate of Percy Fitzgerald, and sold as part of lot 282 by Sotheby's, 14 June 1907. Collation note of Bernard Quaritch on rear endpaper.

Gift of Alexander S. Cochran, December 1911.

STC 22440   Greg 572(a)

SHIRLEY, JAMES, 1596–1666

EC 210
Duke's Mistress
1638

The dvkes mistris, as it was presented by her majesties servants, at the private house in Drury-Lane. Written by Iames Shirly. London, printed by John Norton, for William Cooke, 1638.

4°. A²B–K⁴ 19.2 cm.

The first edition (third variant). Bound by Zaehnsdorf in calf, gold tooling on cover and spine, gilt edges.

Gift of Alexander S. Cochran, December 1911.

STC 22441a   Greg 536(A)

SHIRLEY, JAMES, 1596–1666

EC 211
The Gamester
1637

The gamester. As it was presented by her majesties servants at the private house in Drury-lane. Written by Iames Shirly. London. Printed by Iohn Norton, for Andrew Crooke, and William Cooke. 1637.

4°. A–I⁴K² 18.1 cm.

The first edition. Bound by Lloyd and Wallis in calf, gold tooling on cover and spine, gilt edges. Faded inscription beginning "Dear Mother" on verso of title page.

Gift of Alexander S. Cochran, December 1911.

STC 22443   Greg 523(A)

SHIRLEY, JAMES, 1596–1666

EC 212
Gentleman
of Venice
1655

The gentleman of Venice a tragi-comedie presented at the private house in Salisbury Court by her majesties servants. Written by James Shirley. London, printed for Humphrey Moseley and are to be sold at his shop at the Princes Armes in St. Pauls Church-yard, 1655.

4°. A–K⁴L² 17.6 cm.

The first edition. Bound in blue cloth. Signature of Diana Pigott on title page. Bookplate of Percy Fitzgerald, and sold as part of lot 282 by Sotheby's, 14 June 1907. Collation note of Bernard Quaritch on rear endpaper.

Wing S 3468   Greg 747(AII)

SHIRLEY, JAMES, 1596–1666

EC 213
The Humorous
Courtier
1640

The hvmorovs covrtier. A comedy, as it hath been presented with good applause at the private house in Drury-lane. Written by Iames Shirley Gent. London. Printed by T. C. for William Cooke, and are to be sold by James Becket, in the Inner Temple. 1640.

4°. $A^2B-I^4K^2$ 18.1 cm.

Printed by Thomas Cotes. The first edition. Bound by Rivière in crimson goatskin, gilt edges.

Gift of Alexander S. Cochran, December 1911.

STC 22447   Greg 577(A)

SHIRLEY, JAMES, 1596–1666

EC 214
Poems
1646

Poems &c. by James Shirley. . . . London, printed for Humphrey Moseley, and are to be sold at his shop at the signe of the Princes Armes in St. Pauls Church-yard. 1646.

8°. $A-F^8 A-D^8 A-B^8$ (lacking B_8, blank)   16.3 cm.

The first edition. Bound in contemporary calf, blind tooling on cover. "To Mr. John Bodenham" inscribed on A_1.

Provenance not traced.

Wing S 3481

SHIRLEY, JAMES, 1596–1666

EC 215
The Politician
1655

The polititian, a tragedy, presented at Salisbury Court by her majesties servants; written by James Shirley. London, printed for Humphrey Moseley and are to be sold at his shop at the Princes Armes in St. Pauls Church-yard. 1655.

8°. A–E⁸F² 16.5 cm.

The first edition. A fragment of a catalog of books printed for Moseley, one leaf signed A, follows the text; it lists twenty-two books, and the catchword on the verso indicates that this leaf is a portion of a larger list. Bound by Zaehnsdorf in calf, gold tooling on cover and spine, gilt edges. The Hoe copy (with bookplate) sold by Anderson Auction Co., New York, 4 May 1911, lot 3054.

Gift of Alexander S. Cochran, December 1911.

Wing S 3483

SHIRLEY, JAMES, 1596–1666

EC 216
The Royal Master
1638

The royall master; as it was acted in the new theater in Dublin: and before the right honorable the Lord Deputie of Ireland, in the Castle. Written by Iames Shirley. . . . London, printed by T. Cotes, and are to be sold by Iohn Crooke, and Richard Serger, at the Grayhound in Pauls Church-yard. 1638.

4°. A–K⁴L² 18.1 cm.

The first edition. Bound by Rivière in blue goatskin, gold tooling on cover and spine, gilt edges.

Gift of Alexander S. Cochran, December 1911.

STC 22454   Greg 538(A)

SHIRLEY, JAMES, 1596–1666

EC 217
St. Patrick
1640

St. Patrick for Ireland. The first part. Written by James Shirley. London, printed by J. Raworth, for R. Whitaker. 1640.

4°. A–I⁴   18.5 cm.

The first edition. Bound by Rivière in green goatskin, gold tooling on cover and spine, gilt edges. Nothing is known of the second part suggested by the title.

Gift of Alexander S. Cochran, December 1911.

STC 22455   Greg 593(A)

SHIRLEY, JAMES, 1596–1666

EC 218
Triumph of
Peace
1633

The trivmph of peace. A masque, presented by the foure honourable houses, or Innes of Court. Before the king and queenes majesties, in the banquetting-house at White Hall, February the third, 1633. Invented and written, by James Shirley, Gent. . . . London, printed by Iohn Norton, for William Cooke, and are to be sold at his shop, neere Furnivals-inne-gate, in Holborne. 1633.

4°. a²A–D⁴   17.3 cm.

The first edition. Bound by Rivière in crimson goatskin, gilt edges. Bridgewater Library duplicate stamp on verso of title. This masque, with scenery by Inigo Jones and music by William Lawes, was the most sumptuous ever presented at Court. Its estimated cost was £20,000.

Gift of Alexander S. Cochran, December 1911.

STC 22458.5   Greg 488(a,b+)

SHIRLEY, JAMES, 1596–1666

EC 219
Witty Fair One
1633

The wittie faire one. A comedie. As it was presented at the private house in Drvry Lane. By her maiesties servants. By Iames Shirley. . . . London printed by B. A. and T. F. for Wil. Cooke, and are to be sold at his shop, neere Furnivals-inne gate, in Holborne. 1633.

4°. A²B–I⁴K²   17.9 cm.

Printed by Bernard Alsop and Thomas Fawcet. The first edition. Bound by Rivière in crimson goatskin, gilt edges.

Gift of Alexander S. Cochran, December 1911.

STC 22462   Greg 477(A)

SPENSER, EDMUND, 1552?–1599

EC 220
Colin Clout
1595

Colin Clovts come home againe. By Ed. Spencer. London printed for William Ponsonbie. 1595. [Colophon:] London printed by T. C. for William Ponsonbie. 1595.

4°. A–K⁴   18.2 cm.

Printed by Thomas Creede. The first edition. Bound by Rivière in purple goatskin, gold tooling on cover and spine, gilt edges.

COLIN CLOVTS
Come home againe.

By Ed. Spencer.

LONDON
Printed for VVilliam Ponsonbie.
1595.

Spenser's *Colin Clout*, 1595 (EC 220)
The first edition

Gift of Alexander S. Cochran, December 1911.

STC 23077

SPENSER, EDMUND, 1552?–1599

EC 221
Complaints
1591

Complaints. Containing sundrie small poemes of the worlds vanitie. . . . By Ed. Sp. London. Imprinted for William Ponsonbie, dwelling in Paules Churchyard at the signe of the Bishops Head. 1591.

4°. A–Z⁴ (lacking Z_4, blank)   17.8 cm.

The first edition. Bound by Rivière in blue goatskin, gold tooling on cover and spine, gilt edges.

Gift of Alexander S. Cochran, December 1911.

STC 23078

SPENSER, EDMUND, 1552?–1599

EC 222
Faerie Queene
1590

The faerie qveene. Disposed into twelue books, fashioning XII. morall vertues. London printed for William Ponsonbie. 1590

4°. A–Pp⁸Qq⁴   18.3 cm.

Qq_4 is incorrectly bound in between Pp7 and Pp8. The first edition. Bound by Rivière in purple goatskin, gold tooling on cover and spine, gilt edges. Title page remargined. This first edition contains only books I–III, with an ending that Spenser changed when he added Books IV–VI.

Gift of Alexander S. Cochran, December 1911.

STC 23080

THE FAERIE QVEENE.

Dispoſed into twelue books,
Faſhioning
XII. Morall vertues.

LONDON
Printed for William Ponſonbie.
1590.

Spenser's *Faerie Queene*, 1590 (EC 222)
The first edition, containing only three books

SPENSER, EDMUND, 1552?–1599

EC 223
Faerie Queene,
Part II
1596

The second part of the faerie qveene. Containing the fovrth, fifth, and sixth bookes. By Ed. Spenser. Imprinted at London for William Ponsonby. 1596.

4°. A–Ii⁸Kk⁴   18.2 cm.

The first edition. Bound by Rivière in purple goatskin, gold tooling on cover and spine, gilt edges.

Gift of Alexander S. Cochran, December 1911.

STC 23082

SPENSER, EDMUND, 1552?–1599

EC 224
Prothalamion
1596

Prothalamion or a spousall verse made by Edm. Spenser. In honovr of the dovble mariage of the two honorable & vertuous ladies, the Ladie Elizabeth and the Ladie Katherine Somerset, daughters to the right honourable the Earl of Worcester and espoused to the two worthie gentlemen M. Henry Gilford, and M. William Peter Esquyers. At London. Printed for William Ponsonby. 1596.

4°. A⁴B²   17.9 cm.

The first edition. Bound by the Club Bindery in 1902 in crimson goatskin, gold tooling on cover and spine, gilt edges. The Hoe copy (with bookplate) sold by Anderson Auction Co., New York, 18 January 1912, lot 3120.

Gift of Alexander S. Cochran, February 1912.

STC 23088

SPENSER, EDMUND, 1552?–1599

EC +34
Works
1617

[The Faerie Qveen: The Shepheards Calendar: Together with the other works of England's arch-poet, Edm. Spenser: collected into one volume, and carefully corrected. . . . 1617] [Colophon on reverse of Hh$_5$:] London, printed by H. L. for Matthew Lownes.

Fol. [-]^2(-[-]$_1$)¶^{8}(-¶$_8$)A–P^6(-A$_1$)Q^{4}R–Hh^6(-Hh$_6$) A–E^{6}F^4(-F$_4$)A^{8}A–L^{6}M^2 (lacking [-]$_1$, title-page, and blanks as indicated)   27.2 cm.

The second edition (first, 1611). Printed by Humphrey Lownes. Bound in tree calf, gold tooling on cover and spine, gilt edges. In this copy the leaves signed ¶ have been incorrectly bound in after [-]$_2$; they should appear after Hh. Several leaves have been remargined. Signature of William Wheeler, New Haven, Conn., November 1858, on front flyleaf. There are numerous modern pencil annotations throughout the text.

Provenance not traced.

STC 23085

SUCKLING, SIR JOHN, 1609–1642

EC 225
Discontented
Colonel
[1642]

The discontented colonell. Written by Sir Iohn Sucklin. London, printed by E. G. for Francis Eagles-field, and are to be sold at the Marrigold in Pauls Church-yard. [1642]

4°. A^{2}B–G^{4}H^2 18.5 cm.

Printed by Edward Griffin, Jr. The first edition. Bound by Rivière in crimson goatskin, gilt edges. The first two leaves and the last two leaves have been remargined.

Gift of Alexander S. Cochran, December 1911.

Wing S 6125   Greg 621(a)

SUCKLING, SIR JOHN, 1609–1642

EC 226
Fragmenta Aurea
1646

Fragmenta aurea. A collection of all the incomparable peeces, written by Sir John Svckling. And published by a friend to perpetuate his memory. Printed by his owne copies. London, printed for Humphrey Moseley, and are to be sold at his shop, at the signe of the Princes Armes in St Pauls Churchyard. MDCXLVI.

8°. A⁴A–G⁸H⁴A–E⁸F⁴A–D⁸A–C⁸D⁴   17.7 cm.

The first edition, the issue with the initial letters of *Fragmenta Aurea* in large capitals. Bound by Rivière in purple goatskin, gold tooling on cover and spine, gilt edges.

Gift of Alexander S. Cochran, December 1911.

Wing S 6126

SUCKLING, SIR JOHN, 1609–1642

EC 227
Fragmenta Aurea
1648

Fragmenta avrea. . . . London, printed for Humphrey Moseley, and are to be sold at his shop at the signe of the Princes Arms in S. Pauls Church-yard. 1648.

8°. A⁴A–G⁸H⁴A–E⁸F⁴A–D⁸A–C⁸D⁴ (lacking A$_1$, C$_{3-5}$G$_{4-8}$H$_{1-4}$)   17.4 cm.

The second edition. Bound in half brown leather, marbled-paper-covered boards. Signature of Ann Watkas(?) on the title page. Note and signature of James Crossley on the front flyleaf.

Gift of Charles A. Ryskamp, in memory of Gilbert M. Troxell.

Wing S 6127

SWETNAM, the Woman-Hater

EC 228
Swetnam
1620

Swetnam, the woman-hater, arraigned by women. A new comedie, acted at the Red Bull, by the late queenes seruants. London, printed for Richard Meighen, and are to be sold at his shops at Saint Clements Church, ouer-against Essex House, and at Westminster Hall. 1620.

4°. [-]¹A–K⁴L¹   18.5 cm.

The first edition. Bound in calf, blind tooling on cover, gilt edges. Note and signature of John Mitford, dated March 1817, on front flyleaf. Collation note signed J. G. on front free endpaper. Bookplate of Frederick Locker (*The Rowfant Library,* p. 93), and acquired by Mr. Cochran at the dispersal of that library in 1905.

Gift of Alexander S. Cochran, December 1911.

STC 23544   Greg 362(A)

TACITUS, CORNELIUS

EC +35
Annals
1605

The annales of Cornelivs Tacitvs. The description of Germanie. M. DC. IIII. [Part II:] The end of Nero and beginning of Galba. Fovre bookes of the histories of Cornelius Tacitus. The life of Agricola. The third edition. M. DC. IIII. [Colophon:] Printed at London by Arnold Hatfield for Iohn Norton. Anno 1605.

Fol. ¶⁴A–Y⁶Z⁴
[Part II:] ¶⁶A–S⁶T⁴V⁶   28 cm.

The second edition of the first part (first, 1598) and the third edition of the second (first, 1591). Translated by Richard Greneway and Sir Henry Savile. Bound in contemporary calf, blind and gold tooling on cover and spine, arms of James I stamped on cover. On the verso of the front free endpaper is written in a seventeenth-century hand a recipe for shoe black. On the recto of the first front flyleaf is pasted a sheet bearing a woodblock printed at York "On the frozen River Ouse," 26 January 1740, with a long written description of the event. Beneath is pasted a handbill advertising a school to instruct children "in the Spinning of Worsted," dated York, 16 December 1766. Tipped in after this leaf is a broadside concerning this school. A Latin inscription on the title page is signed Johannes Girdler, 1762. Names have been scored out on the title page and the leaf preceding.

Gift of Alexander S. Cochran, December 1911.

STC 23645

The Great Frost. Which began Martinmas & Continued very severe wt. Continual & Vast Quantity of Snow till Candlemas 1739 & 40 Printed by a Soldier

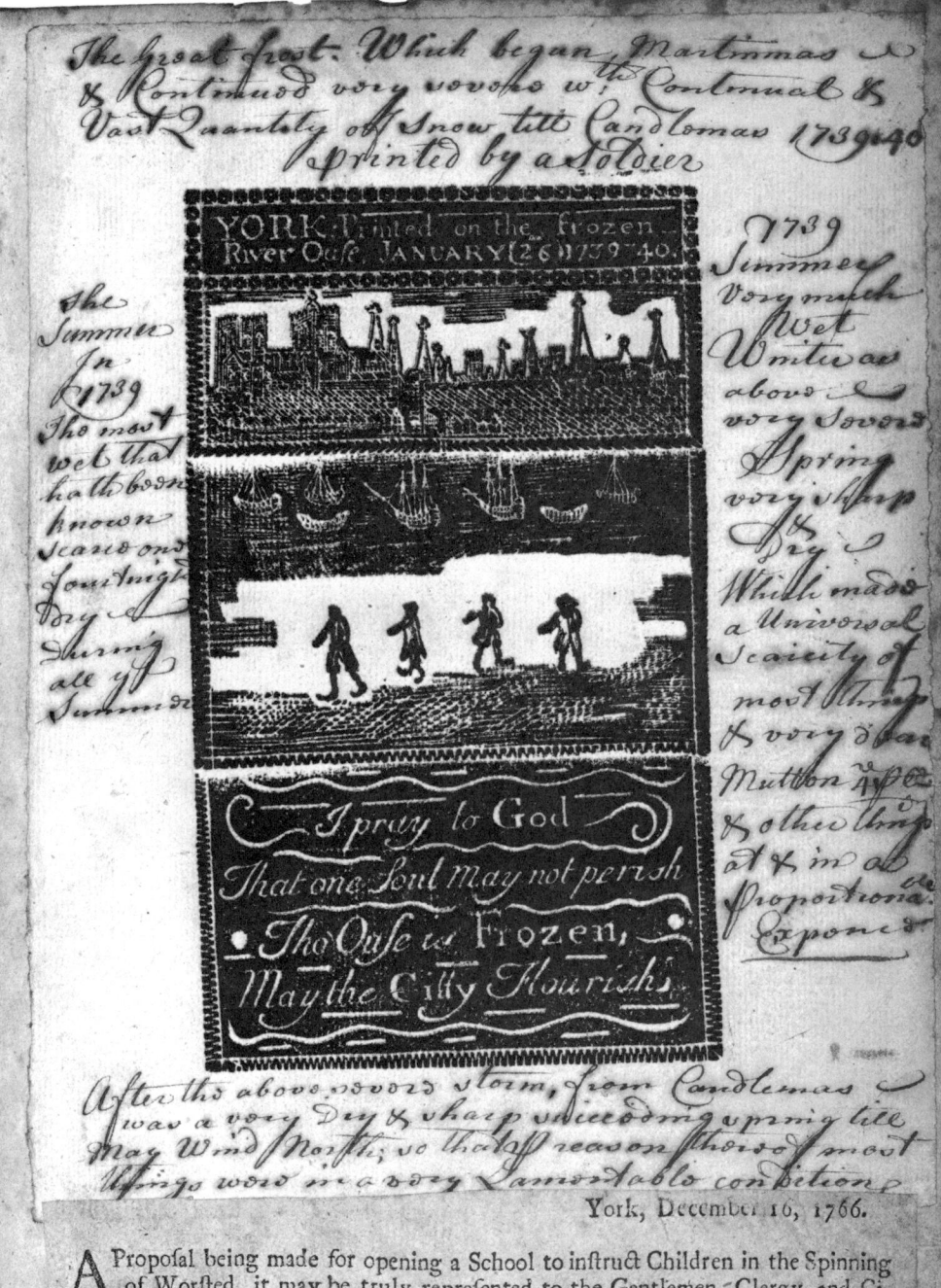

The Summer In 1739 The most wet that hath been known Scarce one fortnight Dry during all ye Summer

1739 Summer very much Wet Winter as above very Severe Spring very sharp & Dry Which made a Universal Scarcity of most things & very dear Mutton 4½d & other things at & in a proportionable Expence

After the above severe storm, from Candlemas was a very Dry & sharp succeeding spring till May Wind North; so that by reason thereof most things were in a very Lamentable condition

York, December 16, 1766.

A Proposal being made for opening a School to instruct Children in the Spinning of Worsted, it may be truly represented to the Gentlemen, Clergy, and Citizens, that it is an Art easily learnt, very advantageous to the Children, their Parents, and the Public; several Children being already taught to gain 1 s. or 1 s. 6 d. per Week, and sent home to their Parents, and several Hundreds more are desirous of being learnt. It is recommended vigorously to support and encourage the Plan by a Subscription, in order to open proper Places in each Ward in the City, to give all an Opportunity of learning that are desirous. Contributions will be received by Mr. Whitaker, in Micklegate; Mr. Tasker, in Stonegate; Mr. Coron, in the Shambles; and Mr. Wyvill, in Coppergate; also by the Churchwardens and Overseers of each Parish, who will collect the said Contributions To-morrow the 17th Instant.

TASSO, TORQUATO, 1544–1595

EC 229
Godfrey of
Bulloigne
1594

Godfrey of Bvlloigne, or the recouerie of Hiervsalem. An heroicall poeme written in Italian by Seig. Torquato Tasso, and translated into English by R. C. Esquire: and now the first part containing fiue cantos, imprinted in both languages. London imprinted by Iohn Windet for Christopher Hunt of Exceter, 1594.

4°. ★²A–Ff⁴Gg² 17.5 cm.

Translated by Richard Carew; the first edition in English. Bound in half red goatskin. Osterley Park bookplate of the Earl of Jersey; lot 1703 in the sale of his books by Sotheby's, 14 May 1885. Bookplate of Frederick Locker (*The Rowfant Library*, p. 123), and acquired by Dodd and Livingston at the dispersal of that library in 1905. Acquired in 1911 by A. Conger Goodyear (his note of acquisition is on the rear free endpaper) from Dodd and Livingston.

Gift of A. Conger Goodyear, February 1916.

STC 23697

TATE, NAHUM, 1652–1715

EC 230
Ingratitude of a
Commonwealth
1682

The ingratitude of a common-wealth: or, the fall of Caius Martius Coriolanus. As it is acted at the Theatre-Royal. By N. Tate. . . . London, printed by T. M. for Joseph Hindmarsh, at the Black-bull in Cornhill. 1682.

4°. A–I⁴ 21.6 cm.

Printed by Thomas Milbourne. The first edition. This adaptation of Shakespeare was first acted in

Facing page: Tacitus' *Annals*, 1605 (EC +35)   Printed souvenir of the frozen River Ouse, at York, 1740, pasted onto the front fly leaf

The Olde, Old, Very Olde Man:

OR

The Age and long Life of *Thomas Par*,
The Sonne of *Iohn Parr* of *Winnington* in the
Parish of *Alberbury*; in the County of
Salopp, (or *Shropshire*) who was Borne in
the Raigne of King *Edward* the 4th. and
is now living in the *Strand*, being
aged 152. yeares and odd
Monethes.

His Manner of Life and Conversation
in so long a Pilgrimage; his Marriages,
and his bringing up to *London* about
the end of *September* last.
1635.

Written by IOHN TAYLOR.

LONDON,
Printed for *Henry Gosson*. 1635.

Taylor's *Old, Old, very old Man*, 1635 (EC 231)

1681. Bound in half calf, marbled-paper boards. First and last leaves closely trimmed, but without loss of text. Signature of W. A. White, and inscription to the Elizabethan Club dated 10 November 1918 on front flyleaf.

Gift of William A. White, November 1918.

Wing T 190

TAYLOR, JOHN, 1580–1653

EC 231
The Old, Old, Very Old Man
1635

The olde, old, very olde man: or the age and long life of Thomas Par, the sonne of John Parr of Winnington in the parish of Alberbury; in the country of Salopp, (or Shropshire) who was borne in the raigne of King Edward the 4th. and is now living in the Strand, being aged 152. yeares and odd monethes. His manner of life and conversation in so long a pilgrimage; his marriages, and his bringing up to London about the end of September last. 1635. Written by Iohn Taylor. London, printed for Henry Gosson. 1635.

4°. A–D⁴   18.1 cm.

The first edition, first issue. Bound by F. Bedford in purple goatskin, gold tooling on cover and spine, gilt edges. Bookplate of Frederick Locker (*The Rowfant Library,* p. 123), and acquired by Dodd and Livingston at the dispersal of that library in 1905. Acquired in 1911 by A. Conger Goodyear (his note of acquisition is on the rear flyleaf) from Dodd and Livingston.

Gift of A. Conger Goodyear, February 1922.

STC 23781

TENISON, THOMAS, Archbishop of Canterbury, 1636–1715, *translator*

See BACON, SIR FRANCIS. *Baconiana*.

TERENCE

EC 232
Andria
1588

Andria the first comoedie of Terence, in English. A furtherance for the attainment vnto the right knowledge, & true proprietie, of the Latin tong. And also a commodious meane of help, to such as haue forgotten Latin, for their speedy recouering of habilitie, to vnderstand, write, and speake the same. Carefully translated out of Latin, by Maurice Kyffin. . . . Printed at London by T. E. for Thomas Woodcocke, at the signe of the Black Beare in Paules Churchyard. 1588.

4°. [-]⁴A–K⁴   18 cm.

Printed by Thomas East. The first edition. Bound by Rivière in crimson goatskin, gold tooling on cover and spine, gilt edges. The Mostyn copy sold at Sotheby's, 1 June 1907, lot 425.

Gift of Alexander S. Cochran, December 1911.

STC 23895   Greg 91(A)

THUCYDIDES

EC +36
History
1550

The hystory writtone by Thucidides the Athenyan of the warre, whiche was betwene the Peloponesians and the Athenyans, translated oute of Frenche into the Englysh language by Thomas Nicolls citezeine and goldesmyth of London. Imprinted the xxv. day of July in the yeare of oure Lorde God a thousande, fyve hendredde and fyftye.

Fol. A–Oo⁶Pp⁴   31.3 cm.

The first edition in English. Bound in contemporary calf, elaborate blind tooling on cover. Inscription: "Tho: Lee his Booke" on front free endpaper.

Provenance not known.

STC 24056

TOURNEUR, CYRIL, 1575?–1626

EC 233
Atheist's
Tragedy
1611

The atheist's tragedie: or the honest man's reuenge. As in diuers places it hath often beene acted. Written by Cyril Tourneur. At London, printed for Iohn Stepneth, and Richard Redmer, and are to be sold at their shops at the west end of Paules. 1611.

4°. [A]¹B–L⁴(-L₄, title page)   18.5 cm.

The first edition, first issue. Bound by Rivière in dark blue goatskin, gold tooling on cover and spine, gilt edges.

Gift of Alexander S. Cochran, December 1911.

STC 24146   Greg 293(A)

TWYNE, THOMAS, 1543–1613, *translator*

See VIRGIL

UDALL, WILLIAM

EC 234
Mary Stuart
1636

The historie of the life and death of Mary Stuart Queene of Scotland. London, printed by Iohn Haviland, and are to be sold by William Sheares in Britaines Burse at the signe of the Harrow. 1636.

12°. A–X^{12}Y^6 13.8 cm.

The second edition (first, 1624), with both engraved and letterpress title pages. Bound in contemporary blind-tooled calf, rebacked. Bookplate of Henry B. H. Beaufoy, F.R.S. Initials of Henrietta Bartlett and date, 1929, on rear paste-down endpaper. Signature cut from title page.

Gift of Henrietta C. Bartlett.

STC 24510

VAILLANT DE GUESLIS, GERMAIN, 1517?–1587, *editor*

See VIRGIL

VIRGIL

EC 235
Aeneid
1553

The xiii. bukes of Eneados of the famose poete Virgill translatet out of Latyne verses into Scottish metir, bi the reuerend father in God, Mayster Gawin Douglas Bishop of Dunkel & unkil to the Erle of Angus. Euery buke hauing hys perticular prologe. Imprinted at Londō 1553.

4°. [A]^{1}B–U^{8}χ^{1}X–Z^{8}a–bb^8 (lacking bb$_8$, probably blank)   20.7 cm.

The first edition in Scottish. Bound in contemporary blind-tooled calf. There are a few annotations in the text, and the signatures of Anna Gordon on Z_1r and Janet Williamsone on u_3^v.

Provenance not traced.

STC 24797

VIRGIL

EC 236
Aeneid
1584

The .xiii. bookes of Aeneidos. The first twelue beeinge the woorke of the diuine poet Virgil Maro, and the thirteenth the supplement of Maphaeus Vergius. Translated into English verse . . . by Thomas Phaer Esquire: and the residue finished, . . . by Thomas Twyne, Doctor in Physicke. Imprinted at London by William How, for Abraham Veale, dwelling in Paules Church yeard, at the signe of the Lambe. 1584.

4°. [-]⁴A–V⁸X⁴ (lacking X_4, probably blank)   18.7 cm.

The first edition. Bound in calf, gold tooling on cover and spine, gilt edges. Signature of Joshua Sylvester (the poet?), dated 1609, on the title page. Collation note, signed and dated G. M., 1 March 1897, on rear free endpaper.

Gift of Alexander S. Cochran, December 1911.

STC 24802

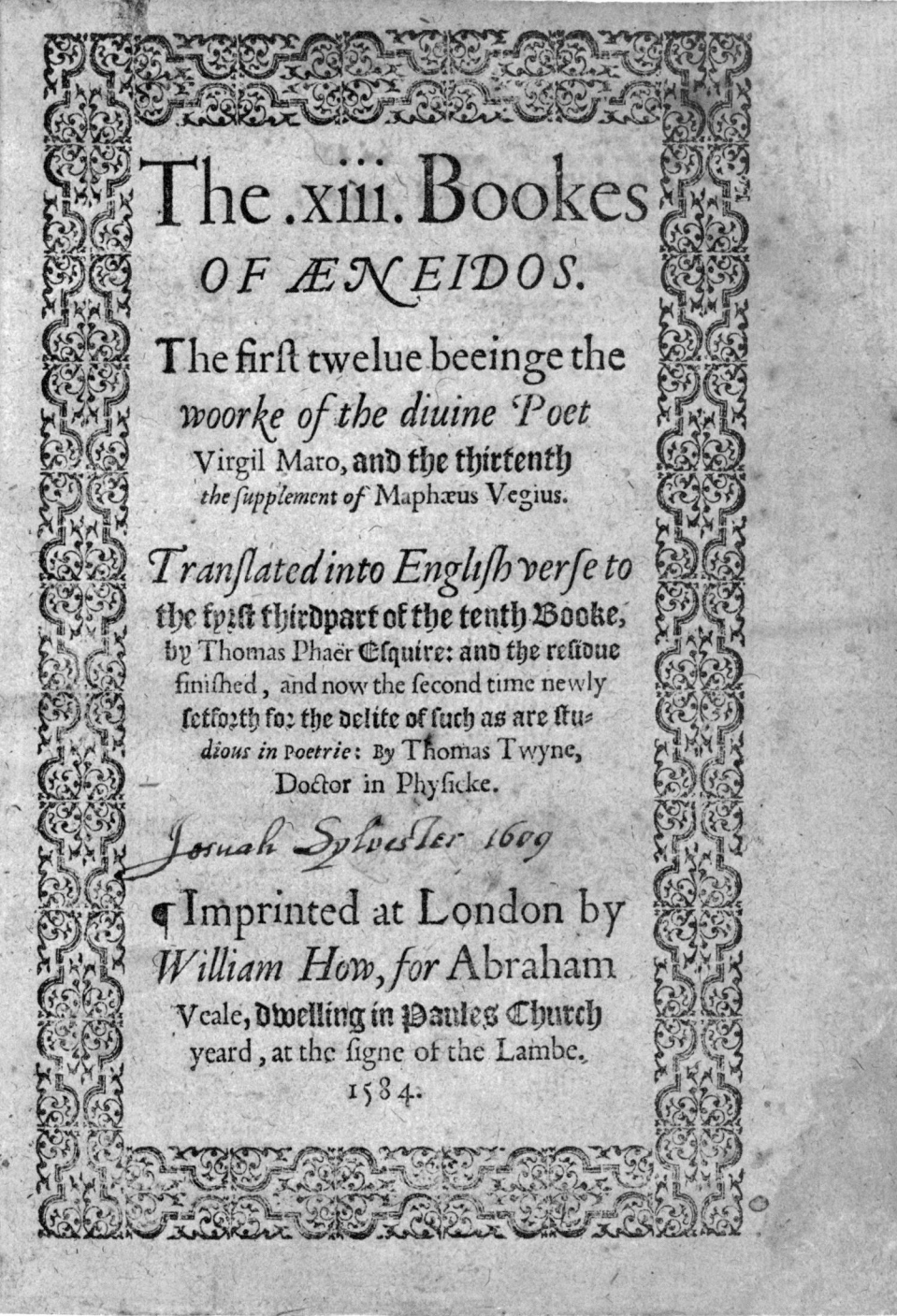

Virgil's *Aeneid*, 1584 (EC 236)
The title page bearing the signature of Joshua Sylvester

EC 237
Bucolics and
Georgics
1589

VIRGIL

The bvcoliks of Pvblivs Virgilivs Maro, prince of all Latine poets; otherwise called his pastoralls, or shepeherds meetings. . . . All newly translated into English verse by Abr: Fleming. Imprinted at London by T. O. for Thomas Woodcocke, dwelling in Paules Churchyard at the signe of the Blacke Beare. 1589.

4°. A–E^{4}A–K^{4}L^1 19.2 cm.

Printed by Thomas Orwin. The first edition. Bound in sprinkled calf, blind tooling on cover. Fleming was the first translator of both the *Bucolics* and the *Georgics* into English.

Gift of Alexander S. Cochran, December 1911.

STC 24817

EC +37
Works
1575

VIRGIL

P. Virgilivs Maro, et in eum commentationes, & paralipomena Germani Valentis Gvellii, PP. Eiusdem Virgilij appendix, cum Josephi Scaligeri commentariis & castigationibus. Antverpiae, ex officina Christophori Plantini, architypographi regii. M. D. LXXV.

Fol. ★^{6}A^{4}B–Z^{6}a–z^{6}Aa–Gg^6★★^{8}aa–hh^{6}ii^4 (lacking ★★$_8$ and ii$_4$, blanks)   33.3 cm.

Bound in contemporary calf, rebacked.

Provenance not known.

VITRUVIUS POLLIO

EC 264
I dieci libri
1584

I dieci libri dell'architettvra di M. Vitrvvio, tradotti et commentati da Monsig. Daniel Barbaro eletto Patriarca d'Aquileia, . . . In Venetia, appresso Francesco de'Franceschi Senese. M D L X X X I I I I.

4°. ★^{4}A–N^{8}O–P^{4}Q^{8}R^{4}S^{1}T^{4}V^{1}X^{8}Y^{4}Z^{8}Aa–Nn^8
24.2 cm.

The third edition in Italian (first, 1566). Bound in contemporary limp vellum. Signature of A. P. Peabody on the front flyleaf.

Gift of Mr. and Mrs. Charles Nagel, in memory of Everett V. Meeks, August 1985.

W., J.

EC 238
Valiant Scot
1637

The valiant Scot. By J. W. Gent. London, printed by Thomas Harper for Iohn Waterson, and are to be sold at his shop in Pauls Church-yard, at the signe of the Crown. 1637.

4°. A–K^4 17.5 cm.

The first edition. Bound by Rivière in crimson goatskin, top edge gilt.

Gift of Alexander S. Cochran, December 1911.

STC 24910   Greg 520(A)

WALTON, IZAAK, 1593–1683

EC 239
Compleat
Angler
1668

The compleat angler or the contemplative man's recreation. Being a discourse of rivers, fish-ponds, fish, & fishing. . . . The fourth edition, much corrected and enlarged. London, printed for R. Marriot, and are to be sold by Charles Harper at his shop, the next door to the Crown near Sergeants-inn in Chancery-lane, 1668.

8°. A–S⁸   14.5 cm.

The fourth edition (first, 1653). Bound by Zaehnsdorf in green goatskin, elaborate gold tooling on cover and spine, gilt edges.

Given to the club in 1912.

Wing W 665

WAPULL, GEORGE, *fl.* 1576

EC 240
Tide Tarrieth
No Man
1576

The tyde taryeth no man. A moste pleasant and merry commody, right pythie and full of delight. Compiled by George Wapull. . . . Imprinted at London, in Fleete-streate, beneath the Conduite, at the signe of Saynt Iohn Euaungelist, by Hugh Iackson. 1576.

4°. A–G⁴   18.5 cm.

The first edition. Bound by Rivière in crimson goatskin, gold tooling on cover and spine, gilt edges.

Gift of Alexander S. Cochran, December 1911.

STC 25018   Greg 70(A)

WEBSTER, JOHN, 1580?–1625?

EC 241
Appius and
Virginia
1654

Appius and Virginia. A tragedy. By John Webster. Printed in the Year, 1654.

4°. [A]¹B–I⁴[-I₄, title page]   19.6 cm.

The first edition. Bound by Rivière in dark blue goatskin, top edge gilt.

Gift of Alexander S. Cochran, December 1911.

Wing W 1215   Greg 733(AII)

WEBSTER, JOHN, 1580?–1625?

EC 242
Devil's Law Case
1623

The deuils law-case. Or, when women goe to law, the deuill is full of businesse. A new tragecomoedy. The true and perfect copie from the originall. As it was approouedly well acted by her maiesties seruants. Written by Iohn Webster. . . . London, printed by A. M. for Iohn Grismand, and are to be sold at his shop in Pauls Alley at the signe of the Gunne. 1623.

4°. A–L⁴   19.7 cm.

Printed by Augustine Matthewes. Bound by Rivière in crimson goatskin, top edge gilt. A few leaves are mended, and some badly stained.

Gift of Alexander S. Cochran, December 1911.

STC 25173   Greg 388

WERRO, SEBASTIAN, 1555–1614

EC 251
Physicorum
Libri X
1581

Sebast. Verronis Fribvrgensis Helvetii, physicorum libri decem. . . . Basileae, ex officina Hervagiana, per Eusebium Episcopium, Anno M. D. LXXXI.

8°. a–s^8 16.8 cm.

The first edition. Bound in contemporary limp vellum, with ties. Upper margin of title page repaired, without damaging text. Initials D. W., and date 6 December 1844 on title page.

Purchased 1980.

WERRO, SEBASTIAN, 1555–1614

EC 248
Physicorum
Libri X
1581

Sebast. Verronis Fribvrgensis Helvetii, physicorvm libri X. . . . Londini, ex officina Henrici Bynneman typographi. M. D. LXXXI. Cum priuilegio regiae maiestatis.

8°. A–N^8 16.2 cm.

The first English edition. Bound in modern quarter leather. Contemporary signature of John Childerley of St. John's College, Oxford, on the title page.

Purchased 1977.

STC 24688

WHITE, WILLIAM, *fl.* 1662

EC 247
Rarities of
Russia
1662

The rarities of Russia with the interest of England in point of trade with that country: which occasioned the magnificent entertainments of the Russian ambassadours; 1. By Queen Elizabeth, anno

SEBAST.
VERRONIS
FRIBVRGENSIS
HELVETII, PHYSI-
corum libri decem.

Nunc primùm in lucem editi.

BASILEÆ,
EX OFFICINA HERVAGIANA,
per Eusebium Episcopium, Anno
M. D. LXXXI.

Werro's *Physicorum*, 1581
The first edition, printed in Basel (EC 251)

SEBAST.
VERRONIS
FRIBVRGENSIS
HELVETII,
PHYSICORVM
LIBRI X.

Nunc primùm in lucem editi.

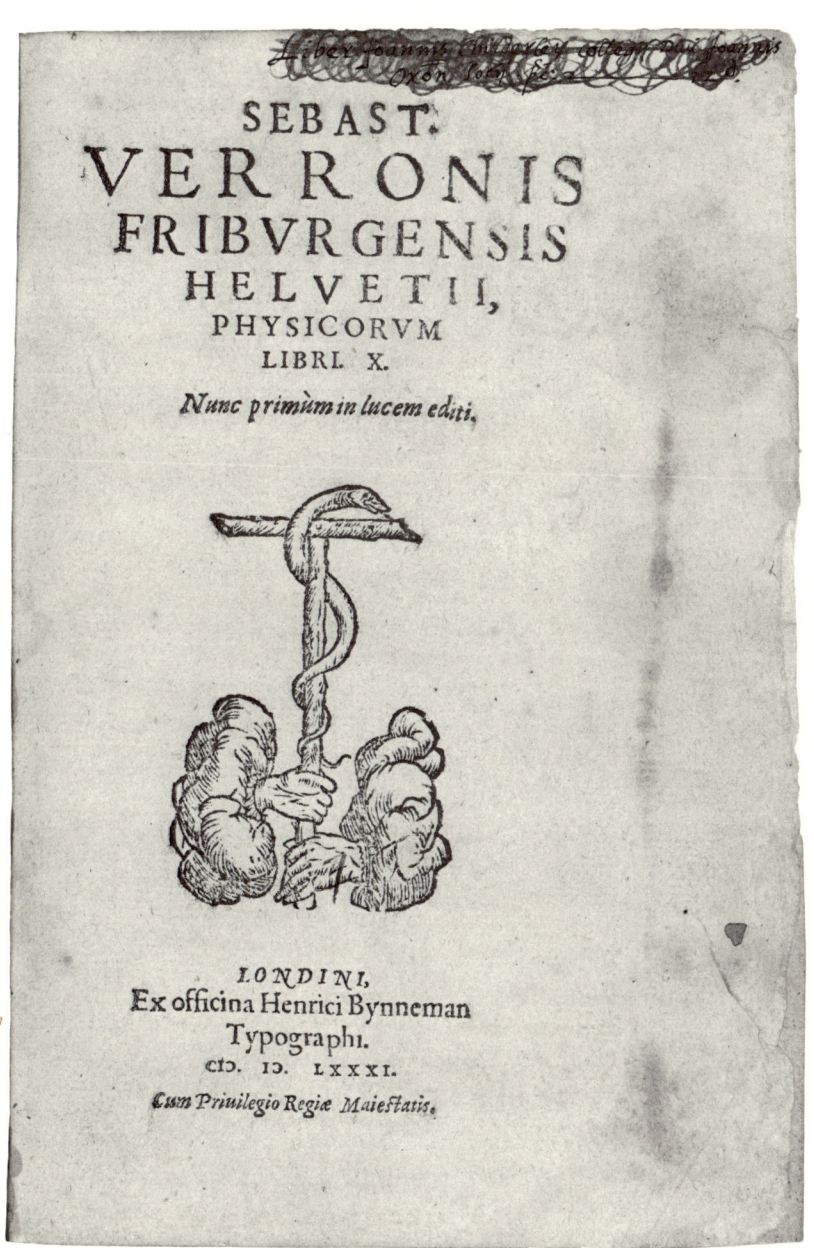

LONDINI,
Ex officina Henrici Bynneman
Typographi.
CIƆ. IƆ. LXXXI.
Cum Priuilegio Regiæ Maiestatis.

Werro's *Physicorum*
The first English edition, printed in London in 1581 (EC 248)

1589. 2. By King James, November 5, 1617. 3. By King Charles the Second, 1662. Which are here described: by Will. White merchant. London, printed for the Author. 1662.

4°. A–B⁴C²D⁴   17.5 cm.

The first edition. Bound by Lloyd in crimson goatskin, gold tooling on cover and spine, gilt edges. Bookplate of Laura K. and Valerian Lada-Mocarski.

Gift of Mrs. Valerian Lada-Mocarski, 1975.

Wing W 1857

WILSON, THOMAS, 1525?–1581, *translator*

See DEMOSTHENES

WOODS, NATHANIEL, *fl.* 1580

EC 243
Conflict of
Conscience
1581

An excellent new commedie, intituled: the conflict of conscience. Contayninge, a most lamentable example, of the dolefull desperation of a miserable worldlinge, termed, by the name of Philologvs, who forsooke the trueth of Gods gospel, for feare of the losse of lyfe, & wordly goods. Compiled, by Natthaniell Woodes. Minister, in Norwich. . . . At London printed, by Richarde Bradocke dwelling in Aldermanburie, a little aboue the conduict. Anno 1581.

4°. A–I⁴   17.4 cm.

The first edition. Bound in straight-grain brown

goatskin, gold tooling on cover and spine, gilt edges. Closely trimmed at top margin, affecting running titles.

Gift of Alexander S. Cochran, December 1911.

STC 25966.5   Greg 78(AII)

WOTTON, SIR HENRY, 1568–1639

EC 244
Elements of Architecture
1624

The elements of architectvre, collected by Henry Wotton Knight, from the best authors and examples. London printed by Iohn Bill. M.DC.XXIV.

4°. ¶⁴A–P⁴Q²   15.9 cm.

The first edition, with cancel signed B_4. Bound in contemporary blind-tooled vellum. Inscribed "Ex dono Authoris" on the title page. Signature of John Poley, dated 1655, on the title page, and signature of Chr. Robinson of Lincoln's Inn, dated 1735, on the front endpaper. Three bookplates of George Cornwall Legh and the High Legh Library. Closely trimmed, affecting title page and some catchwords.

Gift of H. Page Cross.

STC 26011

XENOPHON

EC 245
Treatise of Household
[1550?]

Xenophons treatise of hovseholde. 1534[1550?] [Colophon:] Imprinted at London in Fletestrete, in the house of Thomas Berthelet. . . .

8°. A–H⁸   12.9 cm.

The fourth edition (first, 1532). Bound in straight-grain maroon goatskin, gold tooling on cover and spine. Translated by Gentian Hervet, a French scholar and tutor to the Pole family.

Gift of Alexander S. Cochran, December 1911.

STC 26073

YOUTH

EC 246
Interlude of Youth
[1557?]

[Head-title:] Thēterlude of youth. [Colophon:] Imprinted at London, by John Waley dwellyng in Foster Lane. [1557?]

4°. A–C⁴   18.3 cm.

The second edition (first, ca. 1520). Bound by Rivière in crimson goatskin, gold tooling on cover and spine, gilt edges.

Gift of Alexander S. Cochran, December 1911.

STC 14111a   Greg 20(b)

The Interlude of Youth, ?1557 (EC 246)

Index

*to Binders and Former Owners of Books
described in this Catalog*

INDEX

Abeel, Rev. J. N., 68
Adam, R. B., 57
Adelt, M., of Smigiel, 158
Aiken, T., binder, 55
Aitken, binder, 176
Allen, H., 137
Anderson Auction Co., 48, 57, 61, 82, 85, 90, 91, 106, 109, 130, 131, 132, 168, 175, 176, 191, 243, 249
Anderson, H. H., Jr., 146, 194
Ashburnham, Earl of, 94
Atkinson, J. W., 53
Atterbury, A. H., 95
Augustus Frederick, Duke of Sussex, 117

B., H., 173
B., K., 60
B., R., 80
B., T., 152
Bandinel, B., 204
Bangs and Co., 87
Barlett, P. G., 167
Bartlett, H. C., 41, 60, 104, 260
Battershall, F., 131
Battershall, M., 131
Baynton, binder, 194
Beacon, M., 65
Beadnell, J., 136
Beaufoy, H. B. H., 260
Bedford, F., binder, 79, 83, 131, 139, 156, 159, 167, 180, 184, 199, 204, 205, 206, 209, 210, 215, 218, 224, 228, 229, 235, 237, 257
Beer, T., 101
Benn-Walsh, Sir J., Baron Ormathwaite, 182
Benz, D. L., 187
Bibliotheca Abbatis Fierdepied, 69
Bibliotheca Heberiana, 207, 216
Bibliotheca Turkheimiana, 69

Bindley, J., 216
Blanford, Marquis of, 227
Bodenham, F., 137
Bodenham, J., 242
Bools, W. E., 84, 156
Bowle, J., 163
Bowyer, W., 124
Brandon, J., 87
Bridgewater Library, 115, 244
Briggs, H., 63
British Museum, 225
Britwell Court, 83
Bromley of Hampton, 45
Brown, N., 169
Browne, R., 83

Caldecote, T., 163
Campden, Viscount, 152
Chambolle-Duru, binders, 188
Chase, F. S., 162
Chick, S., 117
Childerley, J., 267
Christ Church, Oxford, 170
Christie's, auctioneers, 187
Christopher, M. F., 63
Choules, J., 169
Clarence, Duke of. *See* William IV
Clarke and Bedford, binders, 93
Club Bindery, 85, 132, 249
Cochran, A. S., 42, 44, 45, 48, 49, 51, 55, 57, 68, 72, 73, 74, 75, 76, 77, 78, 79, 80, 81, 82, 84, 85, 86, 88, 90, 91, 92, 93, 94, 95, 103, 105, 106, 108, 109, 113, 114, 115, 118, 120–21, 124, 125, 126, 127, 129, 130, 131, 132, 134, 136, 137, 138, 139, 141, 142, 145, 146, 147, 149, 150, 151, 152, 153, 154, 155, 156, 157, 158, 159, 160, 165, 167, 168, 170, 174, 175, 177, 178, 179, 180, 182, 183, 184, 188, 190, 191, 192, 195, 196, 199, 200,

Cochran, A. S. (*continued*)
201, 202, 203, 204, 205, 206, 207, 209, 210, 211, 212, 215, 216, 217, 218, 221, 223, 224, 225, 227, 228, 229, 230, 232, 233, 235, 237, 238, 239, 240, 241, 242, 243, 244, 245, 247, 249, 251, 252, 253, 258, 259, 261, 263, 264, 265, 266, 271, 272
Coffin, A. S., 194
Collier, 89
Corser, T., 77, 176, 228
Costeker, D., 61
Cossart, 69
Cotes, J., 194
Crampton, W., 68
Craufurd, C. H., 80
Crawford, J. R., 72
Crawford, W. H., 85, 132
Crisp, D., 41
Crosby, F. M., Jr., 126
Cross, H. P., 271
Crossley, J., 252
Cummyng, J., 203
Cunliffe, H., 178

D., J. M., 131
D., W., 152
Dalrymple, A., 129
Daniel, G., 212, 216, 218, 223, 227, 232, 234
David, S., binder, 91, 106, 109, 153
Davis, J., 196
Davis, T., 87
Davison, L. V., 68
Decaisne, J., 123
Delaune, T., 136
Demander, binder, 52, 138, 139, 144, 173, 194, 197
de Meuron, W. C., 42–43
Dent, J., 142
Dimock, G. E., 131
Dixon, J., 136
Dodd and Livingston, 255, 257
Drake, S. G., 125
Drinkwater, J., 104
Duff, E. G., 156

Earbery, A., 42

Elizabeth I, Queen, arms, 168
Evans, auctioneers, 117, 157, 227

Farr, H. A., 69
Fitzgerald, P., 240, 241
Fitzwilliam, Earl, 43
Fleming, J., 111
Förster, M., 61
Foster, M. B., 63
Foulis, A., 118
Frelinghuysen, Rev. J., 68

G., I., 152
G., J., 129, 252
G., J. K., 58
G., R., 142
Gardiner, F., 41
Gardner, J. D., 197
Gifford, W., 142
Gilbert, B., 172
Girdler, J., 253
Goodyear, A. C., 61, 255, 257
Gordon, A., 261
Gott, W., 142
Greenfield, J., binder, 179
Grimshawe, Rev. T. S., 163
Grove, T., 44
Gunning, Rev. P., 168

Halliwell-Phillipps, J. O., 156, 205, 206, 207, 211
Hamilton, M., 165
Hammond, L. Van der H., 141
Hance, H. F., 163
Hanmer, Sir T., 71
Hargood, R., 194
Harrison, W., 206
Harvey, J., 65
Hasleworth, J., 45
Hatton, Lord Chancellor, 100
Hawkins, R. C., 169
Hawtrey, E. C., 201
Hayday, binder, 206, 232
Heber, R., 207, 216
Hemingway, S. B., 131
Hibbert, G., 197
Hibons, J., 129
High Legh Library, 271

Hill, E. L. H., 188
Hoare, C., 172
Hoare, Sir R. C., 190
Hoe, R., Jr., 48, 57, 61, 82, 85, 90, 91, 106, 109, 130, 131, 132, 168, 175, 243, 249
Hofer, P., 71
Holland, H. W., 157
Holmead, A., 82
Hull, J., 94
Huntington, H. E., 162
Huth, H., 47, 65, 79, 93, 126, 197, 199, 200, 201, 202, 203, 204, 205, 206, 207, 209, 210, 211, 212, 215, 216, 217, 218, 221, 223, 224, 225, 227, 228, 229, 230, 232, 234, 235, 237

Inglis, J. B., 221
Ireland, W. H., 191
Ives, B., 168

Jackson, S. W., 68
James I, 253
James, W. B., 63
Jennings, A. B., 129
Jennings, H. C., 197
Jennings, O. B., 129–30
Jennings, R., 41
Jennings, W., 158
Jersey, Earl of, 255
Jolley, T., 78, 169
Jonson, B., 142

Kemble, J. P., 157
Keogh, A., 75, 77, 194
King, auctioneer, 163

Lada-Mocarski, L. K., 270
Lada-Mocarski, V., 270
Leavitt, auctioneer, 169
Lee, T., 259
Lefferts, M. C., 94
Legh, G. C., 271
le Jay, R., 71
Lewis, binder, 211, 223, 230, 232, 234
Lewis, W. S., 146, 194
Lilly, bookseller, 206
Litchfield, E. H., 43
Lloyd, binder, 121, 270

Lloyd and Wallace, binders, 241
Locker, F., 55, 60, 73, 78, 80, 93, 105, 120, 152, 159, 170, 180, 252, 255, 257
Loos, S., 68
Lortic, binder, 175
Lounsbury, T. R., 52, 89
Luttrell, N., 113

M., G., 261
M., J., 176
MacDonald, binder, 141
Manby, Mr., 172
McDonough, J., 131
McKee, T. J., 176, 178, 191
Meeks, E. V., 264
Mellvill, R., 74
Menzies, T., 194
Mildmay, Sir H. St. J., 238
Milbanke, H. V., 188
Milbanke, R., 188
Milliken, A., 66
Mitford, J., 129, 252
Morgan, J. C., 144
Morgan, J. H., 145
Morrell, binder, 187
Mostyn, Lord, 49, 84, 118, 127, 182, 258
Mudie, G., 75
Murdock, H., 65
Murton, C., binder, 212
Musgrave, W., 173
Myers & Co., 89

Nagel, C., 264
Naunton, R., 172
Newborough, J., 45
Nichols, A. F., 129
Northey, W., 45
Norton, H., 63

Ormathwaite, Baron, 182
Osler, Sir W., 170, 172

Parks, S., 179
Parke-Bernet Galleries, 43
Payne, T., 197
Peabody, A. P., 264
Perkins, F., 74, 79, 151, 178
Pettite, J., 47
Pforzheimer, C. H., 43

Index

Pigott, D., 241
Plummer of Middlestead, 203
Poley, J., 271
Porter, N. T., Jr., 51, 74, 82, 108, 117, 120
Pratt, W., binder, 48, 57, 125, 130, 132
Prouty, C. T., 173
Providence Public Library, 173

Quaritch, B., Ltd., 43, 48, 51, 72, 76, 93, 95, 103, 123, 126, 127, 132, 136, 139, 149, 153, 156, 163, 169, 178, 187, 238, 240, 241

Rehdiger Stadt-Bibliothek zu Breslau, 158
Richards, A. E., 53, 54, 59, 157, 169, 196
Ripley, A. L., 87
Rivière, binders, 44, 48, 49, 50, 59, 63, 68, 73, 74, 75, 78, 80, 81, 84, 85, 88, 92, 93, 94, 101, 105, 108, 109, 111, 113, 114, 115, 118, 125, 127, 129, 133, 134, 137, 138, 139, 140, 141, 147, 149, 150, 151, 152, 154, 155, 158, 159, 160, 162, 165, 167, 173, 174, 177, 179, 182, 190, 191, 192, 195, 202, 217, 233, 242, 243, 244, 245, 247, 249, 251, 258, 259, 264, 265, 266, 272
Robinson, C., 271
Roxburghe, Duke of, 227
Ryskamp, C. A., 252

S., I., 118
Sangorski and Sutcliffe, binders, 75, 77, 146
Scotto, J., 86–87
Seaton, A., 44
Selden, S. H., 194
Sewall, H. F., 87
Shelley, S., 45
Silver, A., 47
Silver, H. P., 47
Simpson, K. F., 51, 74, 82, 108, 117, 120
Simpson, W. K., 51, 74, 82, 108, 117, 120
Slingluff, C. B., 191
Smith, C., binder, 87
Smith, W. H., 124
Sotheby's, auctioneers, 47, 49, 63, 65, 78, 79, 80, 84, 86, 87, 93, 94, 117, 123, 127, 129, 132, 142, 149, 156, 176, 182, 197, 201, 204, 205, 207, 211, 212, 216, 217, 223, 227, 228, 232, 234, 238, 240, 241, 255, 258
Speck, W. A., 47
Squyer, S., 223
Stapfer, M., 204
Starkey, T., 66
Steevens, B. F., 129
Steevens, G., 163, 227
Stevens, P., 172
Storr, R., binder, 71
Story, E., 136
Sutherland, Duke of, 149
Sylvester, J., 261
Syston Park, 71, 117

T., H. W., 63
T., I., 86
T., W. F., 176
Thomas, C., 76
Thorold, Sir J. H., 71, 117
Thorpe, bookseller, 211
Tinker, C. B., 65
Travers, D., 126
Trentham Hall, 149
Troxell, G. M., 252
Twopenny, W., 120

Utterson, E. V., 87

Van Santvoord, A. S., 147
Van Santvoord, G., 163
Vernon, Baron, 65
Volketon, F., 74

W., D., 267
Waith, E. M., 52, 53, 54, 55
Walker, H., 68
Walton, I., 163
Watkas, A., 252
Weld, E., 43
Wendell, B., 58
Wheeler, W., 250
White, B., 163
White, W. A., 60, 66, 87, 123, 163, 169, 175, 257
Whitton, R., 60
Wilks, J., 197
William IV, 96, 97

Williams, G., 49
Williamsone, J., 261
Windus, Mr., 206
Wolseley, W., 42
Woolley, M., 200
Worsfold, binder, 90

Wotton, Sir H., 271
Wright, J., binder, 104

Yale University Library, 144
Young, F., 142

Zaehnsdorf, binder, 82, 240, 243, 265

Thanks are due to Hugh Kennedy for his assistance in preparing this index.

S.P.